Editor's note

For the past three years we've had the pleasure of sharing with honeymooners some of the most romantic hotels in the world – luxurious places that form the perfect backdrop to the first days of your life together. But this year is even more special. Not only is it a poignant time for those of you who are planning your big day, this Millennium year marks our finest issue yet. It is a superb collection – from traditional gems to chic trendsetters – each hotel teeming with character and revelling in uniqueness.

Our goal is to boldly present the world's exceptional hotels and mouth-watering destinations, and I have no doubt that you'll find something here to set your heart racing. Our editorial team – equipped with equal measures of knowledge and enthusiasm – have spared no effort to uncover the most interesting and romantic havens. We're fascinated by the singular charms of each one here. From *grandes dames* city hotels to intimate hideaways; from desert island fantasy-lands to remote safari lodges. At some you may be smack in the middle of the action; at others find yourself miles from civilisation straddling the Himalayan frontier.

On behalf of the Honeymoon Destinations team, our tireless globetrotting researchers, and our senior board directors, James Buchanan and Bill Colegrave, I wish you an unforgettable adventure. I hope our words are an inspiration as you embark on planning your perfect honeymoon. For a more illustrated look at these hotels and travel hot-spots, point your web browser to **www.SpecialHotels.com**. From here you can email us with your own ideas of the perfect romantic getaway. Is it Verona or Vienna, Barbados or Bora Bora? You be the judge. But take it from someone who is forever in search of nirvana: you won't be disappointed with any of them.

Best wishes,

Melanie Garrett, **Editor**

James Buchanan

Bill Colegrave

Special Hotels

Editor
Melanie Garrett
Publishers
James Buchanan, Bill Colegrave
Commercial Director
Debra Doran
Int. Sales & Marketing Manager
Ed Purnell
Editorial/Production Assistant
Jennifer Alcazar

Contributors
Liz Booth, Sandy Cadiz-Smith, Anna Crane, Nigel O'Brien
Production Director
Andrew Wilson
Production Manager
Wendy Bridges
Sales & Marketing
Ivano Palazzi, Serena Martin, NJ Media

Most images provided by
Tony Stone Images Ltd,
101 Bayham St, London NW1 0AG
Cover and additional images by
The Image Bank,
17 Conway St, London W1P 6EE
All other images courtesy of respective tourist organisations.
Reproduction
Colourpath, London
Printed and bound by
Duncan Web Offset Ltd, England

A catalogue record for this book is available from the British Library
ISBN 0-95347-051-2
Published by **Special Hotels Ltd**
Silver House
31-35 Beak Street
London W1R 3LD
Distributed in North America by
The Globe Pequot Press
6 Business Park Road
PO Box 833
Old Saybrook, CT 06475-0833

contents 2000

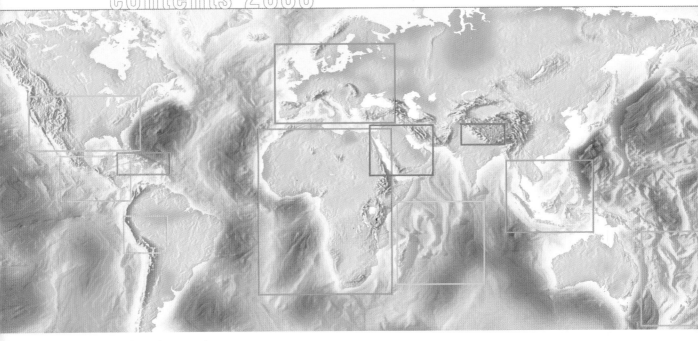

Index by regions

Information & Indexes

hotel listings

hotel listings

hotel listings

you & your
wedding

Britain's best reac

You & Your Wedding is Britain's best read bridal magazine. It is an invaluable guide for thousands of brides as they plan their perfect day. Every issue is packed with inspiration on all aspects of organising a wedding from choosing the right venue to the most romantic honeymoon bedrooms around the world.

Our experts will help you to make informed choices about all your service providers and the fashion team will amaze you with the latest collections of gorgeous dresses and accessories for every member of the bridal party.

All our features are planned with you, the 21st century bride, in mind. We won't tell you what to do, just inspire you with the most original ideas so you can create a day that's truly your own. If you haven't discovered You & Your Wedding yet, treat yourself – it really is the only bridal magazine you need.

bridal magazine

Honeymoons have a lot to live up to, and are viewed by most love-struck couples as the trip of a lifetime with long, lazy days filled with champagne and romance.

It is important that you approach this special holiday with your eyes wide open and your feet firmly on the ground. Great honeymoons do not just happen.

Decisions

First, decide where you want to go. Choose a destination neither of you has visited before. Do not even consider going somewhere you have stayed with a previous lover – your married life should be a fresh place to start.

Work out how much time you can both take off work and how much you can afford to spend. Do not use up all your annual leave with pre-wedding plans, and remember that if you are going to a long-haul destination you will lose about two days of holiday travelling.

Think ahead

Consider carefully about what you both want. That isolated island in the brochure may look like true paradise, but will there be enough to do? A good compromise is to book a two-centre honeymoon. Unwind first at a beach resort and then visit a city for some sightseeing and nightlife.

One way to start the honeymoon ball rolling is to ask your friends and family to recommend destinations they have experience of, and use your travel agent. More and more agents have wedding co-ordinators who will have plenty of ideas and will be able to tell you the best time of year to visit.

If you prefer a more high-tech approach, the Internet is a growing information source. After a few hours' surfing the net, you should have quite a few ideas for your ideal hideaway spot.

There are plenty of opportunities for sporty honeymooners too. Many resorts offer all the usual watersports, and some include scuba diving. Diving holidays offer the best of both worlds – exotic locations and stunning sport – and places like the Red Sea and the Seychelles are hot-spots for divers and honeymooners alike.

Once the decision is made, book as soon as possible so that hotels can reserve the honeymoon suite for you. And remember, don't travel too far on your actual wedding day. Spend a night locally and arrive relaxed and refreshed.

honeymoon

...The little atmosphere of strangeness, of excitement, that only a holiday bedroom brings...

Daphne du Maurier

Travel checklist

Don't leave home without…

Paperwork
Passports
Airline tickets
Car documents, if driving
Hotel booking
confirmations
Tour confirmations
Travel insurance
Foreign currency
Traveller's cheques
Credit cards
Vaccination certificates
Marriage certificate

Health and beauty
Vaccinations
Malaria tablets
Mosquito night-burning
coil/mosquito net
Insect repellent
ting cream
Headache tablets
Sun cream
After-sun lotion
Lip protection

Beauty/skincare products
Haircare products
Make-up

Clothing (hot)
Swimsuit
Shorts
Tops
Sundresses
Sunhat
Sunglasses
Casual eveningwear
Smart eveningwear
Beach shoes
Sports gear

Clothing (cold)
Woolly jumpers
Hats
Gloves
Warm boots
Coats
Sports gear
Casual eveningwear
Smart eveningwear

Off on the right foot

● Pay attention to what is included in any package price. If only breakfast is mentioned, this may be why the hotel sounds like such a bargain. Remember that additional meals at luxury hotels can be extremely expensive.

● Allow extra money for drinks, tips, service charges and airport tax. An all-inclusive resort or hotel may seem expensive at first glance, but the price you pay includes everything.

● Talk to your doctor well in advance about health requirements and what, if any, injections are recommended.

● Some vaccinations need to be given at least a month before you travel, and it may be that you need a course of anti-malarial tablets.

● Make sure everyone involved in your holiday arrangements knows you are on honeymoon. You will be amazed how many gifts and special offers suddenly come your way. Many hotels will offer flowers and a free bottle of champagne on arrival. Most will give upgrades if a better room is available, especially in the low season. Don't forget to take along your marriage certificate as proof of your new status.

● Do take out comprehensive travel insurance. Keep your passports in your hand luggage along with any plane and rail tickets, hotel confirmations and your marriage certificate.

● Think ahead if you are changing your name. Make sure the registrar has signed the relevant form to apply for a new passport in advance. Inform the airline so that the name on your ticket matches the name on your passport.

● Fewer and fewer countries now require British passport-holders to have a visa, but your travel agent will be able to advise you if one is needed.

The thought of a wedding without little arguments over the guest list and the seating plan is more than enough to justify escaping to an exotic clime. Add the spice of a romantic, tropical wedding, exchanging vows on a deserted sandy beach with palm trees rustling in the breeze, and the idea becomes tantalising.

Wherever you get married, the more effort you put in at an early stage, the happier and more relaxed you will be on the day itself. Some tour operators

Remember

● Pack all originals of your required documents.

● Ask the airline in advance if you can carry your dress as hand baggage, and maybe even hang it up during the flight.

● Make friends with the hotel wedding co-ordinator – you are much more likely to have unusual demands met.

● Go easy on the sunbathing – you don't want to be lobster-red in your photos.

● Video the ceremony to appease any relatives and friends who couldn't make the journey with you.

● Do not expect too much of the ceremony. It will be quick and informal, although most registrars will be happy to include a favourite reading or poem. You just have to ask.

Abroad

> *I gave my life to you as soon as I saw you.*

Marrianna Alcoforade

have a weddings department and a dedicated brochure with staff to guide you to the right destination and give you plenty of practical advice.

Countries that are already popular honeymoon destinations have realised they can take advantage of the growing trend to marry overseas and are now changing their local regulations. Even the Far East, where one might have thought strong local culture may have made overseas marriages difficult, has become a relatively easy option.

Bali, Thailand, Fiji and Australia are becoming increasingly popular, along with Kenya and a whole host of Caribbean islands such as Barbados, Jamaica, Grenada and St Kitts & Nevis.

If you're looking to have a wedding with a difference, turn your thoughts first to the USA. Las Vegas reigns supreme in the world of the weird and wonderful wedding stakes. There are drive-through wedding chapels and

kiosks, you can have an Elvis lookalike serenade you, or you can take to the skies in a hot-air balloon. In Florida, you can tie the knot underwater or join Mickey Mouse & Co at Disney World.

The easiest and most efficient way to arrange your wedding is to purchase a package through a tour operator. Typical deals include the services of a minister, all the necessary paperwork, a cake, flowers, accommodation, and often a basic set of photographs. If the two of you want to travel on your own, most hotels will arrange witnesses for you.

Weddings overseas are usually feasible for those with strict religious beliefs, and most ministers are non-denominational if that is a concern. Catholics may face particular difficulties in marrying abroad, and the authorities in some countries such as Bali require that both bride and groom are of the same religion.

Most larger hotels have an on-site wedding co-ordinator who will make sure the day runs perfectly. Normally they will travel with you if you need to visit the local authorities and will arrange the wedding breakfast and any 'extras', such as photographer, videographer, music and flowers, on your behalf.

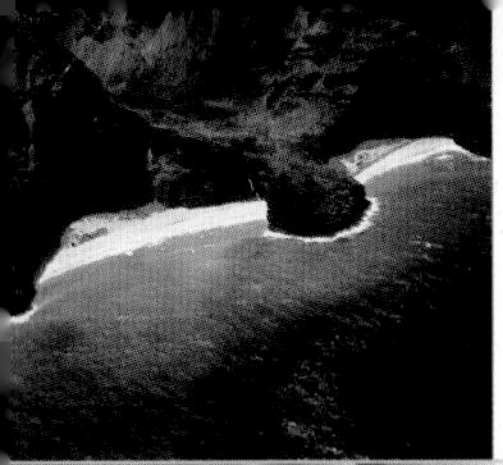

North America

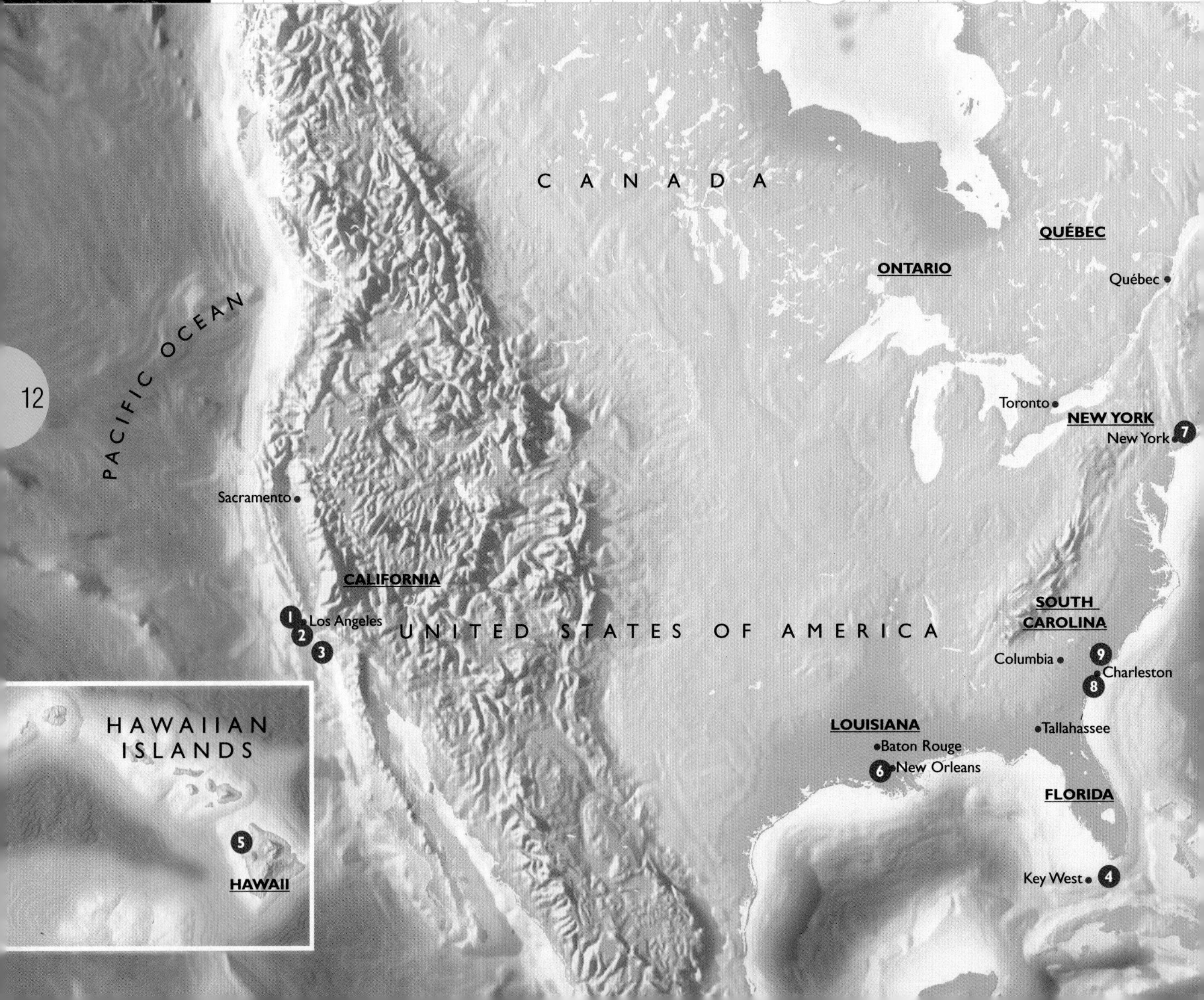

CANADA
QUÉBEC
Québec
ONTARIO
Toronto
NEW YORK
New York
7
PACIFIC OCEAN
Sacramento
CALIFORNIA
1
Los Angeles
2
3
UNITED STATES OF AMERICA
SOUTH CAROLINA
Columbia
9
Charleston
8
LOUISIANA
Baton Rouge
6
New Orleans
Tallahassee
FLORIDA
Key West
4
HAWAIIAN ISLANDS
5
HAWAII

ATLANTIC OCEAN

An American journey embraces not only dramatic and widely varied scenery, but a melting pot of cultures, thanks to generations of immigrants who have been absorbed into the American way of life as we know and love it today.

Not least into the American kitchen with its Italian pizzas, German hot dogs, Chinese noodles, spicy French Creole gumbo... the list goes on and on.

With some of the most spectacular scenery in the world, including the awe-inspiring Grand Canyon, Niagara Falls, the vast expanses of the Great Parks and Lakes and unbeatable mountains and beaches, there is no better place to take up the challenge of nature. Activities like whitewater rafting, ballooning, hiking and riding with cowboys on a dude ranch are all on offer. In California, Colorado, Canada and New England you can combine snowboarding, a bit of skiing and even sunbathing with sightseeing.

There isn't a leisurely option that someone in America hasn't thought of. Take a balloon ride over the plains, cruise the Mississippi in true style on a paddle-steamer, go shrimping around the Lowcountry, or partake of a gourmet wine-tasting tour. It is true... America has it all.

13

key to hotels

California
1 Hotel Casa Del Mar, Santa Monica
2 Shutters on the Beach, Santa Monica
3 Sunset Marquis Hotel & Villas, West Hollywood

Florida
4 Little Palm Island, Little Torch Key

Hawaii
5 Mauna Lani Bay Hotel & Bungalows, Kohala Coast

Louisiana
6 Windsor Court Hotel, New Orleans

New York
7 Hôtel Plaza Athénée

South Carolina
8 Charleston Place, Charleston
9 Litchfield Plantation, Pawleys Island

California

flying time
To: LA/San Francisco
London: 11 hrs
NY: 5-6 hrs

climate
California weather varies from hot desert to distinct seasons in the cooler north.

when to go
The beaches of Santa Monica and along the coast near Los Angeles are gorgeous to visit throughout the year. Theme parks and spots such as Yosemite National Park get crowded in the summer holidays.

getting around
Consider flying in to one Californian city and out of another, driving the distance between.

14

Perhaps the most varied and inspiring of all the American states, from snow-capped mountains and redwood forests, to sunburned deserts and Pacific beaches, California is also the perfect touring destination.

Start off in San Francisco – so picturesque and impossibly hilly that, even if it doesn't steal your heart, it will take your breath away. Let a clanging cable car carry you up to lofty heights for splendid views over San Francisco Bay, then hold on tight as it hurtles downhill towards the irresistible seafood restaurants of Fisherman's Wharf.

Drive north and soon you are in Napa Valley, touring the vineyards, and tasting vintages from California's leading winemakers. And one of America's most scenic drives follows famous Highway 1 south of San Francisco, passing by the craggy coast of Monterey and pretty Carmel, to eventually take you into another world – that of Southern California.

Los Angeles rewards those who brave its smog and sprawl and make time to get to know it. For LA is not only Hollywood, but also the wacky seaside strip of Venice Beach and the elegant Santa Monica, with its hip *nouveau* restaurants, wealth of galleries and museums, and hot-spots for music and dance.

Hotel Casa Del Mar

Information & Reservations
UK 0870 606 1296
INT. +44 870 606 1296

1910 Ocean Front Walk
Santa Monica
California

✈ Los Angeles 8 miles

Tel +310 581 5533
Fax +310 581 5503

reservations@hotelcasadelmar.com
www.hotelcasadelmar.com

Member of:
The Leading Hotels of the World

Situated right on the white sands of Santa Monica Bay, Casa Del Mar, once the grandest of the opulent Santa Monica beach clubs and hotels, has been restored to its former grandeur. Interior designers have created a '20s ambiance with soft lighting, damask and velvet draperies and fruitwood and bronze furnishings.

The luxurious bedrooms are designed to evoke a touch of the Riviera. Gauzy white, floor-to-ceiling draperies and wood Venetian blinds grace the windows and each room features traditional Victorian-style bamboo headboards, furniture in shades of fruitwood and Matisse-inspired art by a local artist. The opulent bathrooms have white Italian marble walls and floors and whirlpool tubs with a window of frosted panes opening onto the room and the panoramas of the stunning Pacific coastline beyond.

Californian cuisine with an emphasis on seafood is served in the casually elegant Oceanfront restaurant where glass walls mean that once again you can revel in the vistas. For more informal dining, relax on the Palm Terrace where there is also a plunge pool, outdoor jacuzzi and *chaise lounges* on an Italian granite deck, all set among a Mediterranean-style garden overlooking the beach.

15

 US$335-600 (112)

 US$775-3,500 (17)

US$15-28

 US$4-14

Honeymoon specials
Champagne welcome in room on arrival.

Sightseeing and leisure
The Spa and Health Club on site offers a wide range of treatments. Golf can be arranged through the concierge.

Shutters on the Beach

Information & Reservations
UK 0870 606 1296
INT. +44 870 606 1296

One Pico Boulevard
Santa Monica
California

✈ Los Angeles Int. 16km

tel +310 458 0030
fax +310 458 4589

Toll Free:
US/Canada 1 800 223 6800
UK 0800 181 123

www.shuttersonthebeach.com

16 Member of:
The Leading Hotels of the World

Shutters On The Beach is the only luxury hotel nestled right on the warm sands of Santa Monica Bay in Los Angeles. Recalling the architecture of historic southern Californian beach resorts of the early 1900s, the hotel has the look and feel of a sumptuous oceanfront home. The structure comprises three separate buildings, linked by elaborate slate-grey shingled siding, flower-covered trellises, balconies and striped awnings.

Each of the rooms and suites has warm walnut desks, lounge chairs and sliding shuttered doors opening onto the balmy ocean breeze and panoramic coastal views. All rooms have large marble bathrooms and whirlpool bathtubs with huge glass windows; while the suites feature wooden flooring and tiled fireplaces.

One Pico, the hotel's intimate restaurant, offers a front row seat to the Pacific Ocean and the stirring sunsets. With the emphasis on local and regionally grown produce, celebrated chef Desi Szonntagh creates entrées with a discreet and unobtrusive quality. Pedals, a casual restaurant at the edge of the beach promenade, has an Italian trattoria feel.

Shutters is situated near the historic pier in this seaside resort and is minutes from fashionable shopping districts, fine restaurants and art galleries.

US$355-595 (186)

US$875-2,500 (12)

US$40

US$14

Honeymoon specials

Two or four night packages include champagne and chocolates, dinner for two, daily breakfast, mountain bike hire, his and her massages and facials, limousine to and from the new Getty Centre and keepsake.

Sightseeing and leisure

Museums (including the new world class Getty Centre), art galleries, Rodeo Drive boutiques and speciality bookshops are just minutes away. On site, enjoy the swimming pool, jacuzzi, health club and spa where aromatherapy, massage, reflexology, facials and nail treatments are available.

Sunset Marquis Hotel & Villas

Information & Reservations
UK 0870 606 1296
INT. +44 870 606 1296

1200 N. Alta Loma Road
West Hollywood
California

✈ Los Angeles Int. 15 miles

tel +310 657 1333
fax +310 652 5300

smhdennis@aol.com
srs-worldhotels.com

The discreet and hip Sunset Marquis is the retreat of choice for many Hollywood types. Tucked away just yards from the glamour of the Sunset Strip, its muted elegance and luxurious ambiance has attracted a loyal clientele since 1963. It even has its own deluxe production studio to keep its musician guests happy and productive.

The cosy, guest-only Whiskey Bar plays host to a happening Hollywood crowd, including Winona Ryder and Leonardo di Caprio, as well as rockers such as Bruce Springsteen and Mick Jagger.

Discover a riot of colour in the lovely, manicured gardens, with koi fish ponds, exotic birds, fountains and palms. At the cabana-lined pool you will undoubtedly find yourself rubbing shoulders with supermodels, rock stars and actors, but remember to stay cool – the atmosphere here is relaxed and definitely understated.

Mediterranean-style villas with canopied beds and woodburning fireplaces add a flourish but in the main building the decor is slick and minimalist. Beautiful custom-designed furniture and luxurious materials such as leather, velvet, mohair, stainless steel and polished wood all point to a dedicated attention to detail. Courteous, attentive staff add to the winning combination.

17

 US$305-550* (102 suites)

 US$600-1,200* (12 villas)

 US$11-27

 US$10-20

 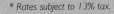

Honeymoon specials

One night up to five night packages in villas and one-bedroom suites include champagne and chocolates, dinner for two, daily breakfast, his and her massages, fresh flowers upon arrival. Airport transfers and on-site car rentals may also be pre-arranged.

* Rates subject to 13% tax.

Sightseeing and leisure

On site there are two outdoor heated pools, whirlpool, sauna and workout room. Nearby, Hollywood attractions include the Sunset Strip, Universal Studios, Mann's Chinese Theater, the Getty Museum, Westwood Village, Santa Monica and Venice Beach, Ahmanson and Shubert theatres.

Florida

flying time
To: Miami, Orlando
London: 9-10 hrs
LA: 4-5 hrs
NY: 3 hrs

climate
Winters are mild:
15-20°C with mainly
sunny days. Summer
is hot and humid,
especially in central
Florida, and you will
be thankful for an
air conditioned car.

when to go
Avoid the busy US
public and school
holidays if visiting
the theme parks.
May, June and Nov
are generally good
months to visit.
Winter months see
the hotel prices fall.

They call it the Sunshine State, but it could easily be known as the Happy State. Yes, it's true... Florida is a fun place.

Every evening is party time in Key West, as street entertainers and visitors from all over the world gather to cheer and celebrate the glorious sunset at Mallory Point. The Florida Keys, hundreds of islands strung together like pearls, offer a glimpse into a laid-back, idyllic way of living. And many miles away at Miami's hip South Beach, the stylish set preen and pose outside the pastel lemon and lilac Art Deco facades.

In the world's theme park capital, Orlando, just as many adults as kids get delightedly dizzy on Disney World's amazing selection of rides.

If sports are your idea of fun, Florida is your dream destination. It has more than a thousand golf courses and excellent tennis centres. All sorts of watersports will tempt you, with scuba diving off the Keys, not to mention exhilarating deep sea fishing trips from here, as well as from Miami, Naples and Fort Lauderdale. The island paradise of Longboat Key, near Sarasota, offers the chance to sample the combination of all of these. And of course there are the legendary beaches – more than 1,800 miles of sugary coastline with something to suit everyone.

Little Palm Island

Information & Reservations
UK 0870 606 1296
INT. +44 870 606 1296

28500 Overseas Highway
Little Torch Key
Florida

✈ Key West 28 miles

Tel +305 872 2524
Fax +305 872 4843

getlost@littlepalm.com
www.littlepalmisland.com

Member of:
Relais & Châteaux

On the lower reaches of the Florida Keys, a string of tropical islands lapped by warm seas, you will find your own miniature paradise at the exclusive Little Palm Island. Accessible only by seaplane or a 15-minute ferry ride from neighbouring Little Torch Key, the secluded private resort is the ultimate in luxury and indulgence.

Beautifully furnished thatched-roof bungalows nestle a mere shell's throw from the sea amidst lush foliage and coconut palms. Inside, the warm, woody tones and elegant colonial-style decor is complemented by spacious baths with whirlpool and private outdoor showers.

You couldn't ask for a more romantic setting: lounge on the powdery beach under a canopy or by the lagoon-style pool with waterfall; relax on your own private sundeck while glorious sunsets suffuse your rooms with a golden glow, or dine by candlelight under the stars. The food here is delicious too: tastes of Florida and the Caribbean with an Asian twist.

If you wish to marry on the island there are a variety of romantic locations – Sunset Dock, Palapa Point Beach, on a yacht, or in the unique Zen Garden. Whatever you do, you'll find the intimate charm of this little island utterly compelling.

19

Honeymoon specials
A choice of packages including complimentary champagne, gourmet meals, massage, unlimited use of non-motorised watersports and various romantic excursions.

Sightseeing and leisure
Outdoor pool, fitness centre, spa, library, full-size chess set. Full watersports amenities include snorkelling and scuba diving. Fishing, sailing and sea plane excursions. Nearby is Looe Key National Marine Sanctuary, the only living coral reef in North America, and the historic — and fun — town of Key West.

 US$550-US$1,500 (30)

 US$20-40

 US$12-30

Hawaii

flying time
To: Honolulu, Oahu
London: 18 hrs
LA: 6 hrs
NY: 12 hrs

climate
Sunshine and mild temperatures all year. Aug-Sept are humid and hottest (25-30°C). Winter (Oct-Apr) is cooler and wetter, rain being most likely Feb-March.

when to go
Avoid Christmas and New Year and school holidays, when rates are high and hotels, golf courses and beaches busy. Try to catch the islanders celebrating during the Aloha Festival (mid Sept-Oct).

getting around
Internal flights link the six main islands. Helicopter trips show off the dramatic scenery.

Hawaii is an excellent choice for a honeymoon destination, a place where American efficiency overlaps with romantic and charming South Seas traditions.

You will be guaranteed a warm welcome – greeted by friendly locals with a garland of flowers, invited to dance the *hula* and to taste the Polynesian barbecue, otherwise popularly known as a *luau*.

Try to visit at least two of the islands during your stay. Of the six main islands – Oahu, Hawaii, Maui, Kauai, Molokai and Lanai – many people vote Kauai the most beautiful. Nicknamed the Garden Isle because of its lush, colourful scenery, it has featured in many movies including *South Pacific* and *Jurassic Park*.

And be sure to surf the swells and make the most of a rare and golden opportunity to go whale-watching. Should one of the islands' volcanoes decide to perform while you are there, count yourself lucky and prepare for a spectacle more grand and thrilling than anything America's theme parks can offer.

Mauna Lani Bay Hotel and Bungalows

Information & Reservations
UK 0870 606 1296
INT. +44 870 606 1296

68-1400 Mauna Lani Drive
Kohala Coast
Hawaii

✈ Kona 37km

Tel +808 885 6622
Fax +808 885 1484

reservations@maunalani.com
www.maunalani.com

Tour operators:
US Pan Pacific Worldwide

Member of:
Preferred Hotels

There's not one but two silver sand beaches on the doorstep of the Mauna Lani Bay Hotel and Bungalows. The resort sprawls out beautifully over 3,200 acres and maintains a secluded atmosphere amid lush gardens and a stretch of shoreline that is home to myriad marine life. Here there is luxury in spoonfuls: two championship golf courses (carved from a 16th-century lava flow), a Tennis Garden, Racquet Club and fitness centre.

If guests opt for one of the luxurious bungalows they will probably believe they've died and gone to heaven. Four thousand square feet of luxury await. Fax through your preferences before arrival and find your favourite CDs in the player, your choice of magazines on the coffee table and your favourite snacks in the fridge (there's even a telescope for star-gazing). To ensure an easy time, discreet staff are on hand to arrange everything: from massages to helicopter rides.

The Big Island of Hawaii offers a diverse tropical paradise to explore, as do the resort's restaurants which, like everything else here, are larger than life and twice as wonderful. Whether it's a hamburger and fruit smoothie on the beach, or Hawaiian Tempura at the award-winning Canoe House, no one leaves disappointed.

21

 US$350-620 (350)

 US$970-4,750 (10)

 US$19-50

 US$14-22

Honeymoon specials
2000 Romantic Interlude Package includes three nights in oceanfront accommodation, champagne and chocolate strawberries on arrival, rose petal turndown on arrival night, daily breakfast in your room, one elegant dinner for two, one romantic picnic basket for two plus Mauna Lani keepsake. Price: US$1,740 inclusive of tax.

Sightseeing and leisure
Two championship golf courses, tennis and swimming pool. Beauty salon, health spa, massage and jacuzzi. The Big Island has the most active volcano in the world, 'Kilauea', which can be viewed brilliantly by helicopter. There are also Monarch Festivals, pro golf tournaments, Cuisines of the Sun in summer months, and historic sites along the Kohala Coast.

Louisiana

flying time
To: New Orleans
via Atlanta
London: 11 hrs
NY: 3½ hrs

climate
It is generally steamy
and sub-tropical. July
is the most humid
month, with an
average 6.73 inches
of rainfall. It's cooler
and less wet from
Oct-March.

when to go
Avoid the summer
if possible, which can
get unbearably hot.
Late winter through
to spring is when
most of the action
is, including the
grand festival of
Mardi Gras.

getting around
There's an extensive
network of buses,
but try streetcars
for more of an
atmosphere. Stroll
or hire a bike during
the day but always
take a cab at night.

Sultry, steamy New Orleans is what most people identify with when they think of Louisiana.

Nestling languidly in a loop of the Mississippi River, it sits on what was once a swamp teeming with alligators. Not the ideal spot for lovestruck honeymooners one might think, but this wildly romantic city just oozes vitality and excitement.

An intriguing blend of influences – French, Spanish, African, native Indian – New Orleans is like nowhere else in the US. From the seedy, dilapidated French Quarter, with its wrought-iron balconies and crumbling colonial architecture, to the palatial Greek Revival mansions of the beautiful Garden District, 'The Big Easy' is a city of contrasts: elegant, exotic, exuberant and mysterious.

There is so much to do and see in New Orleans, but you should try to take in The Old Mint, a branch of the Louisiana State Museum. Here you'll find one of the original streetcars named 'Desire', made famous by the Tennessee Williams play.

Streetcars still run through the streets of New Orleans, but a horse-drawn carriage from Decatur Street near Jackson Square is an even more romantic way to find your bearings. And whatever you do, don't leave without sampling the city's best-known (and aphrodisiac) dish – oysters.

If you visit in late winter you won't fail to get swept up in the world-famous Mardi Gras celebrations. The run-up begins on Twelfth Night (January 6), and culminates in a riotous feast of parades, parties and general hedonism the day before Ash Wednesday – just in time for Lent. Another unmissable event is the annual New Orleans Jazz and Heritage Festival in April/May. So… let the good times roll!

Windsor Court Hotel

Information & Reservations
UK 0870 606 1296
INT. +44 870 606 1296

300 Gravier Street
New Orleans
Louisiana

✈ MSY 20 mins

Tel +504 523 6000
Fax +504 596 4749

resv@windsorcourthotel.com
www.windsorcourthotel.com

Member of:
The Leading Hotels of the World

The Windsor Court Hotel is just 15 years old but already it is a haven for celebrities and the recipient of a host of awards, including the Condé Nast *Traveler* (US) reader's choice award as the 'number one hotel in the world'.

The hotel's strikingly modern architecture rises dramatically above the New Orleans skyline, while inside the interior is deeply traditional, and graced by a fabulous eight million dollar collection of fine arts and antiques spanning the 17th to the 20th centuries, including famous works by Reynolds, Gainsborough, Van Dyck and Huysman.

Surprisingly for New Orleans, the tone is resolutely English throughout – thanks to the hotel's Anglophile founder – from the grand statue of St George in the courtyard to the partaking of high tea every afternoon.

Accommodations are lavish and opulent with plump sofas and rich fabrics, and the bathrooms are fitted with Italian marble. They also boast private balconies or bay windows with stunning river or city views. The accolade-laden Grill room, with its impressive, well-stocked wine cellar and impeccable service, is the only restaurant in Louisiana to be awarded the coveted AAA 'five diamonds' and Mobil Five Stars – truly a romantic setting for a memorable meal.

23

US$230-320 (56)
US$280-460 (268)
US$12.75-300
US$12.75-22

Honeymoon specials
Chilled champagne and seasonal berries on arrival, continental breakfast.

Sightseeing and leisure
Outdoor swimming pool, jacuzzi and complimentary healthclub plus all the heady excitement that New Orleans can offer – the majestic Mississippi River, the French Quarter and the Aquarium are all only two blocks away. Casino and beauty salon nearby. Romantic carriage rides.

New York

flying time
To: JFK/Newark
London: 6-7 hrs
LA: 5-6 hrs
Miami: 3 hrs

climate
Summers can be
very hot, winters can
be bitterly cold with
thick snow. Spring
and autumn are
more pleasant.

when to go
The street parades
are quite a sight;
St Patrick's Day in
March and
Thanksgiving Day
in Nov offer the
biggest and best.
Most travel agents
offer special, low
weekend fares.

getting around
The grid layout of
the streets make
travelling on foot a
good option. Yellow
taxis and buses
abound. The tubes
can be confusing, but
comparatively cheap.

Yellow taxis, flashing neon lights, the classic curves of the Chrysler Building – images of New York are familiar to us all.

There are sights in abundance: the Statue of Liberty; Radio City Music Hall; even the hectic, hustling street life itself. But for most people, the main attraction is in the doing rather than the seeing: shopping like mad in the countless stores and boutiques along Madison and Fifth Avenues and enjoying an evening on Broadway before an unforgettable night in one of the Big Apple's swanky bars and restaurants.

New York can justly lay claim to be the Entertainment Capital of the World. Life here is a distillation of the rest of the planet's most exuberant entertainment played double-time – with jazz, *samba*, cinema, dance, and over 500 galleries and nightclubs to while away the hours.

Nevertheless, there are still opportunities to wind down. Pick the right spots and this can be an extremely relaxing place. Take a romantic carriage ride from The Plaza; stroll round the lake in Central Park and finish up in one of the quiet diners that dot the city; or take a view down First Avenue from the vantage point of the overhead cable cars. New York – it's a world unto itself.

Hôtel Plaza Athénée

Information & Reservations
UK 0870 606 1296
INT. +44 870 606 1296

37 East 64th Street
New York 10021
New York

✈ JFK Int. 16 miles

tel +212 734 9100
fax +212 772 0958

res@plaza-athenee.com
www.plaza-athenee.com

Tour operators:
UK Kirker Holidays, Seasons in Style
US NATS

Member of:
The Leading Hotels of the World

Between the quiet elegance of Park Avenue and the boutiques and art galleries of fashionable Madison Avenue, the Hôtel Plaza Athénée is just one block from Central Park. This prime location provides the perfect base to explore the vibrant city of New York, being within walking from most of the city's main attractions.

The stylish lobby is the last word in elegance with Italian marble floors, lavish French antique furnishing and hand-painted murals. The newly renovated rooms combine European style with meticulous attention to detail.

To underline that feeling of luxury, the sumptous bathrooms in Rose Aurora marble come complete with fresh flowers and bathrobes. Meanwhile, the award-winning Le Régence restaurant is widely considered to offer one of the most innovative menus in New York City. The Sunday brunch has also been rated 'best in the city'. The state-of-the-art Health Lounge gives guests the chance to work off all that good food.

With so much to offer, it's no surprise that Condé Nast *Traveler* (US) voted the hotel 'Best Service in NY City' in its January '99 Gold List.

25

 US$430-620 (117)

 US$990-3,600 (36)

 from US$36

 from US$25

Honeymoon specials

Honeymoon weekend rates from US$295 in traditional room; $355 for deluxe and $525 for a one-bedroom suite, subject to availability. Bottle of champagne included. Same packages available mid-week in Jan, Feb, March, July and August.

Sightseeing and leisure

The Health Lounge offers top-class facilities, including stairmasters, treadmills, lifecycles and free weights. Located on the fashionable Upper East Side of Manhattan, the hotel is within walking distance to Central Park, Fifth Avenue, art galleries, boutiques and New York's finest department stores.

South Carolina

flying time
To: Charleston
via Washington
From: London 11hrs

climate
Pleasant climate all year; sea breezes keep temperatures down in summer (20°-25°C) and up in winter (14°C). Most rainfall occurs in Mar and Nov.

when to go
With such a mild climate, there are fun outdoor activities throughout the year. Except in hurricane season, in Aug and Oct, the beaches are pretty and golden all year long.

getting around
Coach, train and bus services all operate around the state, but car hire is the best way to explore. Also, in Charleston take a horse-drawn carriage around to get a real feel for the quaint city. Ferries operate to the barrier islands.

Magnolia blossoms, rustic wooden porches and cool mint juleps are all part of life in charming, syrupy-sweet South Carolina where the pace is just that bit slower and gentler – the perfect place for total relaxation and long, lazy days.

This state in the Deep South retains the grandeur and elegance of times gone by, combined with a modern outlook and up-to-date amenities that make it a perfect, enviable mix of both old and new.

Whether you visit Charleston, one of the south's best-loved grand old cities which simply oozes grace, beautiful Pawleys Island, or the tiny towns of the Lowcountry where fishermen casually line the marshes and waterways, you will discover the tranquillity of the region. Be sure to tour the many preserved antebellum homes, pretty clapboard churches and town museums.

The south, too, is known for its outdoor lifestyle and the national and state parks are a great place to see it all in action. Find out more about its founders and rich

history at one of the many Civil War sites dotted throughout the state, or search for Indian artefacts along the banks of the winding, and aptly named Salkehatchie, Combahee or Coosawhatchie rivers.

For golfers and those in search of limitless activities, the bright lights and brilliant fairways of Myrtle Beach awaits, while Hilton Head Island offers quiet, upmarket fun, also with a lot of fine golf and kayaking and sailing opportunities to neighbouring islands.

And don't forget the pearl-like coastline with its many tiny islands dotted offshore providing the perfect haven for honeymooners wanting a world all of their own.

Charleston Place

Information & Reservations
UK 0870 606 1296
INT. +44 870 606 1296

205 Meeting Street
Charleston
South Carolina

✈ Charleston Int. 12 miles

tel +843 722 4900
fax +843 722 0728

www.charlestonplacehotel.com
reservations@orientx.net

Member of:
The Leading Hotels of the World

28

Situated in the heart of the beautiful and historical city of Charleston, with its charming cobbled streets, grand antebellum homes, antique shops, museums and piazzas, this recently refurbished, sumptuous hotel offers the highest standards of comfort combined with impeccable service.

From the magnificent lobby with its elegant fountain, grand sweeping double staircase and 12-foot crystal chandelier, to its luxurious, well-appointed bedrooms which boast opulent bathrooms with marble fittings, you'll discover the epitome of luxury – where European-style flair meets with American standards of service.

If you can't bear to venture out of the hotel, you'll find everything you could possibly desire contained under one roof, including a stunning Rooftop Spa offering a state-of-the-art exercise pavilion, rooftop tennis court, sun terrace, a horizon edge pool, sauna, steam room and jacuzzi, and more than a dozen massage and European beauty therapies.

The dining options are irresistibly tempting: indulge in one of their famed 'teatime specials' and feast on freshly baked scones, tea cookies and truffles; or tuck into the award-winning delights of the Charleston Grill as you listen to soothing jazz – all within fabulously plush, opulent surroundings.

🛏 US$189-429 (440)
🛏 US$500-1,700 (42)
🍽 from US$35
☕ US$15-20

🍾 💍 ♿ ⟳

Honeymoon specials
Luxury Honeymoon Package includes *Crabtree & Evelyn* bath amenities, red roses, a private carriage tour and dinner for two at the Charleston Grill. Rose petals strewn around the bed with heart-shaped Godiva chocolates on your pillow. Chilled champagne and lighted tea candles wait next to a recently drawn bath. Parting gift of a personally engraved silver travel candle and a special framed photo.

Sightseeing and leisure
The hotel has a fitness centre, swimming pool and steam room and on-site speciality shopping. Nearby there are championship golf courses, fishing, tennis courts, plantation homes and gardens, and all the delights of historical Charleston.

Litchfield Plantation

Information & Reservations
UK 0870 606 1296
INT. +44 870 606 1296

PO Box 290
Kings River Road
Pawleys Island 29585
South Carolina

✈ Myrtle Beach Int. 25 miles

tel +843 237 9121
fax +843 237 1041

vacation@litchfieldplantation.com
www.litchfieldplantation.com

Tour operators:
UK Whole World Golf Travel
American Way
US North American Travel Service

Member of:
Small Luxury Hotels of the World
Johansens

South Carolina's famous Grand Strand is home to 60 miles of wide sandy beaches, more than 100 championship golf courses, and, for the discriminating traveller, historic and charming Litchfield Plantation in Pawleys Island.

A member of Small Luxury Hotels of the World and Zagat's highest-rated property on the Grand Strand, the Plantation welcomes guests through grand, wrought-iron gates and a quarter-mile avenue of moss-draped, centuries-old live oaks.

The original 1700s plantation house offers four historically decorated suites brimming with fine artworks, fireplaces and antique furniture. There are 34 other luxurious suites and rooms dotted throughout the 600-acre resort hideaway featuring distinctive decor, charm and luxury, overlooking acres of creeks, ponds and lush rice fields.

The Carriage House, the Plantation's gourmet restaurant and social centre, serves a variety of beautifully presented fare ranging from continental cuisine to South Carolina Lowcountry specialities and favourite libations.

Abundant recreational amenities include tennis courts, oceanfront beach clubhouse, private marina, heated pool, romantic carriage rides and concierge-arranged tee times.

 US$168-210 (20)

 US$184-582 (18)

 US$18-40

 US$7-20

Honeymoon specials

Complimentary champagne on arrival. Honeymoon and romantic getaway packages available. On site wedding package.

Please note: meal plan available on request.

Sightseeing and leisure

Tennis, heated outdoor pool, beach clubhouse, gourmet restaurant, 100 golf courses to choose from. Historic tours in Georgetown and Charleston. Brookgreen Gardens, river tours, plantation tours, museums. Factory outlet shopping, theatre and shows.

key to hotels

Costa Rica
1 Hotel Makanda by the Sea, Quepos
2 Hotel Punta Islita, San José
3 Lapa Rios, Pto. Jimenez

Mexico
4 Hotel Villa del Sol, Zihuatanejo
5 Las Brisas Acapulco, Acapulco

Peru
6 Hotel Monasterio, Cusco

30

MEXICO

GULF OF MEXICO

•Mexico City

4 •Zihuatanejo

5 •Acapulco

SOUTH AMERICA

PERU
Lima• 6 •Cusco

PACIFIC OCEAN

H ere, at 'the sweet waist of America', a fantastic range of political, ethnic and environmental forces have collided, creating a magical hybrid.

In the big cities, a version of Coca-Cola culture moves to the rhythm of Colombian *salsa*. Deep in the forests, species of birds, beasts and plants from north and south live beside local species that are found nowhere else in the world.

There are places where it is not wise to travel, but the beautiful bays and rainforests of Costa Rica, and the soaring, creeper-clad ruins of the ancient Mayan Indian civilisation in Guatemala, are truly unforgettable honeymoon locations. Neighbouring Mexico, a more cosmopolitan country with long, gorgeous beaches, pulsating resorts and magnificent monuments, is already a mainstream holiday destination.

The whole region is incredibly romantic: for its scenery of smouldering volcanoes rising above green and gold highland valleys; for its dark lakes and mysterious swirling mists; for its tropical jungles hiding ancient pyramids; for its crumbling, elegant colonial architecture; for its thrilling music and certainly for its kind, passionate people.

The great driving forces here are land, family and religion, and throughout the whole length of Central America a fiery and unforgettable Latin heart beats just below the surface of all things.

STA RICA
● San José

3

flying time
To: San José
via Bogotá
London: 12 hrs
Miami: 3 hrs
NY: 7 hrs

climate
Tropical country with two seasons: wet and dry. Dry between late Dec-Apr, wet for the rest of the year. Temperatures vary little between seasons. In San José the climate is eternal spring (15°-25°C), coastal areas are hotter (30°C+).

when to go
Late Dec-Apr is drier but prices are higher. Note that hotels book up early.

currency
Costa Rican colón. But be sure to take US dollars with you.

getting around
By air to almost all the main towns. The bus service is the best on the isthmus but services are scarce off main routes. Car hire can be expensive.

The second smallest of the Central American nations, Costa Rica is an increasingly popular destination with travellers.

Nature-lovers and sports enthusiasts in particular are finding this country of such diversity a terrific place to explore. But it is still relatively undiscovered – and cleaner, greener and more relaxed than its neighbours.

No less than 20% of the country has been set aside for nature conservation in a superb network of national parks, all alive with the overwhelming fertility of the tropics, and offering a unique and intriguing opportunity to see wildlife in the raw. The country is home to more than 750 species of bird, and protected areas include steaming volcanic peaks, undisturbed tropical forests, vast lakes, islands, dry grassland, superb beaches, mountains and rambling pre-Colombian ruins.

In this country of great wonders, highlights include Corcovado National Park, diving off the Cocos Islands, Arenal Volcano, and a whole raft of sports. The deep sea fishing is superb; Pacific rollers keep surfers happy; the gruelling ascent of a volcanic peak is not to be missed, and wildlife viewing is in a league of its own.

Hotel Makanda by the Sea

Information & Reservations
UK 0870 606 1296
INT. +44 870 606 1296

Apartado 29
Quepos
Manuel Antonio
Costa Rica

✈ San José 3 hrs
(San José to Quepos 20min flight)

Tel +506 777 0442
Fax +506 777 1032

makanda@sol.racsa.co.cr
www.makanda.com

Member of:
Small Luxury Hotels of the World

33

Makanda by the Sea is located on the lush Central Pacific Coast, between the port town of Quepos and Costa Rica's smallest and most beautiful park, Manuel Antonio National Park. This exclusive, adults-only hotel overlooks the tranquil waters of a dazzling Pacific Ocean bay, and offers five villas and four luxury studios, accommodating 18-21 guests.

The elegant interiors, with vaulted ceilings, hand-crafted tiles and exotic hardwoods, invite the cool Pacific breezes and brilliant sunsets in. Relax in a bubbling jacuzzi or lounge by the cascade of the infinity pool. Breathe in the fragrance of tropical flowers and the wild sounds of the surrounding forest. Monkeys, sloths, brightly coloured birds and flickering butterflies are always close by.

The hotel's fabulous Sunset Poolside Bar and Grill is a must. Beneath the flowing curtains of tropical tents dine on fresh seafood such as grilled jumbo shrimp, octopus and Pacific Coast lobster. Treat yourself to delicious seared breast of duck, rack of lamb, range-fed steaks or one of the mouth-watering salads. Freshly baked pastries, chocolates, fruits and ice creams round off the perfect dining experience.

Here the theme is 'romance in nature' and Makanda's attentive staff will make your wedding or honeymoon a tropical dream come true.

 US$135-175 (4)

 US$175-250 (5)

 US$5-25

 included

Honeymoon specials

Special packages include candlelight dinners, champagne on arrival, rose petals on the bed, tropical floral arrangements, in-room spa service, complimentary fruit plate and mariachi serenade. A certified on site wedding planner will ensure your ceremony runs smoothly.

Sightseeing and leisure

Horseriding through rainforest trails, explore the waters of the Savegre and Naranjo rivers by river raft or kayak. Snorkelling, surfing and scuba diving off volcanic reefs of nearby islands. Boat trips to view whales, dolphins, sea turtles and the occasional manta ray, or fishing for sailfish & marlin. Jungle canopy tours, birdwatching, tours of Manuel Antonio National Park and guided rainforest tours are available.

Hotel Punta Islita

Information & Reservations
UK   0870 606 1296
INT. +44 870 606 1296

Islita Beach
Guanacaste
Costa Rica

✈ Punta Islita airstrip 3km

tel +506 231 6122
fax +506 231 0715

ventas@hotelpuntaislita.com
www.hotelpuntaislita.com

34   Member:
Small Luxury Hotels of the World

Leave the trials of life well and truly behind and escape to a tropical hideaway nestling in the forested hills of the Nicoya Peninsula, overlooking the sparkling ocean of Costa Rica's exotic Pacific coast.

This intimate and romantic oasis, with its air of rustic elegance, provides the perfect opportunity to lounge in a hammock taking in the stunning vista or sip a cocktail on the private beach. For those more energetic moments, you will also have the chance to really get back to nature with nature tours as well as boating, mountain biking, horseback riding and walking through the exotic, tropical forest that surrounds the hotel.

Choose from beautifully appointed bungalows with ocean or mountain views and private terrace complete with hammock, or spacious junior suites with private deck that look out over the blue sea with your own romantic outdoor jacuzzi.

The open-air restaurant that overlooks the hotel's spectacular pool offers fresh seafood, inventive international cuisine and exotic native dishes, all expertly prepared by the hotel's highly acclaimed chef. If you're feeling adventurous, hire a four-wheel drive vehicle at San José and really experience the beauty of the countryside on your way to the hotel.

 US$132-165* (20 bungalows)
 US$175-275* (8)
 US$22-35**
 included

Honeymoon specials

Flowers in room on arrival. Three-night package includes: sparkling wine, welcome cocktail, honeymoon breakfast, a romantic candlelight dinner, air transfer with domestic airline (San José/Islita/San José) – US$919 per couple with taxes included. Specials apply in Green Season (May-Nov).
* Plus tax of 16.39%.
** Plus 23% service & sales taxes.

Sightseeing and leisure

Tennis courts, a fully equipped gym and a spa offering natural products. Activities available include horseback riding, nature trails, mountain biking and birdwatching tours. Boat tours including in-shore and off-shore sportfishing and snorkelling. Jeep safari and A.T.V.'s guided tours to nearby towns and beaches.

Information & Reservations
UK 0870 606 1296
INT. +44 870 606 1296

Lapa Rios

Pto. Jiménez
Costa Rica

✈ Pto Jimenez 12 miles

tel +506 735 5130
fax +506 735 5179

Contact:
PO Box 025216
SJO-706
Miami, Florida 33102-5216

info@laparios.com
www.laparios.com

Set in a thousand acres of private, lush rainforest, high up on the Osa Peninsula overlooking the vast Pacific Ocean, owner-operated Lapa Rios is one of the most deluxe jungle and beach hideaways in all of Costa Rica.

Fourteen luxury thatched bungalows are dotted throughout the jungle. Each has a private deck and patio garden with magnificent views over the ocean, showers with solar-heated water, and two queen-sized beds. The bungalows are furnished in wood and bamboo with tropical printed fabrics. Constant breezes pass through the screened window walls. Although isolated (no phones), service at Lapa Rios is sophisticated. Staff are outgoing and experienced. Electricity is provided 24 hours a day. The main lodge, soaring 50 feet into the air, has a full service bar and restaurant serving quality cuisine, with the accent on fresh fruits, vegetables and meat, and local seafood.

While here, you can relax on safe, unspoiled sandy beaches, watch the continuous parade of colourful birds, butterflies and animals native to Costa Rica, and take part in adventurous organised activities – from jungle hikes to sea kayaking.

35

US$151-205* pppn (14)

 from US$31

 from US$12

 (incl)

Honeymoon specials

Flower arrangement on bed and welcome cocktail on arrival.

Rates are per person per night staying in a double room and including three multi-course meals daily, taxes and service.

Sightseeing and leisure

On site there is a romantic swimming pool set in tropical rainforest and a private tropical plant and orchid garden. Massages also available. Resident naturalists give guided tours around the private reserve and the famous Corovado National Park. Orchid Garden and Mangrove River tours. Guided hiking, horseriding, kayaking, fishing, surfing.

Mexico

Mexico's famous shimmering coastline along the Pacific, the Caribbean and the Gulf of Mexico is just one element of this vast country's extraordinary range of attractions.

The captivating landscape varies from snow-capped mountains to arid deserts, and lush, tropical forests to temperate valleys, while numerous archaeological sites inspire visitors with their mysticism and beauty.

Mexico City is rambling, cosmopolitan and modern, and a tribute to earlier civilisations with its magnificent Aztec temples and the floating gardens of Xochimilco, where people still live on the canals as the Aztecs did 500 years ago. The city is also an ideal base from which to visit the pyramids of Teotihuacan, one of the world's most impressive archaeological sites, the temple of Tlahizcalpantecuhtli in Tula, with its gigantic Atlantes statues, and the colonial cities of Toluca and Tepotzotlan.

The southern area of Mexico was home to the Maya, one of the greatest of the country's civilisations dating from 3,000 years ago. Chichen-Itza is the most renowned of all Mayan cities, with some of the greatest monuments, including the great pyramid known as El Castillo.

Heading north, Guadalajara is hailed as the essence of Mexico, upholding traditions like the *charreadas* (rodeos) and *jaraba tapatlo* (hat dance), while the famous *mariachis* create amazing amounts of atmosphere in Plaza Tapatio.

Acapulco offers glittering nightlife and beaches surrounded by tall mountain ranges, with the famous divers of la Quebrada soaring from a cliff 45m high.

Stunning scenery, including pine forests, can be seen from the Chihuahua-Pacifico train, which joins the high plane of Mexico with the Sea of Cortez. The train travels through historic towns like Bahuichivo, a good base from which to explore the staggering Copper Canyon. And try travelling down to the southern tip of the Baja Peninsula, where you'll be mesmerised by cactus-laden desert meeting spectacularly with the Sea of Cortez, and, perhaps, by the glitzy crowd who zoom down from LA for long, lazy weekends.

Rich flavours of the native cuisine are also a trademark, with three indispensable elements: *tortillas*, beans and chillies. And no meal is complete without Mexico's other homegrown staple: tequila.

flying time
To: Mexico City
London: 10-12 hrs
LA/Miami: 3 hrs
NY: 5 hrs

climate
Generally the north west coast, northern Baja California and central plateau are coolest. Overall, the weather is temperate and dry Nov-May, with temperatures rising and rainfall heavier June-Oct.

when to go
High season, with crowds and action, is Dec, Feb, July-Aug. The quiet months are Apr-May.

currency
Mexican peso

getting around
Frequent flights between major cities, together with a vast bus network and a rather slow rail system.

Information & Reservations
UK 0870 606 1296
INT. +44 870 606 1296

Hotel Villa del Sol

Playa la Ropa
Zihuatanejo
Guerro 40880
Mexico

✈ Ixtapa Zihuatanejo 5 miles

tel +52 755 4 2239
fax +52 755 4 2758

hotel@villasol.com.mx
www.hotelvilladelsol.com

Member of:
Small Luxury Hotels of the World

38

Peeping through the tops of swaying coconut palms, the terracotta-tiled and thatched palapa roofs of the charming Villa del Sol are a welcoming sight. In the luxuriant tropical gardens, twisted tree trunks support little red-tile roofs, hibiscus bushes adorn every turn, and vibrant pink bougainvillea rambles across earthen walls and romantic stone arches.

Dressed in warm colours and chic decor, the rooms and suites are located in adobe-like villas and, for true character, no two are alike. On private terraces beautiful mosaic-tiled minipools glint in the afternoon sun as you sway contentedly in a comfortable hammock, margarita in hand.

Fringed by vibrant green palms, Zihuatanejo's mile-long, crescent-shaped Playa la Ropa is one of Mexico's most striking beaches. Step off the hot sands and a cooling dip is in easy reach – try the enticing infinity pool which spills into the azure sea. Lounge chairs with wooden pergolas ensure your total relaxation and tranquillity. Or for the active among you, there is sailing, beach horseriding, diving, deep sea fishing, tennis and golf.

Two restaurants cater for your every culinary desire and mood. For elegant sophistication try The Restaurant at Villa del Sol, and for informal dining, La Cantina Bar & Grill will more than satisfy.

 US$220-300 (31)

 US$350-900 (24)

[○] from US$45

 US$18.50

Honeymoon specials
Fruit basket, welcome drink, early morning coffee, honeymoon gift. Romance Package includes: Lagoon or Beach Suites, fresh roses, one candlelight dinner with champagne, full American breakfast every day, transfers to/from airport, one massage. Four nights US$2,010-2,750, seven nights US$3,350-4,650, extra nights US$443-630 (valid April 1-Nov 14).

Sightseeing and leisure
Beauty salon with facials and massages. Spanish and Mexican cooking courses available. Two 18-hole golf courses. Traditional fishing village of Zihuatanejo. Tours of the nature reserve on Ixtapa Island and the local countryside. Great opportunities for shopping (gold can be bought at reasonable prices). Trip to Mexico City. Deep sea fishing, sailing, diving, luxury private yacht for hire.

Information & Reservations
UK 0870 606 1296
INT. +44 870 606 1296

Las Brisas Acapulco

Carretera Escénica 5255
Fracc Las Brisas Acapulco
Guerrero 39868
Mexico

✈ Juan N Alvarez 15km

tel +527 469 6900
fax +527 446 5328

brisa@westin.com
www.westin.com

Set in 110 acres of lush hibiscus gardens on a hillside high above Acapulco Bay on Mexico's southwest Pacific coast, Las Brisas Acapulco offers the perfect spot to get away from it all. But its location is perfect: for when you've fully recharged those batteries, the sizzling nightlife of Acapulco, just 20 minutes away, is waiting to be explored.

The unique village of 300 spacious pink *casitas* each have private pool and stunning, sweeping views of the turquoise sea. And when you're ready, pink and white jeeps will whisk you to the La Concha Beach Club which, with two salt water lagoons and a huge freshwater swimming pool, is Mexico's only private beach club.

Or you can sample any of the other many facilities at and around the hotel. Guests can take to the water where you can choose from snorkelling, scuba diving, deep sea fishing, jet-skiing or sailing. There is also a championship 18-hole golf course nearby at Club Tres Vidas, plus five floodlit tennis courts and a fantastic spa on the premises.

And then there's the food. Whether you want a spectacular sprawling tropical buffet, a 10-course dinner served to you at your table, or an authentic Mexican fiesta prepared from the finest local ingredients, the Las Brisas chefs can do it for you at one of the two highly renowned restaurants, both with stunning views over Acapulco.

39

 US$240-400 (263)

 US$520-1,260 (10)

US$45-60

 US$15-30

Honeymoon specials
Welcome cocktails and flower petals in the pool.

Sightseeing and leisure
Private beach club, jeeps for rental, watersports and tennis. Golf courses available nearby. The legendary nightlife of Acapulco with dancing, shows and world-renowned restaurants. The world-famous cliff divers at La Quebrada are a fabulous spectacle.

Peru

High up in the dense cloud forests of the spectacular Peruvian Andes lies the Lost City of the Incas – Machu Picchu.

Abandoned by its 15th-century Inca founders following a scourge of smallpox and the first wave of Spanish *conquistadores* in the early 16th century, the sacred and royal site lay undiscovered until 1911. Arrive by train from nearby Cusco, or follow at least part of the 33km Inca Trail, to view the magnificent terraced gardens, canal systems and imposing ruins which perch vertiginously above sheer drops to the canyon below. Dizzying altitudes and rolling mists only add to the enchantment of this magical place, which even the thousands of tourists that flock here can't spoil. Its atmosphere and grandeur is seriously intoxicating.

Deeply traditional ways of life continue, and the mountains are home to millions of highland Indians who still speak the ancient tongue of Quechua. To the east of Machu Picchu is the old Incan capital of Cusco, an archaeological honey pot. Share in the excitement as you explore the ancient city streets, still lined with Inca-built stone walls.

Peru has plenty to offer the adventurous spirit. Trekking and mountaineering are favourite pastimes in the dry season; while the most popular hike is the Inca Trail which, if completed, will take you three days. Whitewater rafting is also an option, and, if you're feeling in the mood, try the local Inca delicacy – roast guinea pig.

Information & Reservations
UK 0870 606 1296
INT. +44 870 606 1296

Hotel Monasterio

Calle Palacio 136
Plazoleta Nazarenas
Cusco
Peru

✈ Cusco Airport 5km

tel +51 84 24 1777
fax +51 84 23 7111

www.orient-express.com

Member of:
The Leading Hotels of the World

High in the Andes, perched more than 11,000ft above sea level, lies the Inca city of Cusco and, within it, the magnificent Hotel Monasterio.

As the name suggests, it was built as a monastery in 1592 on the site of the Inca Amaru Qhala Palace. It was given a royal seal of approval back in 1692 and only became a hotel four years ago. Now managed by the exclusive Orient Express hotel group, this is a jewel from which to explore the land of the Incas and the ancient ruins of Machu Picchu. The hotel reflects the ancestry of the city with its Cusco Baroque architectural style and provides an oasis of peace and calm.

It has 105 guest rooms, 16 junior suites and a presidential suite all combining modern and colonial Spanish styles while first floor rooms have particular flair and open on to airy galleries.

The ornate Chapel of San Antonio Abad is available for weddings while the vaulted Tupay Restaurant is perfect for receptions or for intimate candlelit dinners for two.

Head north to the ancient Inca citadel of Machu Picchu to the Sanctuary Lodge – one of the only hotels within the boundaries of the sanctuary itself. Set in its own gardens overlooking the deep valley, the Lodge offers 32 character rooms and suites.

41

🧳 US$135-270 (111)

🛏 US$270-320 (12)

🍽 US$5-28

☕ included

🍾💍

Honeymoon specials
Flowers, fruit, one bottle of Peruvian champagne.

Sightseeing and leisure
The ancient ruins of Machu Picchu can be reached via a three-hour train journey or a short, spectacular helicopter trip from Cusco. Also worth exploring is Sacsayhuanan and the Cusco historical centre.

key to hotels

Antigua & Barbuda
1   Galley Bay, St John's, Antigua
2   Siboney Beach Club, St John's, Antigua
3   St James's Club, Mamora Bay, Antigua
4   Palmetto Beach Hotel, Barbuda

Barbados
5   Colony Club Hotel, St James
6   Glitter Bay, St James
7   Royal Pavilion, St James

Bermuda
8   Cambridge Beaches, Sandys
9   Horizons & Cottages, Paget
10 Waterloo House, Pitts Bay

Grenada
11 Secret Harbour Resort, St George

Guadeloupe
12 Le Meridien La Cocoteraie,
    St Francois

Jamaica
13 Couples Negril
14 Couples Ocho Rios
15 Half Moon Golf, Tennis & Beach Club,
    Montego Bay
16 Swept Away, Negril
17 Trident Villas & Hotel, Port Antonio

Nevis & St Kitts
18 The Hermitage, Gingerland, Nevis
19 Montpelier Plantation, Nevis
20 Ottley's Plantation, Basseterre, St Kitts

St Barts
21 Hotel Guanahani, Anse Grand Cul de Sac

St Lucia
22 Mago Estate Hotel, Soufrière

St Martin
23 La Samanna, Marigot

St Vincent & The Grenadines
24 Palm Island

Tobago
25 Blue Waters Inn, Speyside

42

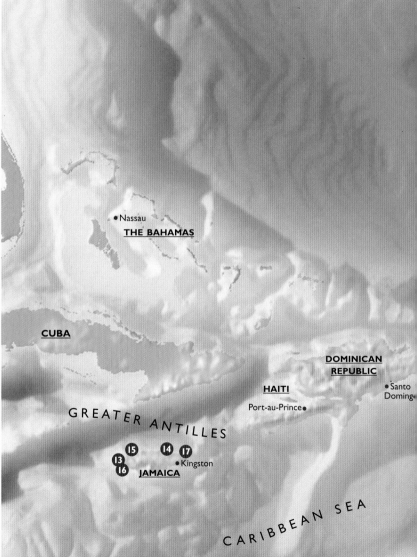

Nassau

THE BAHAMAS

CUBA

DOMINICAN
REPUBLIC

Santo
Domingo

HAITI

Port-au-Prince

GREATER ANTILLES

15 14 17

13

Kingston

16 JAMAICA

CARIBBEAN SEA

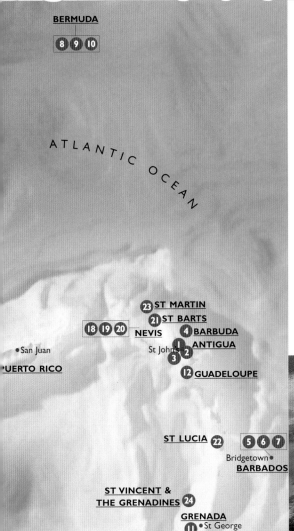

BERMUDA
⑧ ⑨ ⑩

ATLANTIC OCEAN

㉓ **ST MARTIN**
㉑ **ST BARTS**
⑱ ⑲ ⑳ **NEVIS**   ④ **BARBUDA**
                    St John's ① **ANTIGUA**
•San Juan   ③ ②
PUERTO RICO
                    ⑫ **GUADELOUPE**

ST LUCIA ㉒   ⑤ ⑥ ⑦
            Bridgetown •
            BARBADOS

ST VINCENT &
THE GRENADINES ㉔

GRENADA
⑪ •St George

TOBAGO ㉕

The Caribbean is the world's most popular honeymoon destination by far – and so it should be...

Here you are bombarded by intense sensations – the sweet flavours of ripened fruits, the fragrance of jasmine in the night air, the impossibly bright plumage of a scarlet ibis and music played loudly, everywhere.

You can dive in crystal seas to a glittering extravaganza of colourful corals and tropical fish, take an unforgettable trip on a catamaran, feel the surge of a windsurfer beneath you as you race off on the trade winds, or simply lie back and absorb the sun's warmth.

The region is an extraordinary melting pot of cultures including Parisian chic, English country churches, American-style cable television and large cruising cars, Hindu prayer flags, Moslem minarets and the spirit of Africa.

In places it can be difficult to find an isolated beach, and would-be island-hoppers should plan their route with care. Elsewhere there are sugary, quiet beaches from paradise, and certainly some of the most romantic and exclusive resorts to visit in the world.

43

Antigua & Barbuda

The largest of the Leeward Islands, Antigua is famous for cricket matches, yachting parties, soft manners and gentle shores, and of course rum parties and soaring frigate birds.

And it is one of the prettiest. Within the sweeping curves of bays on the protected shores of the Caribbean Sea, gentle wave action on the reefs has pushed up miles of blinding white sand. Between the main beaches there are any number of small coves, and reefs on all sides with plenty of wrecks to dive.

In Antigua's capital, St John's, many of the old wood and stone buildings with overhanging balconies remain, and traditional West Indian life can still be seen – in the chaos of the market, and by the water where fishermen mend their nets. And at English Harbour, a pretty enclave in the southeast, Nelson's Dockyard is a centre for tourism and yachting that is touristy but nevertheless charming.

In the 18th century the island bristled with forts and fortlets, and today many visitors enjoy rooting around the ruins, now 15 feet deep in scrub, and taking in the glorious views for which the forts were originally built.

Yachting is a big activity, with a major regatta at the end of the winter season that attracts sailors from everywhere, and is a good excuse for a 'jump-up'.

Barbuda's great attractions are marine life and beaches. The contours of the island are even gentler than Antigua's, and the pace of life slower. There are a few sights, but a visit to Codrington Lagoon to see thousands of frigate birds from a boat in amongst the mangroves is quite an experience.

flying time
London: 8 hrs
Miami: 3 hrs
NY: 4 hrs

climate
Warm year-round with temperatures from 20°-25°C.

when to go
Apr for regattas, July for carnival, Oct for the jazz festival.

currency
Eastern Caribbean dollar, fixed to the US dollar. Life can be expensive; the government raises taxes through sales of food and goods.

language
English

getting around
Daily flights to the other islands. No scheduled boat services and few local buses, but an abundance of taxis, bicycles, hire cars. Rent a 4-wheel-drive to venture off main routes.

45

Information & Reservations
UK 0870 606 1296
INT. +44 870 606 1296

Galley Bay

Five Islands
Antigua

✈ VC Bird Int. 25 mins

tel +561 994 4733
fax +561 994 9597

UK reservations:
tel +44 (0) 1244 355300
fax +44 (0) 1244 355309

res@palmislandresorts.com
www.palmislandresorts.com

46

First discovered in 1964, Galley Bay is an enchanting hideaway where casual island life and luxury exist in perfect harmony. This elegant resort is a mix of West Indian charm and Gauguin-inspired Tahitian architecture, situated on a perfect white sand beach. All rooms overlook the sparkling, turquoise sea and reflect the splendour of their natural surroundings.

The huge baths and showers provide plenty of opportunities for indulgence and the patios and balconies are the ideal spot to relax in complete privacy. You could even choose to stay in one of the stunning thatched-roof cottages, which capture the essence of Gauguin's Polynesian legacy.

Start your evenings with cocktails in the lounge to the soft rhythm of a steel band before heading to the Sea Grape restaurant, with its dramatic beachfront location. Revel in the sumptuous dishes, brimming with the exotic flavours of the Caribbean while enjoying impeccable service.

Spend the days soaking up the sun and seclusion on the three-quarter-mile stretch of beach, or take to the sea for some sailing, kayaking or snorkelling. And if you need a break from the beach, take a plunge in the swimming pool that appears to have grown naturally out of the Caribbean landscape.

🛏 US$520-860* (70)

🛏 US$730-1,010* (16)

🍽 included

☕ included

🍾 💿 🚶 Ⓢ (incl)

Honeymoon specials
Champagne, flowers and a complimentary boat trip.

* All inclusive per night for two people.

Sightseeing and leisure
Beauty salon, fitness centre, tennis court on property. Ten minutes from downtown shopping market and the attractions of Shirley Heights, Nelson's Dockyard and Devil's Bridge. Also, Cedar Valley Golf Course is just 15 minutes away.

Siboney Beach Club

Information & Reservations
UK 0870 606 1296
INT. +44 870 606 1296

PO Box 222
St John's
Antigua

✈ VC Bird Int. 10km

tel +268 462 0806
fax +268 462 3356

www.caribbeanhighlights.com/
siboney
siboney@candw.ag

Tour operators:
UK Unique Hotels
US Go Go

"How pleasant it would be," wrote the naturalist Charles Darwin, "to pass one's life in such quiet abodes." In Antigua, it is not only the fittest that have survived but the most beautiful as well. Brightly-coloured papaya, mangoes and guava abound, growing under flamboyant trees and palms, and amidst this miniature jungle beside a sheltered mile of white sand and emerald waters is the intimate Siboney Beach Club.

Suites are individually decorated in rich, earthy colours and furnished with tropical prints, comfortable sofas and king-size beds. Balconies afford glimpses of the Caribbean through a profusion of palm fronds and bougainvillea.

The food is a riot of colour and taste and attests to the Antiguan proverb 'Better man belly bust than good food waste'. Delicious concoctions of fresh lobster and seafood, spicy curries, thick steaks, bright salads, baby back ribs and even Conch Fritters are available at the Coconut Grove on the water's edge and at other nearby restaurants.

Weddings are easily arranged. Couples can exchange vows barefoot in the sand or, for a more formal ceremony, at the Siboney Beach Club itself. Wedding extras can include anything from cake and champagne to steel pan soloist.

47

 US$130-190* (1)

 US$160-310* (12)

|◌| US$11.50-30

US$6.50-9.50

Honeymoon specials
Welcome cocktail, bottle of wine and flowers in suite, car to St John's for shopping, use of snorkels, mask, beach lounges and towels, plus full day of sailing. Or an evening of revelry, dancing with the steelband at Shirley Heights with transport and dinner included. Packages cost from US$1,085* per couple for a seven-night stay.
* Prices subject to 18.5% gratuity and government tax.

Sightseeing and leisure
Sailing, scuba diving, snorkelling, golf, tennis, windsurfing, fitness club, cycling. Also, trips to Nelson's Dockyard, Devil's Bridge, Betty's Hope, Redcliffe Quay, Museum of Antigua and Barbuda, English Harbour, Jolly Harbour and Indian Town. Antigua sailing week takes place in April.

Information & Reservations
UK 0870 606 1296
INT. +44 870 606 1296

PO Box 63
Mamora Bay
Antigua

✈ VC Bird Int. 12 miles

tel +561 994 4733
fax +561 994 9597

UK reservations:
tel +44 (0) 1244 355300
fax +44 (0) 1244 355309

res@palmislandresorts.com
www.palmislandresorts.com

48

St James's Club

If it's glitz and glamour that compels, the world-class St James's Club on the southeastern coast of Antigua is the hotspot for you. Classy, but fun and unpretentious, this colourful resort will cater to your every whim. Set on a 100-acre private peninsula, with swaying coconut palms and glorious bougainvillea of every hue, St James's Club has two beaches as well as a full-service marina, providing the ultimate Caribbean holiday with all the trimmings.

Wake to the gentle lapping of waves, as the scent of frangipani wafts through your window on trade winds. Spend balmy days on the beach or riding on horseback through the densely wooded landscape.

Take a swim in the clear, azure waters, windsurf in stunning Mamora Bay, or paddle idly in the protected cove from the comfort of a little ocean kayak or paddle boat.

Should the sun, sea and sand become too much for you, rejuvenate at the luxurious spa or seek refuge in one of St James's fabulous restaurants, offering you the finest epicurean treasures.

As night falls, a thousand glimmering lights are reflected at the water's edge and the resort really comes alive. Spend exhilarating evenings at the casino, or dance the night away at the glittering Jacaranda night club.

US$235-740 (113)

US$530-1,650 (73 villas)

US$10-50

US$10-30

Honeymoon specials
Champagne, flowers and complimentary boat trip.

Sightseeing and leisure
Beauty salon and spa on property, as well as horseback riding and fantastic walks. 18-hole Cedar Valley golf course 40 minutes away. English Harbour, Shirley Heights and Nelson's Dockyard are among some of the splendid sights of Antigua.

Palmetto Beach Hotel

Information & Reservations
UK 0870 606 1296
INT. +44 870 606 1296

Palmetto Point
Barbuda

✈ Codrington 6km

tel/fax +268 460 0440

info@palmettohotel.com
www.palmettohotel.com

The island of Barbuda lies within the Antilles in the Caribbean Sea, just 27 miles north of Antigua. Here you'll find 108sq miles of wild, untouched paradise, and the tranquil Palmetto Beach Hotel, which occupies one of the loveliest spots in the Caribbean. The pace of life is easy here, and the hotel's welcoming, laid-back approach and intimate atmosphere ensure an unforgettable holiday.

The azure-coloured sea is the focal attraction on Barbuda. There are stunning coral reefs to explore, watersports and deep sea fishing on offer. If you want to stay on the beach, the hotel benefits from 11 miles of sparkling, pristine white sand, where you can spend days basking in the warm sun and hardly see another person. If it's privacy you desire, you will certainly find it on Barbuda – although the friendly, inviting clubhouse is a good way to socialise with other guests.

The comfortable suites are stocked with every comfort and amenity you could require. Take in the spectacular views from your own private verandah, and be sure to enjoy a delicious Mediterranean meal – prepared specially by the hotel's Italian chef – either inside or outdoors by the pool overlooking the sparkling sea. The perfect end to another perfect day!

49

 US$160-210* (22)

 US$260-310* (2)

 included

 included

Honeymoon specials
Villa upgrade upon availability plus excursion with romantic lunch on the beach.

* Prices are fullboard but exclusive of 18.5% service & government tax.

Sightseeing and leisure
Local activities include tennis and volleyball. There is also snorkelling, scuba diving, windsurfing and horseriding. The great long pink beach is a must; and there are daily excursions by boat to the barrier reef and caves. Plus, deep sea fishing and visits to the bird sanctuary.

Barbados

flying time
London: 3¹/₂ hrs by
Concorde, or
8 hrs by jet
LA: 9¹/₂ hrs
Miami: 3¹/₂ hrs
NY: 4¹/₂ hrs

**climate/
when to go**
You can visit the
island any time,
but May-June and
Oct-Nov are wet
seasons with fewer
festivals and regattas.

currency
Barbados dollar,
fixed to US dollar.

language
English

getting around
There are frequent
air and sea services
to other islands. On
Barbados use the
friendly local buses
or taxis. Car hire is
expensive.

Barbados stands alone, out in the azure Atlantic, about a hundred miles beyond the rest of the Eastern Caribbean islands.

It's a small coral island with some of the finest golden sandy beaches anywhere and a most agreeable climate. The island is long established as a winter getaway, and its famous west coast, second home to a crowd of international celebrities and sophisticates, has given it the nickname 'millionaires' playground'.

The island's decidedly British heritage has left a delightful and often old-fashioned charm in its manners, buildings and even its language. (You can hear distinct traces of a West Country accent in Bajan speech.) Gorgeous and very well-preserved plantation houses stand in swathes of sugar-cane, cricketers in whites play beneath palm trees. In the thriving capital of Bridgetown, grand old colonial structures with filigree metal balconies jostle happily with glass-fronted shops and offices.

Festivals are big here, and the highlight is Cropover, held every August (the crop being sugar-cane). This is a major blow-out with calypso-singing, steel band music and carnival bands made up of hundreds of costumed players who strut to soca music. There is also a jazz festival in early January, while the Holetown Festival (in Feb) celebrates the first settlement of the island in 1627 with a week of exhibitions and jamborees.

Colony Club Hotel

Information & Reservations
UK 0870 606 1296
INT. +44 870 606 1296

Porters, St James
Barbados

✈ Grantley Adams 35km

Tel +246 422 2335
Fax +246 422 0667

UK contact:
Tel +44 (020) 7910 8240
Fax +44 (020) 7910 8248

Tour operators:
UK British Airways Holidays, Kuoni
US Liberty GoGo, Travel Impressions

Member of:
Elegant Hotels Group

One of the Caribbean's premier hotels, Colony Club is set in seven acres of resplendent gardens on the famous platinum coast of Barbados, shaded by coconut palms and cooled by the waters of four twisting freshwater lagoons.

Once a gentleman's club, today the hotel is the epitome of sophisticated elegance. With breathtaking views of the turquoise seas, Colony Club's facilities are unrivalled. Here, you have state-of-the-art sports equipment and complimentary activities from waterskiing to catamaran sailing, windsurfing to tennis. Horseriding along the beach and even a submarine tour can be arranged.

Impeccable service complements award-winning cuisine. Dine in the Laguna restaurant, which stretches two stories high, and sample both international and Caribbean fare. Or choose Colony's *à la carte* restaurant, the Orchid Room, and three cocktail bars which provide refreshments Caribbean-style. Or you may choose to take the complimentary day-time water taxi to make use of one of Colony's sister hotels on the island.

Colony Club is a popular choice for weddings and honeymoons alike. The hotel's own wedding co-ordinator is more than happy to deliver and meet your every expectation.

51

US$140-340* (64)

US$167-384* (34)

US$55-65

US$15-22

Honeymoon specials
Tropical flowers and bottle of sparkling wine on arrival. Champagne breakfast served on balcony, romantic dinner with photos of the evening. Special gift from hotel. Luxury and Ultimate Wedding Packages available, please enquire for further information.
* Prices quoted are per person per night, based on double occupancy. Half board or room only available.

Sightseeing and leisure
Waterskiing, sailing, snorkelling, windsurfing, tennis, fitness centre, golf, biking, horseriding, deep sea fishing, shopping tours, helicopter tours, submarine tours, and trips to neighbouring Caribbean islands.

Glitter Bay

Information & Reservations
UK 0870 606 1296
INT. +44 870 606 1296

Porters
St James
Barbados

✈ Grantley Adams 12 miles

tel +246 422 5555
fax +246 422 3940

reserve@rpv.cphotels.com
www.fairmont.com

The aptly named Glitter Bay lies on the west coast of Barbados within 19 acres of lush, tropical private gardens – a veritable oasis on this jewel of Caribbean islands. The former home of shipping magnate Sir Edward Cunard, who regularly entertained a dazzling array of celebrities here, this beautiful hotel still retains an air of gracious living and refined charm.

The tone is relaxed and friendly but definitely one of sophistication. Modelled on the family palazzo in Venice, the beach house on this Platinum Coast is now Glitter Bay's reception, while guests stay in delightful Andulacian-style accommodation,

with snow-white stucco walls and Spanish red clay roofs lending a warm, old-world atmosphere.

Every room has a private balcony, many with stunning views of the sparkling white sands and glittering azure sea. Cool terracotta floors, tropical fabrics, elegant rattan furniture and gently whirring ceiling fans complete the colonial feel, and you can even take traditional afternoon tea, as well as indulge in many other culinary pleasures. So enticing is the romantic allure, you might feel you never want to leave the magnificent hotel grounds, but tear yourself away and you'll find much to amaze and delight you on this charming island.

 US$255-600* (26)

 US$280-750* (36)

 US$20-61

 US$20-30

Honeymoon specials
Complimentary bottle of champagne and floral arrangements in room on arrival. Room upgrade subject to availability.

Plus 10% service charge and 7.5% tax to be added.

Sightseeing and leisure
The hotel offers tennis and a fitness and massage centre. Championship golf is available at the nearby Royal Westmoreland club. All watersports, such as sailing, windsurfing, waterskiing and snorkelling are complimentary. Nearby attractions include St James parish church, the Sugar Machine Museum and Folkestone Underwater Park and Museum.

Information & Reservations
UK 0870 606 1296
INT. +44 870 606 1296

Royal Pavilion

St James
Barbados

✈ Grantley Adams 12 miles

tel +246 422 5555
fax +246 422 3940

reserve@rpv.cphotels.com
www.royalpavilion.com

Located in the parish of St James, overlooking a half-mile stretch of pink and white beach on the stunning west coast of Barbados, the Royal Pavilion has everything you could possibly need for that perfect Caribbean getaway.

From the moment you drive down the avenue of majestic royal palms and get your first glimpse of the Pavilion – a magnificent building of the palest rose which rises above the gardens of lily and bougainvillea – it will seem impossible to tear yourself away. All of the magnificent guest rooms, decorated in the vibrant colours of the Caribbean, have awesome views across the limitless azure sea and sky. Set in 30 acres of stunning tropical gardens, facilities include a swimming pool, restaurant, cafe, exclusive boutiques, tennis courts, an extensive watersport centre and of course the glorious Caribbean beach for you to soak up the sun.

The Palm Terrace restaurant, with breathtaking views of the ocean, serves tantalising food, a fantastic fusion of exotic Caribbean flavours and fine, classic cuisine.

And for the golfers among you, the renowned Royal Westmoreland Golf Club, designed by Robert Trent Jones Jnr, is close by and welcomes all hotel guests.

53

Honeymoon specials
Free champagne and flowers in room on arrival.
Honeymoon packages available.

Sightseeing and leisure
Many natural wonders including Harrisons Cave, Welchman Hall Gully, Flower Forest, Barbados Wildlife Reserve, Farley Hill National Park and numerous historic homes and churches. Watersports, tennis and beauty salon on site. Royal Westmoreland and Sandy Bay Golf Clubs nearby. Fitness centre at sister hotel next door.

US$280-750 (75)

US$20-61

US$20-30

Bermuda

flying time
London: 7 hrs
Miami: 3-4 hrs
NY: 2 hrs

climate
Summers (May-Oct) can be hot and humid. Winters are quite mild.

when to go
For watersports the summer months are best. Golf and riding are best enjoyed in spring and autumn. In June of alternate (even-numbered) years go for the great Newport to Bermuda Ocean Yacht Race.

currency
Bermuda dollar, on a par with the US dollar.

getting around
Distances are small, and buses and taxis abound. Visitors hire bicycles and mopeds rather than cars. For a romantic jaunt, there is no better way to see Hamilton than from a horse-drawn surrey with a fringe on top.

A sub-tropical paradise set in the warm Atlantic some 600 miles off America's east coast, Bermuda actually comprises a 21-mile curve of linked islands.

Blessed with lush green countryside, a profusion of colourful flowering shrubs and beautiful beaches of fine coral-pink sand, Bermuda is a special place indeed.

Discovered by Spanish mariner Juan de Bermudez in 1503, the islands were claimed in England's name in 1609 and remain English speaking and loyal to Britain to this day. Their proximity to North America has given them a New World feel and made them a popular cruise ship destination, while the mild climate, safe environment, top hotels and excellent sports facilities continue to attract many repeat visitors.

History buffs will love St George's Town, the island's first capital. A stroll through the narrow streets is a walk back in time. At the other end of the islands visit Gibbs Hill Lighthouse, which affords wonderful sweeping views across the whole archipelago.

And be sure not to miss Scaur Hill Fort Park, with its 19th-century fortress and the old Royal Navy Dockyard, beautifully restored and now one of Bermuda's main attractions.

Cambridge Beaches

Information & Reservations
UK 0870 606 1296
INT. +44 870 606 1296

30 Kings Point
Sandys MA 02
Bermuda

✈ Bermuda Int. 35km

Tel +441 234 0331
Fax +441 234 3352

cambeach@ibl.bm
www.cambridgebeaches.com

Tour operators:
UK Elegant Resorts
Caribbean Connection

This elegant cottage colony, situated at the western end of Bermuda on a stunning 25-acre peninsula and surrounded by five private, soft pink, sandy beaches, is the perfect romantic getaway.

Individually decorated rooms and suites offer privacy and comfort and include balcony or terrace. Many have spectacular ocean views.

Award-winning gourmet cuisine can be enjoyed in a variety of settings, both indoor and outdoor. Afternoon tea is served daily at four o'clock in the Clubhouse. For a truly magical evening, guests can dine *al fresco* beneath the stars on the beautiful Mangrove Bay Terrace.

The resort offers a wealth of activities and all watersports imaginable. Guests can choose to take a private shuttle to Hamilton, Bermuda's charming capital, for a day's shopping, or simply escape to one of the many beaches and coves which provide romantic, secluded locations for swimming, sunbathing and snorkelling. And don't miss the European Health Spa.

This is also an absolutely ideal setting for both weddings and receptions for up to 50 guests. These can be arranged by the hotel and take place on the grass terraces or in the lounge overlooking picturesque Mangrove Bay.

55

 US$280-585* (62)

US$420-680* (19)

included

included

Honeymoon specials
Heart and Soul Honeymoon package includes six nights deluxe accommodation, breakfast, afternoon tea and dinner, fruit basket and champagne on arrival, double moped for a day, sunset sailing trip, personalised photo, massages, use of all facilities. Price: $445 extra per couple. Wedding packages are also available for an additional $2,200 per couple.
Plus gratuities of $16pppn and 11.25% tax & surcharge.

Sightseeing and leisure
Ferry excursions to Hamilton. Visits to historic dockyard, maritime museum, arts and crafts centre and galleries. Private beaches, pool, croquet, tennis, marina, reef snorkelling. Moped and bicycle hire is also available. European solarium and spa with a range of treatments, sauna, steamroom. Access to nearby golf courses, deep sea fishing and scuba diving.

Horizons & Cottages

Information & Reservations
UK 0870 606 1296
INT. +44 870 606 1296

33 South Road
Paget PG04
Bermuda

✈ Bermuda Int. 15km

tel +441 236 0048
fax +441 236 1981

www.bermudasbest.com
horizons@ibl.bm

Member of:
Relais & Châteaux

56

As its name suggests, Horizons & Cottages is famed for its views, sitting on a hilltop with panoramic vistas of the countryside and ocean beyond. One of the oldest plantation estates in Bermuda and a Relais & Châteaux member, the hotel was originally owned by the Middleton family, made famous by Captain Lewis Middleton who saved the Turks Islands from the French and Spaniards in 1710.

The Horizons' house itself is typical Bermudian architecture with whitewashed keystone corners, knee-high cedar fireplaces and tray ceilings.

Outside guests can enjoy 25 acres of rolling lawns and beautifully landscaped, stylish gardens.

Horizons has its own nine-hole golf course, three tennis courts and a swimming pool.

All the rooms and cottages are air conditioned and some bathrooms are equipped with private jacuzzi. And of course all the rooms have their own individual stunning views.

With the emphasis on personal service, guests can dine on the terrace during the summer months enjoying uninterrupted sea views and step inside to the warmth of open log fires in the stonewashed dining room in the winter. And those staying in one of the cottages even get their cooked breakfast prepared fresh right in their own kitchen.

 US$360-470* (45)

 US$545-735* (3)

🍽 included

☕ included

Honeymoon specials

Seven-day package includes accommodation for two, full English breakfast, afternoon tea, dinner, champagne on arrival, cocktail party, tennis, golf, use of freshwater pool, privileges at the exclusive Coral Beach & Tennis Club across the road with luxurious fitness facilities, European spa and private beach. From US$2,532 inclusive of taxes.
* Room rates subject to 17.25% government & service taxes.

Sightseeing and leisure

Own mashie golf course, putting green, freshwater pool, tennis, fitness facilities with personal trainer, newly-opened European spa, private beach, watersports, plus championship golf courses nearby. Around the island are the beautiful pink sands of the South Shore beaches, Gibbs Hill Lighthouse, St George's, Dockyard, Aquarium. There are also festivals, pro golf & tennis tournaments and sailing events throughout the year.

Waterloo House

Information & Reservations
UK 0870 606 1296
INT. +44 870 606 1296

00 Pitts Bay Road
Hamilton
Bermuda

✈ Bermuda Int. 15km

Tel +441 295 4480
Fax +441 295 2585

waterloo@ibl.bm
www.bermudasbest.com

Member of:
Relais & Châteaux

Colonial elegance is the hallmark of this historic hotel, which sits in four acres of terraced gardens right on Hamilton Harbour.

One of only two Relais & Châteaux properties in Bermuda, the hotel dates back to 1815 when it was built as a sumptuous manor house. Today it retains the elegance of days gone by and is filled with fine antiques and elaborate soft furnishings, while providing the very latest in amenities to ensure every visit is truly luxurious.

Known around the world for its fine cuisine, the hotel offers the choice between the relaxing waterside Poinciana Terrace, where diners can enjoy stunning views of the bustling harbour, or the more formal, but magnificent, Wellington Room.

As a waterfront hotel, the choice of sports is excellent, varying from charter deep sea fishing boats to windsurfing or swimming in the hotel's sparkling freshwater pool.

But for romantic beach picnics, take advantage of the hotel's private launch which will ferry you to uninhabited and unspoilt islands that surround Bermuda, or spend the evening aboard for a cocktail cruise with beautiful sunset views.

57

 US$280-410* (20)

 US$420-700* (10)

US$45-55

included

Honeymoon specials

Seven-day package incl. accommodation for two, full English breakfast, afternoon tea, airport transfers, welcome gift for bride, champagne on arrival, cocktail party, one day free tennis or golf, picnic lunch, use of pool, privileges at the exclusive Coral Beach & Tennis Club with luxurious fitness facilities, European spa & private beach. From US$2,216 incl. taxes.
* Room rates subject to 17.25% government & service taxes.

Sightseeing and leisure

Freshwater pool, Har-Tru tennis courts, putting green, fitness facilities with personal trainer, newly-opened European spa, private beach, watersports, championship golf courses nearby. Shopping, historical sites, private launch for harbour cruises or champagne cruises to secluded islands. South Shore beaches & Gibbs Hill Lighthouse. There are also pro golf & tennis tournaments, festivals and sailing events throughout the year.

Grenada

flying time
Direct to Port
Salines or via St
Lucia, Trinidad or
the Bahamas
London: 8-9 hrs
Miami: 3-4 hrs
NY: 4-5 hrs

**climate/
when to go**
Warm, constant
temperatures all
year. Travel in Aug
for Carnival and the
island's most lively
sailing regatta.

currency
Eastern Caribbean
dollar, fixed to the
US dollar.

language
English

getting around
Local buses, taxis,
ferries and island-
hopping planes offer
frequent services.
Hiring a car is a
good way to see
the island if you are
prepared to brave
the somewhat
erratic roads.

Grenada, in the far south of the Windward Islands, is typical of this chain of islands in its tropical beauty.

It has excellent beaches and the capital, St George's, is the prettiest harbour town in the whole Caribbean. Set in a massive volcanic bowl, its slopes dotted with red-tiled roofs that descend to the edge of the way, where yachts and old-fashioned schooners have long lined the waterfront. In the valleys of the interior there are large fruit and spice plantations.

Grenada sees a steady stream of tourists to its broad range of hotels. The nightlife is generally pretty quiet, but most hotels and restaurants have bars and there are clubs that attract a young crowd. The island is also well positioned for exploring the Grenadines, by yacht, ferry and island-hopping plane.

Information & Reservations
UK 0870 606 1296
INT. +44 870 606 1296

Secret Harbour Resort

Lance aux Epines
St George's
Grenada

✈ Point Saline 10km

tel +473 444 4439
fax +473 444 4819

www.secretharbour.com

Tour operators:
UK Hayes & Jarvis
US Go Go Tours

The hideaway resort of Secret Harbour is tucked into a tropical hillside overlooking Mount Hartman Bay on the island of Grenada. This is an island of outstanding natural beauty with stunning mountain vistas, cascading waterfalls that invite bathers, palm-fringed beaches and picturesque harbours.

The rooms retain the Mediterranean influence of the early explorers and feature four-poster beds, sunken sitting rooms, vaulted brick ceilings, and sumptuous bathrooms with Italian-tiled tubs. French windows lead out onto private balconies with views overlooking the ocean, dotted with sailing boats, and the busy little harbour.

Guests can dine *al fresco* at the restaurant, with Moorish arches framing the ocean views, or relax casually at the poolside terrace restaurant.

There are a wealth of activities on offer from windsurfing along the shores of the private beach to the new PADI five-star dive operation on site. The resort also offers excursions to local islands on skippered or self-skippered yachts, and can arrange 'Sail and Stay' packages combining four days on a yacht with three days at the resort.

Wedding ceremonies are also staged under a rustically tiled archway with a canopy of local flowers, or at one of the village churches.

59

  US$130-230* (20)

US$14-30

US$8-14

Honeymoon specials
Sparkling wine or champagne in room on arrival. Room upgrade subject to availability. Wedding packages available.

* Rates subject to 18% government & service taxes.

Sightseeing and leisure
Waterfalls, mountains and beaches. Annual carnival and sailing festivals. Trips to daily farmer's market. Tennis and watersports including sailing, kayaking and windsurfing. Fitness centre and beauty salon, plus 9-hole golf course nearby. Also, private beach and swimming area.

Guadeloupe

flying time
London: 9 hrs
NY: 3 hrs

**climate/
when to go**
A tropical climate
tempered by trade
winds; very similar
year-round. It can
get busy during
summer months.

currency
French franc,
although US dollars
are also accepted.

language
French but English
is widely spoken.

getting around
A variety of links
via sea plane and
ferries. Local bus
services are good.

Legend has it that when Christopher Columbus first glimpsed Guadeloupe, he placed the island in a casket to be presented to the king and queen of Spain.

The island's romantic history continued when it was used as a base for 16th-century pirates to store their cargoes of rum and sea-booty. Since that time, this jewel of the French Caribbean has developed into a thoroughly modern, chic and, above all, thoroughly French tropical playground. Sun, sea, surf and of course champagne combine deliciously in these extravagant fantasy islands to produce an exciting and unique mix of cultures and nationalities.

The Gallic influence is overt: shops are filled with Lacroix and Givenchy, *boules* is played in dusty town squares, and bakeries provide a daily supply of *baguettes* and *croissants*. And under-pinning all this is a Caribbean sensibility. Leisure and pleasure are actively pursued – sunbathing, snorkelling and windsurfing throughout the day, dining and dancing all night.

Guadeloupe also abounds in natural beauty. Lush vegetation frames the waterfalls and rivers. Norfolk pines and great ferns surround the sleepy towns where fresh sea breezes gently rock the boats moored by the wharf. Numerous little restaurants serve up fantastic local produce like breadfruit, plaintains, congo peas and salted pork to create the rich and wonderful Creole cuisine for which the region is justly famous.

Le Meridien La Cocoteraie

Information & Reservations
UK 0870 606 1296
INT. +44 870 606 1296

Avenue de L'Europe
97118 St Francois
Guadeloupe

✈ Pôle Caraibes 30km

tel +590 887 981
fax +590 887 833

cocoteraie@wanadoo.fr
www.antilles-info-tourisme.com/
guadeloupe/coco.htm

Nestled between one of the most beautiful lagoons on Guadeloupe and the impressive golf course designed by Robert Trent Jones, La Cocoteraie combines the charm of a colonial habitation with the luxury of a first-class hotel.

Each of the suites is exquisitely decorated in typical Creole style. The bathrooms are spacious with hexagonal-shaped, raised baths offering magnificent views of the sun setting over the lagoon. Bright living rooms give way to flowered terraces overlooking the pool and sea beyond.

At La Varangue restaurant chefs prepare refined and imaginative local specialities based on local produce, such as fish and shellfish freshly landed at the port of Saint Francois.

Sail away on a catamaran, play a round of golf, or just relax in the magnificent swimming pool decorated with Chinese vases while enjoying traditional rum-based cocktails at the Indigo Bar.

The hotel is happy to organise anything from a Corsair party with a steel band or a full-blown carnival party to the rhythm of a *zouk* band, which comes complete with limbo dancers. A sailing excursion discovering the neighbouring island of Petite Terre, will add the finishing touch to a truly unforgettable honeymoon.

61

US$250-1,180 (52)

US$45-90

included

Honeymoon specials
Champagne and flowers in room on arrival, plus complimentary t-shirts and beach bag. Room upgrade subject to availability.

Sightseeing and leisure
18-hole championship golf course designed by Robert Trent Jones, parachuting, windsurfing, swimming, two tennis courts. The hotel also has its own private beach. There is also land and sea sightseeing in Guadeloupe and on four of its neighbouring islands.

Jamaica

flying time
To: Montego
Bay, Kingston
London: 11 hrs
Miami: 1½ hrs
NY: 3½ hrs

**climate/
when to go**
The weather is fairly
perfect (27°C at sea
level, 13°C in the
mountains), with
overcast periods in
winter and rainfall all
year. April is carnival
time; the big reggae
festivals happen in
Feb and Aug.

currency
Jamaican dollar, but
US dollars are widely
accepted, even in
markets.

language
English

getting around
There are regular
internal flights.
Frequent if chaotic
buses; taxis and
minivans abound.
Hire cars are pretty
expensive and not
recommended due
to driving conditions.

Jamaica is one of the liveliest islands, its allure the strongest of all the former British territories.

Physically the island is spectacular. Greenery bursts into life everywhere. You might almost expect a pencil to take root. And the scenery is fantastic; within a few hundred yards of the sea you can be at an altitude of 1,000 feet with stunning mountains all around you.

For the visitor, Jamaica has the most romantic allure of all the Caribbean islands. Neglected stone gateposts and decaying walls of abandoned plantation houses are witness to times when the island was the focus of British dreams, and source of fortunes for the planters.

Noel Coward, Winston Churchill, Ian Fleming and Errol Flynn all fell in love with the place.

There is something for everyone here: humming resorts that specialise in sun, sea, sand and golf, elegant hotels, and huge plantation hideaways that preserve a glorious air of old colonial Jamaica.

The tourist areas are on the north coast, between Negril and Ocho Rios. This is where the beaches and main facilities are, and the liveliest crowds. Be sure to climb Dunns River Falls while you are here. In the west, Negril has all the trappings of a resort, but without the frantic atmosphere. Ocho Rios is more developed, with some outstanding hotels. Close by, there are exotic botanical gardens, and a genuine

Jamaican countryside of steep valleys watered by numerous rivers and falls.

Montego Bay, the tourist capital, is large and busy, with beaches and watersports, and a lively nightlife. The most famous great houses are here; and historic Falmouth, which is site of some of the finest Georgian architecture on the island.

Port Antonio is a charming, dozy town in the far east, the loveliest and most strikingly fertile part of the island. From here you can venture up into the Blue Mountains, a region of spectacular natural beauty.

The capital of Kingston is well worth a visit. Check out the wonderful mayhem of the markets downtown that beat to the pulse of ever-present reggae sounds. This is definitely the Jamaicans' Jamaica – energetic, lively, noisy, and sometimes volatile – so take care.

Information & Reservations
UK 0870 606 1296
INT. +44 870 606 1296

Couples Jamaica

Jamaica

Couples Negril
Norman Manley Blvd
Westmoreland
✈ Montego Bay 55 miles

Couples Ocho Rios
Tower Isle, St Mary
✈ Montego Bay 65 miles

UK contact:
Group Promotions
tel +44 (020) 8795 1718
fax +44 (020) 8795 1728

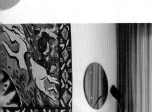

Couples Ocho Rios is Jamaica's original all-inclusive resort, set on 19 acres of breathtaking beachfront. Couples Negril, its sister property, is Jamaica's latest all-inclusive resort located on a seven-mile crescent of white sand beach in Bloody Bay. Both resorts provide the best in all-inclusive luxury with beautifully appointed rooms with balcony or patio overlooking the exotic tropical gardens or sparkling Caribbean Sea.

Special suites also include personal jacuzzis. A wide range of restaurants provide 24-hour food service from gourmet dining in the *à la carte* restaurants to the beachfront grill to ensure your taste buds are constantly tantalised. Wine is served with dinner and all bars serve premium brand drinks.

For sun worshippers, both resorts have the opportunity for *au naturel* sunbathing – at Ocho Rios you can do so on the hotel's very own private island. For the energetic, the facilities are fantastic with state-of-the-art gym, squash, tennis (also lit for night play), cycle tours, golf nearby and horseriding is available at Couples Resort's own equestrian centre. For the more adventurous, pursuits such as scuba diving, sailing and waterskiing are included, and professional instruction is available for all sports.

US$128-230*

US$190-300*

🍽 included

☕ included

Honeymoon specials

Half-hour massage for the bride and groom. Champagne on arrival. Free weddings include ceremony, marriage licence, wedding flowers, two-tier cake, sparkling wine, live music and commemorative t-shirts.

* Rates are per person per night.

Sightseeing and leisure

Excursions are included at both Couples Resorts – catamaran cruise, shopping trips to the local town and plantation tours. Dunn's River Falls is included at Couples Ocho Rios and Rick's Cafe, which is famous for cliff diving at Negril. A free flight between resorts is offered for those wishing to experience both Couples Ocho Rios and Couples Negril.

Half Moon
Golf, Tennis & Beach Club

Information & Reservations
UK 0870 606 1296
INT. +44 870 606 1296

Half Moon PO
Rose Hall
Montego Bay
Jamaica

✈ Donald Sangster 6 miles

tel +876 953 2211
fax +876 953 2731

sales@halfmoonclub.com
www.halfmoon.com.jm

Tour operators:
UK Elegant Resorts, ITC

Located on the northern coast and within easy reach of Montego Bay is the Half Moon club, long renowned as one of the island's finest villa hotels, set amid green hills and nestling behind one of Jamaica's finest crescent-shaped beaches.

The accommodation is simply elegant – all rooms and suites have splendid sea views and are individually designed and decorated in crisp, bright colours and fabrics that reflect the cool, laid-back style of the island and its culture. For those seeking true romance, the villas, with their canopied beds, private pools, and their own gardeners, maids and cooks, are ideal.

A shuttle bus links the villas to the main resort where you can choose from the six gourmet restaurants serving everything from local Caribbean fare with a spicy twist to international dishes such as Japanese and Italian. After dinner, relax to the sounds of calypso bands, sip Jamaican rum at the terrace bar, and end another perfect day with a moonlit stroll along the beach.

Weddings can be arranged in the lush tropical gardens or a gazebo perched right on the edge of the Caribbean. Parties of all kinds are catered for at every stage – from the provision of a marriage officer, to the entertainment and floral decorations.

65

 US$120-145 (145)

US$175-595

US$30-100

US$25

Honeymoon specials
Complimentary welcome bouquet and fruit basket on arrival.

Please note: There are also Royal Villas at Half Moon, prices from US$780 per night. Packages are also available on request.

Sightseeing and leisure
On site is an 18-hole championship golf course and David Leadbetter Golf Academy, tennis courts, squash, horseriding, all watersports, deep sea fishing, swimming, plus health and fitness club with massage, sauna and herbal body wraps. Nearby are sunset cruises along the coast of Montego Bay, tropical bird sanctuary, Dunn's River Falls.

Swept Away Resort

Information & Reservations
UK 0870 606 1296
INT. +44 870 606 1296

PO Box 3077
Long Bay
Negril
Jamaica

✈ Montego Bay 60 miles

tel +876 957 4061
fax +876 957 4060

UK contact:
Group Promotions
tel +44 (0) 20 8795 1718
fax +44 (0) 20 8795 1728

66

As the name suggests, you should be prepared to be swept away into a dream world. This all-inclusive Jamaican resort is set among a stunning tropical botanical garden. The gentle sea breeze through the lush foliage, the melody of the tree frogs at night...the complete serenity of it all will make you believe that modern life no longer exists.

Set in the grounds you'll find a small pool for that quick dip and a large one for swimming laps and plenty of shaded nooks and romantic spots for those special moments.

For dining you can choose between the open air beachside restaurant, the beachside grill and the gourmet Feathers restaurant where you'll sample such local specials as Jamaican pumpkin soup and curry conch with green mango chutney. And there are four bars – all serving premium brand drinks – where you can quench your thirst.

Sports facilities are outstanding as well, with a fully-equipped gym, aerobic studio, 10 floodlit tennis courts, squash and racquetball courts, sailing and scuba diving and more, all with professional instructors on hand. Unlimited golf is also available nearby at Negril Hills.

 US$152-330* (134)

 included

 included

Honeymoon specials

Bottle of champagne on arrival. Half-hour massage for the bride and groom. Weekly honeymoon party.

* Rates are per person per night.

Sightseeing and leisure

Visit Rick's Cafe, a rooftop bar and restaurant, famous for its cliff diving. Massage, beauty salon and spa facilities available on site. A wide range of sporting activities both on land and water.

Information & Reservations
UK 0870 606 1296
INT. +44 870 606 1296

Trident Villas & Hotel

PO Box 119
Port Antonio
Jamaica

✈ Port Antonio 6 miles

tel +876 993 2602
fax +876 993 2960

trident@infochan.com
www.tridentvillas.com

Nestled between the tall blue mountains of Jamaica's lush interior and the palm-fringed sapphire sea, Port Antonio is a photographer's fantasy land, with majestic waterfalls, blue lagoons and winding rivers. It is a place of natural beauty and it's where you'll find the romantic Trident Villas & Hotel.

Trident's 14 gazebo-dotted acres meander along the Jamaican coastline just to the east of Port Antonio. Each of its 27 antique-furnished rooms has uninterrupted views of the sea from their private balconies and verandahs. Large paddle fans reminiscent of a bygone era provide a soft breeze and beautifully accent the cool, soft furnishings.

A trip to Trident will be one of intimacy and relaxation, cultivation and grace. It's perfect for honeymooners and for those wishing to marry in such a place of fine European tradition tempered by the melodic lilt of Jamaica. Breakfast is served in your room or on the dining terrace; and afternoon tea is a daily ritual not to be missed.

Nearby, plan to spend hours on Trident's private beach, or venture a little further and explore the pristine beauty of Reach and Somerset falls. And a visit to Jamaica wouldn't be complete without visiting Noel Coward's house, known as 'Firefly'.

67

 US$220-340 (11)

 US$320-620 (15)

🍽 included

☕ included

Honeymoon specials

Upgrade, breakfast, dinner, private car transfer from Kingston, welcome drink, bottle of Jamaican cologne, complimentary tennis, croquet, snorkelling, plus fruit plate & champagne. There is also a private wedding chapel in the grounds and the hotel can arrange weddings, including a marriage officer, a bottle of champagne, wedding cake, flowers and a photographer to shoot one roll of film.

Sightseeing and leisure

Massages on site; beautician will come to the hotel to tend to nails, hair, etc. Watersports, horseriding on the beach, tennis. Local town of Port Antonio, sightseeing and shopping in Kingston. Rafting on the Rio Grande.

Nevis & St Kitts

flying time
London: 8 hrs
Miami: 3 hrs
NY: 4 hrs

climate
Warm year-round
with temperatures
from 20°-25°C.

when to go
St Kitts: Dec
for Carnival and
Christmas
celebrations.
Nevis: July for the
Carnival parades
and the festivities
of Culturama.

currency
The Eastern
Caribbean dollar,
which is fixed to
the US dollar.

language
English

getting around
Flights to other
islands take place
throughout the day,
but are often fully
booked. The local
inter-island 'bus' is
really a ferry. Taxis
are readily available;
car hire gives you
the most mobility.

St Kitts and Nevis stand side by side, with strikingly beautiful views of one another across a channel just two miles wide. Both are welcoming and laid-back in classic old-Caribbean style and there is a strong and vibrant West Indian culture here.

These two islands share far and away the finest collection of plantation house hotels in the Caribbean. Many are surrounded by sugar cane fields as they were 200 years ago, and they retain the relaxed grace and hospitality of that genteel, intriguing era loved by so many.

St Kitts is the larger of the two islands. In the mountainous northern areas, beaches are mostly of black sand, but in the southern peninsula there are a number of good strips of golden-brown sand, usually deserted.

Nevis was once so illustrious it was known as the Queen of the Caribbees. The 'old-time' elegance of the West Indies is still just about visible in the finely crafted bridges and dark stone walls that poke out of the ever-encroaching jungle.

There is the normal range of watersports on both islands. Most of the diving takes place off Nevis, where there are submarine volcanic vents for explorations as well as the usual reefs. On land, there are excellent hikes into the jungle.

Information & Reservations
UK 0870 606 1296
INT. +44 870 606 1296

The Hermitage

Gingerland
Nevis

✈ Newcastle 10 miles

tel +869 469 3477
fax +869 469 2481

nevherm@caribsurf.com
www.hermitagenevis.com

69

Surrounded by lush rainforest and acres of stone terraces, The Hermitage slumbers peacefully on the island of Nevis. Romance wafts on the air among its pastel cottages scattered among fruit trees, which sway to songbirds by day and a chorus of crickets by night.

This truly is a special place. Every evening, guests congregate for drinks and just when the aroma of local specialities makes its way from the kitchen, two rings of the bell announce the call to dinner, a West Indian tradition that has stood the test of time for many years. You can dine on the verandah of the 250-year-old Great House, with its 18th-century furnishings, or dine *à deux* on the balcony of your very own cottage.

The individual cottages surround the Great House and are designed to catch the prevailing sea breezes. Sprinkled among acres of flowering gardens, the cottages are classic Nevisian Colonial, with beautifully romantic canopy beds and a full range of amenities.

For the more adventurous guests, there's tennis, nature hikes, riding stables and most watersports nearby. But, if relaxation and romance is more your cup of tea, lob yourselves into a hammock strung between a mango and a breadfruit tree, sip on a cocktail and let the trade winds gently rock you. Heavenly.

US$170-790* (7 cottages)

US$50-75

included

Honeymoon specials

Honeymoon Packages available: a seven night stay from Dec 15-April 15 starts at US$2,900 per couple. And from April 16-Dec 14 prices start at US$1,950 per couple for seven nights.

Rates are subject to 18% service charge and taxes.

Sightseeing and leisure

On site there is a tennis court, freshwater pool and sun terrace. You can go trail riding on horseback, take carriage rides through historic Gingerland, nature walks and history hikes through Charlestown and New River Plantation. Rental cars and jeeps are available for self-hire to explore the island. Other activities include the Museum of Nevis History, deep sea fishing, sailing, snorkelling and scuba diving.

Montpelier Plantation Inn

Information & Reservations
UK 0870 606 1296
INT. +44 870 606 1296

Montpelier Estate
Nevis

✈ Newcastle 12 miles

tel +869 469 3462
fax +869 469 2932

montpinn@caribsurf.com
www.montpeliernevis.com

70

Located in the foothills of Nevis, this award-winning hotel – ranked one of the top-10 privately owned and managed hotels worldwide by *Tatler Travel Guide* – offers the ultimate get-away-from-it-all experience. The Inn was created from a historic converted sugar estate and hosted the wedding of Horatio Nelson (later Admiral Lord Nelson) and Fanny Nisbet in 1787.

In splendid seclusion and offering panoramic views at 750 feet above sea level, the 17 rooms are scattered among 10 acres of stunning landscaped gardens. They have all been recently refurbished with fresh tropical-style fabrics and enjoy sea facing views and a patio.

The focal point of the intimate hideaway is The Great House, with the bar, the Western Verandah, and the library and card room for relaxing. Dinner is served on the Western Verandah, with lovely views of the floodlit gardens, the ocean and the distant sparkling lights of St Kitts. Enjoy meals with an imaginative use of local produce, including fresh lobster, fish and organically reared pork.

And for fun in the sun, the hotel will whisk you off to their private three-acre beach with landscaped lawns and flowering trees, sun shelters and a quaint pavilion with tables for intimate barbecue lunches.

 US$210-330 (17)

🍽 US$48-59

☕ included

🍾 💍

Honeymoon specials

Upgrade to four poster premier room, subject to availability. Bottle of champagne and fresh flowers on arrival. Picnic lunch on Montpelier's private and romantic three-acre beach.

Sightseeing and leisure

Tennis court plus professional coach. Scuba diving, deep sea fishing, horseback riding, mountain biking, windsurfing, sailing and rainforest hikes are all available nearby and there is an 18-hole golf course at the Four Seasons resort, which must be pre-booked to ensure availability. Historic tours of the island are available, as are day trips to the neighbouring islands of St Kitts, St Barts and St Martin.

Ottley's Plantation Inn

Information & Reservations
UK 0870 606 1296
INT. +44 870 606 1296

PO Box 345
Basseterre
St Kitts

✈ St Kitts 10km

tel +869 465 7234
fax +869 465 4760

ottleys@caribsurf.com
www.ottleys.com

Tour operators:
UK Elegant Resorts, Kuoni Airwaves
US GoGo Worldwide Tours

Lovingly transformed from the ruins of a 17th-century sugar plantation, Ottley's Plantation Inn has risen from the depths of neglect to the height of beauty. Family run, it snuggles in the foothills of Mount Liamuiga, a dormant volcano surrounded by lush rainforest, tropical gardens and rolling lawns.

Accommodation is in the majestic Great House or one of the stone cottages. The rooms are sensual and cool, decorated in colourful chintzes with polished wooden and wicker furniture. All have a balcony or private patio with spectacular ocean and mountain views. Royal Suites and Supreme rooms in the incomparable new cottages feature jacuzzis and private plunge pools on ocean-view patios.

The award-winning restaurant, The Royal Palm, is set into the old stone walls of the sugar mill, where guests can discover delightful New Island cuisine served in an *al fresco* setting.

Guests can relax by the spring-fed pool sipping rum punches, or venture out onto the cobbled trails of the property's own rainforest ravine – home to some of the island's green vervet monkeys. Enjoy a game of tennis on the new hard surface court or a round of croquet on the newly added croquet lawn. Ottley's provides daily shuttles to two beaches and to Basseterre, the historic capital.

71

 US$225-450 (22)

 US$510-695 (5)

 US$60-70

 included

Honeymoon specials
Seven-night package starting at $2,150 and 10-night package starting at $2,995 are available for direct bookings. Packages include accommodation, some dinners and island activities. Honeymooners choosing either of these will also receive a complimentary 'champagne and flowers welcome'. Wedding packages are also available. Please contact the hotel for details.

Sightseeing and leisure
Visits to Independence Square, where slaves were once sold in the days of the working sugar plantation. Brimstone Hill and the capital, with its West Indian architecture. Batik demonstrations. Carnival in December and music festival in June. Rainforest, volcano and historic tours and hikes. Spa services, swimming and watersports. Golf 20 mins away.

flying time
London: 13-14 hrs
via Antigua
Miami: 3$\frac{1}{2}$ hrs
NY: 4$\frac{1}{2}$ hrs

**climate/
when to go**
There is hardly any
rain here but July
and Aug still have
the best weather.
Temperatures range
from 20°-25°C.
There is a great
music festival in Jan.

72

currency
French franc,
although US dollars
are usually accepted.

language
French, but English is
widely spoken.

getting around
Linked to other
islands by a variety
of plane and sea ser-
vices.

The exclusive and very French St Barts provides an idyllic environment for transient millionaires and glamour-seekers, with glorious sandy beaches and luxury Riviera-style hotels.

At only 10sq miles, St Barts (St Barthélémy) is little more than a pebble in the midst of French Antilles, but for all its Lilliputian proportions it manages to cram a lot in and attests to the maxim that less is more. Steep-sided mountains laden with cactus and fragrant frangipani, a coastline full of rugged cliffs, exceptional beaches and kaleidoscopic panoramas combine to create a feeling of endless variation.

The island's capital and only town, Gustavia, has a harbour as calm as a pool but is lively and welcoming, with a stylish mix of restaurants and nightlife. With a population of mainly French and Swedish origins, St Barts has less of the hot pepper sauce and steel bands about it, but the welcome is entirely Caribbean.

Hotel Guanahani

Information & Reservations
UK 0870 606 1296
INT. +44 870 606 1296

Grand Cul de Sac
97133
St Barts

✈ St Jean Airport 15 mins

Tel +590 276 660
Fax +590 277 070

www.guanahani-hotel.com
guanahani@saint-barths.com

Member of:
The Leading Hotels of the World

Resting among the lush grounds of a 16-hectare peninsula, set between two white sandy beaches and clear aquamarine seas, the Hotel Guanahani is the only full-service hotel on the tropical island of St Barthélémy.

Bungalows painted in cheerful colours, with terracotta floors and wooden-rafted ceilings, reproduce the genteel ambiance of the island's colonial past. Most of the rooms offer panoramic views of the Atlantic on one side or, on the other, wide expanses of deep ocean bordered by picturesque coconut groves.

The hotel has two freshwater swimming pools and a large jacuzzi – the perfect place to unwind. For tennis enthusiasts, there are two floodlit courts with a professional instructor on hand to help guests improve their game. And down on the sugary beach, the hotel provides complimentary use of all non-motorised watersports.

The Indigo, a charming *al fresco* restaurant situated on the beach, is a delight, serving perfect light salads and fresh local seafood, while at The Bartolomeo expect more of an intimate experience. This renowned French restaurant offers delicious local specialities to the romantic accompaniment of the resident jazz pianist.

73

US$270-750 (47)

US$570-1,180 (28)

US$50-70

US$15

Honeymoon specials

Visit the Guanahani website (www.guanahani-hotel.com) for very attractive Honeymoon Packages, valid from April 26 through October 2000.

Sightseeing and leisure

On site is a Clarins Institute Beauty Salon, fitness room, two tennis courts, two restaurants, Beach Bar and boutique. Watersports activities include windsurfing, jetskiing, waterskiing, snorkelling, kayaking and jetboats. Island tours can be organised, as can trips to Gustavia Harbor and shopping excursions.

St Lucia

flying time
London: 8-9 hrs
Miami: 3-4 hrs
NY: 4-5 hrs

when to go
Feb for celebrating
Independence Day
and a real carnival
blast; May for the
jazz festival; Dec for
National Day.

currency
Eastern Caribbean
dollar, which is fixed
to the US dollar.

language
English

getting around
By local bus, taxi
or car. Ferries and
hopping planes
connect islands.
Yacht charters are
especially popular.

Swapped between the French and British no less than 14 times, St Lucia has a unique mix of Anglo-French culture.

One of the Caribbean's hottest destinations, it is a charmed isle – for her people, among the friendliest anywhere, the natural beauty of her hidden coves, her tropical abundance and her twin volcanic pyramids, or Pitons as they are officially known.

The majority of hotels are on the Leeward coast, facing the calm sea and the romantic orange glow of the sunset. Some of the charming smaller hotels offer seclusion in dramatic settings, tucked away in coves or in view of the Pitons.

The luscious French heritage extends to the food, and West Indian ingredients take on a new life here in such Creole dishes as treacle and coconut chicken stew.

St Lucians delight in throwing a party and the island's nightlife is renowned for its liveliness, with every little town hosting its own weekly dance. The best-known party is the 'jump-up' on Friday nights in Castries, when clubs open their doors and let people – and speakers – spill into the street, both at full volume.

Mago Estate Hotel

Information & Reservations
UK 0870 606 1296
INT. +44 870 606 1296

Soufrière
St Lucia

✈ Hewanorra 40 min

Tel +758 459 5880
Fax +758 459 7352

monica@candw.lc
www.mago-hotel.com

Member of:
Charming Hotels
Independent Luxury Hotels

Once a private residence, the Mago Estate Hotel is now an intimate and secluded hotel with only six bedrooms, each of which overlooks the bay and the striking mountains of St Lucia.

This is a place to really get away from the crowds and become enveloped in a tropical dream in the beautiful rainforest surroundings, where mango trees, mahogany, papaya, maracuya, banana, bougainvillaea and hibiscus flourish. You can enjoy your cocktails in the Polar, nestled in the roots of a huge mango tree, or climb two floors higher into the mango tree house. The open air Rainforest restaurant serves up tasty creole fish and fresh, exotic Caribbean vegetables and fruit.

The hotel was designed, built and furnished by the owner who took his inspiration from the colours, materials and shapes of the culture and lifestyle of the local people. The overall effect combines tropical dark wood furnishings crafted by local artists, tapestries and sculptures by contemporary artists, cushions in chromatic tones and antique Persian carpets to create a wonderfully comfortable and harmonious setting.

The hotel also offers their Healthpath Yin and Yang therapy, with luxurious mineral baths, massage, healthy food and drink.

75

US$100-350* (6 rooms & units)

US$35-60

included

Honeymoon specials

Honeymoon package: champagne, flowers, fruit basket, breakfast, evening meal for seven nights US$1,980 plus 8% tax and 10% service.

* Prices range from US$100-250 during low season (April 1-Dec 15) and from US$150-350 in high season (Dec 16-March 31).

Sightseeing and leisure

Visit the nearby markets, botanical gardens, waterfalls and the world's only 'drive-in volcano'. Watersports include sailing, boating, surfing, fishing, deep sea fishing and scuba diving. Golf and horse back riding can also be arranged.

St Martin

flying time
London: 8-9 hrs
via San Juan or St
Thomas
Miami: 2½ hrs
NY: 3½ hrs

climate
Sunny and warm all
year-round, with an
average temperature
of 27°C.

when to go
Late Feb to April is
carnival-packed and
March is particularly
lively. Schoelcher Day
in July celebrates the
abolition of slavery
on the French side.

currency
French franc in
St Martin/Antillean
florin or guilder in
St Maarten – US
dollars are accepted
everywhere.

language
English, French and
Dutch

getting around
Try hopping aboard
a 'jitney', a colourful
little van that can be
hailed by the road-
side, and take day
trips by boat to
neighbouring islands.

A beguiling and eclectic blend of cultures, the jewel-like island of St Martin is an earthly paradise for honeymooners.

Encapsulated in this Caribbean haven is everything one could wish for in a holiday – history, adventure, beauty, and romance. Lapped by clear, gentle waters and refreshed by cooling trade winds, St Martin enjoys a deliciously warm and sunny climate all year round.

The island is divided harmoniously between the French and the Dutch, and although you can travel unhindered across the barely perceptible borders, each half happily retains a separate and distinct character, so that it's almost like enjoying two holidays in one.

French St Martin is relaxed and elegant, with quiet bays, secluded beaches and an emphasis on fine food. The sweeping beach at Grand Case is noted for its restaurants and pretty, gingerbread style pastel-coloured houses, and there is some lush and romantic scenery nearby. Visit the beautiful, tropical valley of Colombier, half way between Grand Case and the charming French capital of Marigot, or walk in luxuriant Eden Park, thronged with exotic birds and flowers and offering breathtaking views across the bays to neighbouring islands.

If you crave bright lights and bustle, then go Dutch: St Maarten is friendly and informal and great for shopping. Its capital, Philipsburg, has a busy port and lively nightlife, and the majority of the island's activities can be enjoyed here: from a round of tennis or golf to snorkelling, waterskiing, or fishing for marlin, tuna, barracuda, and kingfish.

La Samanna

nformation & Reservations
UK 0870 606 1296
NT. +44 870 606 1296

The Lowlands
BP 4077
St Martin

✈ Princess Juliana 8 mins

el +590 876 400
ax +590 878 786

www.orient-express.com

Member of:
The Leading Hotels of the World

La Samanna is a palm-fringed paradise boasting 55 acres of powdery soft sands and panoramic ocean views. Just minutes from the charming French capital of Marigot, the resort has a distinctive Mediterranean-style ambiance.

Pretty, white stucco villas overlook impossibly blue seas, their private walled gardens and patios opening directly onto the beach. The lush vegetation, tropical flowers in every room and the welcoming wooden-decked Beach Bar all lend an air of casual, relaxed elegance to the surroundings, and are the perfect antidote to any prenuptial stress you might have suffered!

Whether you stay in an exclusive three-bedroom villa, luxurious suite or one of the lovely rooms, all the choices you'll have to make here will be pleasant ones. Chill out by the glorious pool with a fruit punch, drink in the view from your private terrace or take a dip in the dazzling Caribbean.

If you tire of soaking up the rays there are plenty of activities to keep you busy and St Martin has many areas of outstanding beauty and historical sights to experience. There are plenty of amenities on site – sailing, windsurfing, waterskiing and tennis can all be enjoyed on the house – and be sure to pamper yourself at the Health and Beauty Spa.

77

 US$360-675 (83)

 US$655-3,650

 US$95

 included

Honeymoon specials

Seven-night Passion in Paradise package includes oceanfront accommodation, return transport to hotel, a bottle of champagne, flowers and fruit on arrival, breakfast daily, one candlelight dinner on your terrace or in The Restaurant, a sunset champagne cruise, massage or personal training session, rental car for two days, watersports, tennis, use of fitness pavilion. Prices from US$2,760-8,040 excl. 5% tax.

Sightseeing and leisure

Elysée Health and Beauty Spa, Fitness Pavilion. Golf, complimentary sailing, windsurfing, waterskiing and tennis, cruises for sightseeing, diving, deep sea fishing. Butterfly farm, museum, twice-weekly markets and shopping in Marigot.

St Vincent &
the Grenadines

flying time
London: 8-9 hrs
NY: 4 hrs
Miami: 3 hrs

when to go
June is a great
time when Vincie
Mas is on.

currency
The Eastern
Caribbean dollar,
fixed to the US
dollar. (US dollars
are also widely
accepted).

language
English

getting around
By local bus, taxi
or hire car. Ferries
and hopping planes
make getting to
neighbouring
islands easy.

St Vincent and the Grenadines offer a classic Caribbean combination: the staggering lushness and friendly character of the Windward Islands, and the slow-time, easy life of the tiny Grenadines.

St Vincent is dominated by the mighty Soufrière, a volcano which last blew in 1979. And although a thoroughly delightful place, with the perfect amount of atmosphere and quaint charm, there are comparatively few tourists here – making it the ideal romantic and secluded retreat for honeymooners. The capital, Kingstown, sits on a sweeping bay, surrounded by steep ridges, from where Fort Charlotte commands a magnificent view of the 30 islands of the Grenadines. Each island is just a short hop from the next, strung out over 60 miles of strikingly blue sea.

The Grenadines, not as developed as other Caribbean islands, are simply magical. This is a part of the world seemingly suspended in time and where the water is impossibly clear and the beaches as white as snow. And there are some lovely places to stay: luxury villas perched on peninsulas; rooms in fine old buildings and small hotels; and perhaps most spectacularly, private island resorts comprising just a few rooms on an isolated cove.

Palm Island

Information & Reservations
UK 0870 606 1296
INT. +44 870 606 1296

Palm Island
St Vincent &
the Grenadines

✈ Union Island 1 mile

Tel +561 994 4733
Fax +561 994 9597

UK reservations:
Tel +44 (0) 1244 355300
Fax +44 (0) 1244 355309

res@palmislandresorts.com
www.palmislandresorts.com

At the southern end of the strand of magical islands that make up St Vincent and the Grenadines lies the secret hideaway of Palm Island, a luscious 150 acres of jewelled coastline, ragged palms and wooded, miniature-scale mountains. Uniquely, aside from a few private homes owned by rarely-seen, international jet-setters, the whole island is yours, and at an all-inclusive price. With only 40 guest accommodations, and five glorious white sand beaches on which to while away the golden hours, you're sure to find peace and solitude.

A typically laid-back island pace ensures tranquil days, where time seems suspended. Spend your life in the water or on it: there's sailing, kayaking, windsurfing, and neighbouring Tobago Cays has fantastic beaches and renowned snorkelling locations. And of course, the weather is perfect – the sun beats through the palm fronds by day and stars shine like diamonds in the clear night skies.

Rooms are furnished with bamboo and rattan furniture, soft cotton bedspreads and local artwork. Choose from cottages that open right onto the beach, 'palm views' that boast gardens of tropical colour, or even a romantic 'coconut treehouse', six feet off the ground on stilts with your own hammock on the balcony for those lazy moments.

79

Honeymoon specials
Champagne, flowers and fruit basket on arrival. Choice of either breakfast in bed on the first morning or a candlelight dinner one evening of your stay.

Sightseeing and leisure
Tobago Cays for snorkelling, watersports, tennis, nature trails – all included in the price.

 US$520-830 (40)

 included

 included

Trinidad & Tobago

flying time
London: 8½ hrs
via San Juan
NY: 7 hrs

climate
In the rainy season
(June-Dec) it is hot.
It is cooler in the
dry season (Jan-
May). Temperatures
range from 20-30°C.

when to go
In 2000 the main
carnival falls on
March 6/7. There are
regattas throughout
the year, but The
Great Race takes
place in early Aug.

currency
Trinidad & Tobago
dollar, fixed to the
US dollar, which is
also accepted.

language
English

getting around
Taxis are cheap and
more reliable than
buses. Car hire is
not too expensive
and neither are the
small planes that
hop between the
islands.

On the eastern boundary of the Caribbean lie tranquil little Tobago and her boisterous big sister Trinidad — famous among the islands for hosting the wildest, most popular carnival of them all...

Tobago, by contrast, is a place for rest and relaxation: serene and unhurried, it's the ideal environment in which to lay back in a hammock, sip on a rum punch and watch the sun slip gently below the horizon. It has to be one of the most perfect destinations for lovers, seemingly created for lingering moonlit walks and romantic escapades.

The azure blue seas and white sands are not the only lure of this largely undeveloped, friendly island, with its nostalgically named villages — Pembroke, Speyside, Glamorgan — more than hinting at a colonial past. Tobago is also cherished for its fascinating

ecological diversity — its abundant wildlife and awe-some scenery, both above ground with its waterfalls and rivers, forests and flora, and beneath the waves with its magical coral reefs, are a feast for the senses.

Bird watching is particularly fruitful in Tobago and the names are almost as exotic as the creatures themselves — look out for White-Tailed Tropicbirds, the Magnificent Frigatebird and Crested Oropendolas

There are monkeys everywhere, too, and if you visit between March and July, you might just be witness to a giant, endangered leatherback turtle laying her eggs in the sand, a memorable and magical experience.

Blue Waters Inn

Information & Reservations
UK 0870 606 1296
INT. +44 870 606 1296

Batteaux Bay
Speyside
Tobago

✈ Piarco Int. 26 miles

Tel +868 660 4341
Fax +868 660 5195

wi@bluewatersinn.com
www.bluewatersinn.com

If you wish to find seclusion and romance in the midst of spectacular natural beauty, Blue Waters Inn fits the bill nicely. Nestled reassuringly away from the main tourist resorts of Tobago, its secluded white sand beach and mountainous backdrop are brimming with dazzling flora and fauna of all descriptions. Colourful birds grace the trees, and further rare and exotic breeds can be discovered at the protected Main Ridge forest reserve and also at Little Tobago, where the largest seabird colony in the Caribbean has chosen to nest.

A nature-lover's paradise, the Blue Waters Inn is also a prime spot from which to explore the wonderful marine life that Tobago has to offer, including giant manta rays, turtles, moray eels, eagle rays and at least 70 species of coral. The on-site scuba diving facilities or glass-bottomed boat rides are a great way to experience this magnificent underwater world.

Guest rooms are charming and well-equipped, with private balconies or patios commanding stunning views of Batteaux Bay, Glover's Island and Little Tobago. Along with great seafood, and a cooling bottle of Carib Beer at the welcoming Shipwreck Bar, you'll find everything you could ask for at this fantastic, friendly resort.

81

US$95-210 (35)

US$195-330 (3)

US$6-25

US$6-12

Honeymoon specials
Flowers, wine and fruit basket on arrival.

Sightseeing and leisure
Aromatherapy on site. Tennis, glass-bottomed boat rides, kayaking, windsurfing and scuba diving. Main Ridge forest reserve is nearby.

Europe

IRELAND
Dublin •
(61)

NORTH SEA

ATLANTIC
OCEAN

ENGLAND
(59) (60) London
(58)
(6) BELGIUM
Brussels • GERMANY
(62) Berlin •
Paris • (18)
(20)

Prague • (10)
(11)
CZECH REPUBLIC

FRANCE
SWITZERLAND (5) (3) Vienna • (2)
Bern • (12) (1) AUSTRIA
(13) (54) (53) (55) (56) (4)

(16) (30) (32)
(31)
(15) (19) (34) (28)
(14) (17) (37) (26) (33)
PORTUGAL (52) (27)
(42) Lisbon • (35)
Madrid • Rome • ITALY
SPAIN
(41) (43) (45) (46)
(47)
(48) (51) (29)
(49) (50) (36)
(44)
MEDITERRANEAN SEA GREECE
• Athe
(39)
(38) (23)

MALTA (25)
(40) CRETE

key to hotels

Austria
1 Arlberg Hospiz Hotel, St Christoph
2 Hotel Im Palais Schwarzenberg, Vienna
3 Hotel Schloss Monchstein, Salzburg
4 Hoteldorf Gruner Baum, Badgastein
5 Thurnhers Alpenhof, Zurs

Belgium
6 Montanus Hotel, Bruges

Cyprus
7 Four Seasons Hotel, Limassol
8 Le Meridien Limassol, Limassol
9 Paphos Amathus Beach Hotel, Paphos

Czech Republic
10 Hotel Hoffmeister, Prague
11 Hotel Pariz, Prague

France
12 Château de Bagnols, nr Lyon
13 Château des Vigiers, Monestier
14 Château Eza, Eze
15 Hôtel de la Cité, Carcassonne
16 Hotel du Palais, Biarritz
17 Hotel Martinez, Cannes
18 Hotel Royal Monceau, Paris
19 Oustau de Baumanière, Les-Baux-de-Provence

Germany
20 Krone Assmannshausen, Assmannshausen

Greece
21 Elounda Mare Hotel, Crete
22 Kivotos Clubhotel, Mykonos
23 Santa Marina Hotel, Mykonos
24 St Nicolas Bay, Crete
25 The Tsitouras Collecton, Santorini

Italy
26 Albergo Pietrasanta, Lucca
27 Brufani Palace, Perugia
28 Excelsior Palace Hotel, Rapallo
29 Grand Hotel Excelsior Vittoria, Sorrento
30 Grand Hotel Fasano, Lake Garda

31 Hotel Gabbia D'Oro, Verona
32 Hotel Londra Palace, Venice
33 Hotel Lungarno, Florence
34 Hotel Splendido & Splendido Mare, Portofino
35 Romantik Hotel le Silve, Assisi
36 Romantik Hotel Poseidon, Positano
37 Royal Hotel, Sanremo
38 San Domenico Palace, Taormina
39 Villa Igiea Grand Hotel, Palermo

Malta
40 The Xara Palace, Mdina

Portugal & Madeira
41 Hotel Quinta do Lago, Almancil
42 Lapa Palace, Lisbon
43 Monte Do Casal County House Hotel, Faro
44 Reid's Palace, Funchal, Madeira

Spain
45 Casa No.7, Seville
46 Hotel Alfonso XIII, Seville
47 Hotel La Bobadilla, Loja
48 Hotel Puente Romano, Marbella
49 Kempinski Resort Hotel Estepona, Estepona
50 Las Dunas Beach Hotel & Spa, Estepona
51 Marbella Club, Marbella
52 Mas De Torrent, Girona

Switzerland
53 Grand Hotel Zermatterhof, Zermatt
54 Palace Hotel Gstaad, Gstaad
55 Park Hotel Delta, Ascona
56 Suvretta House, St Moritz

Turkey
57 Ciragan Palace Hotel Kempinski Istanbul

UK & Ireland
58 The Beaufort, London, England
59 Chewton Glen Hotel, New Forest, England
60 Taplow House Hotel, Berkshire, England
61 Ballylickey Manor House, Bantry Bay, Ireland
62 Longueville Manor, St Helier, Jersey

BLACK SEA

• Ankara

TURKEY

CYPRUS
• Nicosia
9 7 8

83

Austria

flying time
To: Vienna/Salzburg
London: 2 hrs
NY: 9 hrs
Miami: 10 hrs

climate
There are four distinct seasons, with warm summers and cold winters with widespread snow.

when to go
Tourist areas are very busy July-Aug. Ski resorts operate Dec-April. From May-June, Sept-Oct it is quieter and good for touring.

currency
Austrian schilling

language
German, although many Austrians also speak some English, French or Italian.

getting around
By train, bus and tram. Scenic boat trips on lakes and the River Danube.

If you are seeking a perfectly romantic setting for a winter honeymoon, Austria fits the bill.

The weeks leading up to Christmas see the streets come to life, bright with the lights of the Christkindl – Christmas markets that sell gifts and Christmas decorations, fresh local produce for the festive season, and warming cups of spicy gluhwein. And on New Year's Eve in Vienna, the grand Imperial Ball kicks off a season of lavish, glittering, full-dress balls that last throughout January and February.

On a snowy winter's day, you can escape the cold and join the locals over their coffee and cake in a Viennese coffeehouse such as the Cafe Sacher, which gave its name to the wickedly rich chocolate cake.

Forget calorie-counting and fuel up on a hearty lunch of paprika-peppered goulash, and apple strudel with lashings of cream. Try the Austrian wines, too, which are as praiseworthy as many French varieties.

Austrian ski resorts are renowned for their charm and apres-ski jollity. In the late afternoon, still in your ski gear, you can party to the music at a tea-dance and, after an ample dinner, try a sleigh ride or toboggan racing by moonlight. There are resorts to suit everyone, from fashionable Zurs, Kitzbühel, St Anton and Lech, to lively Söll and Schladming.

In summer, the carpets of alpine flowers attract a more sedate kind of visitor. Others arrive for activity holidays. Hiking, climbing and mountain-biking are all popular, amid the spectacular mountain scenery of Austria's lakes and rivers.

Information & Reservations
UK 0870 606 1296
INT. +44 870 606 1296

Arlberg Hospiz Hotel

Familie Werner A-6580
St Christoph
Tirol
Austria

✈ Innsbruck 100km
✈ Zurich 210km

tel +43 54 46 26 11
fax +43 54 46 35 45

info@hospiz.com
www.hospiz.com

Member of:
Relais & Châteaux

The award-winning, family-run Hospiz, that dates back to 1386, offers a very warm welcome in a traditional Austrian ski resort. Situated in the village of St Christoph, the smallest village on the Arlberg in western Austria, this skiing paradise benefits from its high altitude (1,800m) and enjoys snow from the end of November to the beginning of May.

Immediately opposite the hotel is access to the vast skiing area of St Christoph, St Anton, Zurs, Lech and Stuben, with 85 cable cars and lifts providing access to 260kms of groomed slopes and roughly 185kms of off-piste routes.

Aprés-ski, the fine food and excellent wines are waiting to tempt your palate in the charming, early 19th-century Hospiz farmhouse. You'll be more than impressed with the wine list – it holds one of the world's largest collections of Bordeaux wines.

Soak up the sun on the terrace until it disappears, then retreat to the comfort of the crackling open fire to enjoy the local specialities such as roast wild duck with red cabbage. Suites also have open fireplaces. To relieve those post-ski aches and pains, rejuvenate yourself in the whirlpool and sauna or enjoy the sheer luxury of a specialist massage.

85

 US$75-290 (78)

 US$80-665 (120)

🍽 US$16-125

☕ US$20-40

Honeymoon specials

Champagne in room on arrival, large in-room breakfast, special candlelit dinner with wine. Upgrade upon availability. Also, 5% discount off package rates for stay of one week or longer. Please phone for details.

Sightseeing and leisure

On site is a wellness centre with sauna, sunbed, spa, massage and indoor pool. The hotel also boasts its own church. Situated on a mountain, there is some of the country's best skiing on the hotel's doorstep. Also, try horseriding, mountain biking, tobogganing, trekking and horse-drawn sleigh rides. Old cities of Innsbruck and Bregenz. Summer classical music festival on Lake Constanz.

Hotel im Palais Schwarzenberg

Information & Reservations
UK 0870 606 1296
INT. +44 870 606 1296

Schwarzenbergplatz 9
A-1030
Vienna
Austria

✈ Vienna-Schwechat 25km

tel +43 1 798 45 15
fax +43 1 798 47 14

palais@schwarzenberg.co.at
www.palais-schwarzenberg.com

86

Member of:
Relais & Châteaux

The Palais Schwarzenberg is surrounded by 18 acres of stunning private park; a park which has a reputation as the ultimate pleasure garden, featuring groups of sculptures and stone vases. An avenue of majestic chestnut trees leads on to more intimate corners, a secluded pool and croquet lawn and finally to five tennis courts.

In 1697 the famous baroque architect Lucas von Hildebrandt was commissioned to build a palace with orangerie and gardens. After being acquired by the Schwarzenberg family, the interior was completed in 1727 and from this day on the palace was intermittently used as a summer residence. In the early '60s, an exclusive *hotel-pension* was opened and the stately rooms of the Palais were occasionally used for entertainment purposes.

Since then, development and restoration has continued to reach the luxury and style that now exists. All rooms and suites are individually decorated with traditional period furniture and pieces of art; however, six Park Suites are designed in modern style which blend wonderfully with the 300-year-old exterior.

A combination of classical Viennese and French cuisine is served in the elegant restaurant and you can relax to the strains of piano music every night.

 US$285-485 (36)

 US$485-1,070 (8)

🍽 US$60-120

☕ US$18-26

Honeymoon specials

Transfer to and from the airport or station or free parking upon arrival. Fruit, flowers and a bottle of champagne on arrival. Breakfast daily and one dinner for two in the Terrace Restaurant.

Sightseeing and leisure

Within walking distance of the State Opera and most of Vienna's famous sites including Belvedere Castle and St Stephan Cathedral. Jogging paths, croquet lawn, five clay tennis courts in a unique location next to Belvedere Castle and outdoor swimming pool all on site. Several golf courses in the surrounding area.

Information & Reservations
UK 0870 606 1296
INT. +44 870 606 1296

Hotel Schloss Mönchstein

Mönchsberg Park 26
A-5020 Salzburg
Austria

✈ Salzburg Int. 5km

tel +43 662 848 5550
fax +43 662 848 559

salzburg@monchstein.at
www.monchstein.at

Member of:
Relais & Châteaux
Johansens

This enchanting castle hotel, above the rooftops of Salzburg in Mönchsberg Park, was originally built in 1358 to house the guests of archbishops and later became a popular venue for musical soirées by Haydn and Mozart. Hotel Schloss Mönchstein today has the reputation of being the 'Urban Sanctuary of the World' (Hideaway Report, USA).

Towers and turrets cloaked with ivy in summer and sparkling with snow in winter, renaissance-style furnishings and precious paintings adorn this splendid building. Most rooms are spacious and decorated in pastel shades with gilt-framed mirrors.

Authentic dishes are served in the award-winning Castle-Restaurant, Paris Lodron, which has outstanding views of the city below. A lift and a romantic 7-minute walk through the park links the hotel to the baroque buildings of the old town, and to various entertainment.

The castle chapel, where couples have exchanged vows since 1531, still provides a perfect setting for a fairytale wedding. 'Salzburg's Wedding Wall', in front of the chapel, is covered in brass plates bearing the names of couples married inside. Receptions of up to 80 guests are catered for in the restaurant, cafe or castle grounds and staff can arrange cocktail parties and concerts.

87

US$235-528 (9)
US$439-2,439 (7)
US$43-105
US$13-22

Honeymoon specials
Complimentary wine on arrival. Room upgrade upon availability.

Sightseeing and leisure
The historic city of Salzburg, castles, lakes, mountains. Visits to Mozart's birthplace, Castle Mirabell and an underground glacier. Music festivals and events in the castle grounds and the city. Beauty treatments and massage by appointment. Tennis, golf and jogging.

Hoteldorf Gruner Baum

Information & Reservations
UK 0870 606 1296
INT. +44 870 606 1296

Kotschachtal 25
A-5640 Bad Gastein
Austria

✈ Salzburg 95km

tel +43 64 34 25 160
fax +43 64 34 25 1625

info@grunerbaum.com
www.grunerbaum.com

88 Member of:
Relais & Châteaux

In the heart of the wild and romantic Kotschach Valley, the Hoteldorf Gruner Baum is a place of fairytales and where dreams come true.

The hotel is designed like a small village deep in the heart of the picturesque valley where guests can choose between the charm and elegance of the main house, the romantic and traditional country house, or the magnificent Villa Solitude which lies within the health spa of Bad Gastein and has six luxury suites.

Whether winter or summer, the hotel has something to offer everyone, with such stunning views and picturesque surroundings. Choose between the open-air pool and sunbathing meadow, a game of tennis or a round of golf.

After the hectic run-up to your wedding day, indulge in the many beauty and spa treatments before enjoying the thermal indoor pool. Staff can design a treatment especially for you.

Winter brings its own magic with fairytale settings of ice and snow. Travel by horse-drawn sleigh or take to the slopes on skis or snowboards. And afterwards indulge in the resort's no-holds-barred gastronomy, combining traditional Austrian dishes with international cuisine, washed down with locally produced wines.

🛏 ATS1,120-1,880 (73)

🛏 ATS1,520-2,120 (12)

🍽 incl in half-board rates

☕ incl in half-board rates

🍾 👜 ✈

Honeymoon specials

Three nights in superior room on half-board basis. Visit to the hairdresser & beautician for the bride. Civil ceremony in chapel or Villa Solitude. Flowers. Photographer plus 70 photos. Drive in Rolls Royce. Music. Glass of sparkling wine at waterfall, plus wedding meal with champagne, wine and wedding cake. Horse-drawn coach through park, champagne & salmon breakfast. Price for two ATS26,020.

Sightseeing and leisure

Waterfall in Bad Gastein. Museum of Gastein. Thermal fountains and stalactite caves. Tours to Salzburg.

Information & Reservations
UK 0870 606 1296
INT. +44 870 606 1296

Thurnhers Alpenhof

A-6763 Zurs
Arlberg
Austria

✈ Zurich 150km

tel +43 5583 2191
fax +43 5583 3330

www.thurnhers-alpenhof.at
www.skihotel.at
mail@thurnhers-alpenhof.at

Open 11 December-25 April

Member of:
Leading Small Hotels of the World

In 1999, the American Academy of Hospitality Sciences awarded Thurnhers Alpenhof with the Five Star Diamond Award for extraordinary achievement. Situated in the centre of Zurs am Arlberg, which is one of the most beautiful and fashionable wintersports resorts in the world, it is a private hotel with familiar tradition, rural luxury and *l'art d'hospitalité* on an international level.

Exquisite antiques and artworks abound, and highly comfortable and beautifully furnished rooms and suites – some with their own whirlpool or fireplace – characterise this charming hotel. There is also an outstanding gourmet restaurant and piano bar and excellent sporting facilities, such as swimming pool, sauna, steambath, solarium, massage and fitness corner.

Room rates include a welcome cocktail and fruit basket on arrival, gourmet breakfast and afternoon snack daily, five to seven-course gourmet dinner and use of the wellness area. A further highlight is 'Little Dream', a small shop with specially selected accessories for home and table. Ski runs (from 1,700m to 2,800m) and the famous ski school of Zurs are directly next to the hotel.

89

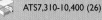 ATS5,610-7,360 (23)

 ATS7,310-10,400 (26)

🍽 included

☕ included

🍾 💍

Honeymoon specials
Champagne, flowers, fruit basket in the room on arrival. The hotel will organise your entire wedding with the ceremony in the romantic church in Lech built in the 14th century and afterwards a horse-drawn sleigh ride to an original ski hut.

Sightseeing and leisure
Snow-covered landscape, beautiful mountain world of the Arlberg region, small Austrian villages, skiing paradise with 180km of prepared ski pistes. The house-own sports and activity trainer offers romantic torchlight hikes, exciting downhill toboggan rides, paragliding, heli-skiing and more.

Belgium

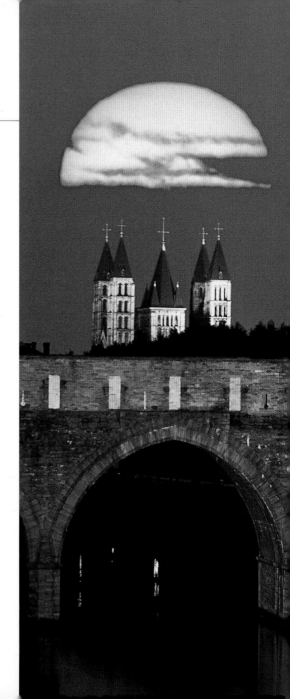

flying time
London: 1hr 10mins
NY: 8 hrs
(via London)

by rail
Eurostar from
London to Brussels
takes 2hrs 45mins;
Bruges is another
45mins by train.

**climate/
when to go**
Much like that in the
UK – mild and often
damp. April-Sept is
the warmest time.
Winter is popular
for skiing in the
Ardennes. Summer is
better for festivals.
Belgium's National
Day is July 21, which
marks the start of
the month-long
Brussels Fair. Bruges
is picture-perfect
throughout the year.

currency
Belgian franc

language
Flemish, French and
German.

getting around
There are trams and
a metro system in
Brussels, and the rail
network is extensive
and well-priced.

Belgium, land of Tintin and Hercule Poirot, is full of surprises. With ancient cities and a rich landscape, Belgium has plenty to offer the traveller.

Discover the golden dunes and sandy beaches of the Ostend coast, tour through the canal-laced lowlands of Flanders, or head to the Belgian Ardennes, famed for its rolling hills and forests that attract walkers in summer and skiers in winter.

The ancient city of Bruges, with its miles of hidden canals, is known as the 'Venice of the north' and is a perfect romantic honeymoon retreat. Here you can wander through narrow streets lined with gabled mansions and happen across delightful squares brimming with cafes and chic boutiques.

Amble through bustling weekly markets or glide serenely along the miles of hidden canals, sailing under charming hump-backed bridges and past miles of beautiful homes.

Brussels, now at the political heart of Europe, also has centuries of history to inform and intrigue the visitor. The magnificent Grand Place is still the focal point. Dating back to the 1500s, it remains a charming cobbled square surrounded by exquisite 15th-century Guild buildings and teeming with period antiques and characterful shops.

But there is more than history to lure you to Belgium. Brussels is also home to the famous Comic Strip Centre, celebrating the fictional life of Tintin, while the Atomium takes a leap into the future.

Montanus Hotel

Information & Reservations
UK 0870 606 1296
INT. +44 870 606 1296

Nieuwe Gentweg 78
8000 Bruges
Belgium

✈ Oostende 20km

tel +32 50 33 11 76
fax +32 50 34 09 38

info@montanus.be
www.montanus.be
www.hotelbel.com/montanus.htm

This charming character hotel combines glamour, sophistication and romance and is located right in the heart of the historical town of Bruges.

Nearby lies the enchanting Beguinage, literally 'The Vineyard', a community of houses around a small garden where nuns have lived and worked since the 16th century. Also, just a stone's throw away is the Minnewater (Lake of Love), a canalised, swan-filled lake set in idyllic parkland.

The Montanus is a listed mansion house that once belonged to a prime minister of Belgium, and has been renovated to the highest standards. The decor is delightful: cool, relaxed and contemporary, with stylish Lloyd Loom chairs and muted, modern textures and colours. Outside, there are 1,200sq metres of private gardens, colonial pavilion rooms and a sun terrace. Most compelling of all, however, is the secluded honeymoon suite, decorated in cedar wood, with its own private terrace facing onto lovely water fountains.

And for more pampering you can have a basket delivered to your room, brimming with chocolates, wine, luxury Roger & Gallet soaps, and the promise of more to come: a ticket for a romantic evening ride in a horse-drawn carriage or a champagne and lobster breakfast next morning.

91

 US$100-170 (17)

 US$165-350 (7)

 US$44-118

 included

Honeymoon specials

The hotel will automatically upgrade you to the honeymoon suite; if this is not available another suite will be offered. Champagne and Belgian chocolates are complimentary.

Sightseeing and leisure

The seaside is just 15km from the hotel. There is also horesriding and the delights of historic Bruges to take in.

Cyprus

flying time
To: Larnasa
London: 4 hrs
NY: 11 hrs
LA: 16-17 hrs

climate
Hot, dry summers
with mild winters.
Rainfall mainly in
Oct-Mar.

when to go
In summer for
swimming, boating,
watersports and
nightlife. In spring
and autumn for
sightseeing and
touring. In winter
for skiing in the
Troodos Mountains.

currency
Cyprus pound.
Credit cards are
generally accepted in
hotels but take cash
for excursions.

getting around
With limited public
transport, car rental
is the best option.
Remember to take
out insurance.

Cyprus is the mythical birthplace of Aphrodite, goddess of love. Discover her presence still today, in the crystal-clear Med and the fascinating remains of ancient civilisations.

Marvel at splendid Roman mosaics at Paphos. Climb the ruins of Crusader castles in the Kyrenia mountains and explore Venetian bastions in Nicosia and Byzantine monasteries in the Troodos Mountains, where Mount Olympus rises to 6,450 feet. The wooded slopes and foothills are ideal for rambling. In spring, hikers are rewarded with carpets of wildflowers. In winter, Platres and Kakopetria are good bases for uncrowded skiing.

Old Paphos, the centre of the cult of Aphrodite, dates back to Mycenaean times. New Paphos, founded in the 4th century BC, is now a popular resort with modern hotels and restaurants alongside archaeological remains.

Limassol is a busy port city, and its attractive suburbs have a number of good hotels. The ancient fishing village of Ayia Napa is now a bustling resort, with development along the coast and non-stop nightlife.

Wherever you are in Cyprus, you are never more than a couple of hours from Nicosia, the island's spiritual heart. Walk the narrow streets, shop for local bargains, explore the Archbishop's Palace, then relax at a pavement cafe and feel the true pulse of this enigmatic and romantic island.

Four Seasons Hotel

Information & Reservations
UK 0870 606 1296
INT. +44 870 606 1296

PO Box 57222
Limassol
Cyprus

*Owned and operated by
Muskita Hotels Ltd*

✈ Larnaca 75km

tel +357 5 310 222
fax +357 5 310 887

inquiries@fourseasons.com.cy
www.fourseasons.com.cy

Tour operators:
UK Thomson a la Carte
Cyplon Holidays

Long known as the 'island of love', Cyprus is a favourite destination for wedding couples and honeymooners alike. On a sandy beach not far from the legendary birthplace of Aphrodite, the Greek Goddess of Love, stands the remarkable Four Seasons Hotel, one of the island's finest, and where personal comfort and discreet service go hand in hand.

The hotel's variety of exclusive suites attracts guests who are aiming for a holiday of a lifetime. The Honeymoon Suite welcomes newlyweds with the kind of romantic detail and service a couple usually only dreams about. Equally tempting are the garden studios and suites. With their own pool area and bar, they constitute a separate complex reserved just for adults. Here guests enjoy the privileges of private jacuzzis, butler service, private check-in, as well as complimentary pre-dinner drinks.

Three gourmet restaurants provide an enviable choice of dining options in-house or under the stars. Music and dance are a daily must. An array of sports and leisure facilities allow you to make the most of the Mediterranean weather conditions, while beauty and relaxation are yours to enjoy with the help of marine-based treatments in the exclusive Thalasso Spa.

93

 CY£143-170 (323)

 CY£196-750 (32)

🍽 CY£17-34

☕ included

Honeymoon specials

Honeymoon couples are welcomed with champagne, fruit basket and flowers, to be followed by a romantic candlelight dinner. If possible, room upgrades will be granted with the hotel's compliments.

Sightseeing and leisure

Facilities include two freeform pools, one indoor seawater pool, leisure club with tennis, squash, gym, sauna, jacuzzi, massage, aerobics and more. Diving centre and watersports on the beach. Theme nights. Exclusive Thalasso Spa offers marine-based treatments, including relaxation and beauty packages. Nearby: the 9th-century city of Amathus, medieval fortress, Kolossi castle and the ancient city of Curium.

Le Meridien
Limassol Spa & Resort

Information & Reservations
UK 0870 606 1296
INT. +44 870 606 1296

Old Limassol-Nicosia Road
PO Box 56560
CY 3308 Limassol
Cyprus

✈ Larnaca 55km

tel +357 5 634 000
fax +357 5 634 222

sales@lemeridien-cyprus.com
www.lemeridien-cyprus.com

Member of:
Le Meridien Hotels and Resorts

94

Located directly on the beach on the south side of the island, Le Meridien Limassol combines the very best of French style and service with the warmth of friendly and attentive Cypriot hospitality.

Accommodations include the 265 lavish double rooms, which are the largest on the island. Those requiring even more luxury and privacy can choose from the many suites and villas that are available. But wherever you choose to lay your head you'll be assured of spacious quarters and refined decorations.

Gourmands will relish the hotel's myriad dining opportunities. Choose from delicious Cypriot or French cuisine in a variety of stunning surroundings. Le Vieux Village Taverna offers open air dining and Le Nautile is reputed to be the best French restaurant on the island.

Highlight of the hotel's many leisure facilities is the free-form pool, one of the largest in Cyprus. A unique Thalassotherapy Spa Centre with indoor and outdoor seawater pools, 17 treatment rooms and four relaxing areas is also available. Daily shuttles allow you to explore the surrounding area calling at the public gardens, the shopping centre and the local market. And don't forget to pick up some of the fine leather goods that Cyprus is famous for.

🛏 CY£110-155 (265)

🛏 CY£230-750 (18)

🍽 CY£15-60

☕ included

🍾 🍽 ♿ 🔲 🚁

Honeymoon specials

Champagne, flowers and fruit on arrival. Room upgrade when available. Package deals are available through various tour operators.

Sightseeing and leisure

Fitness club with gym, pool, sauna, jacuzzi, steambath. Tennis, badminton, watersports centre plus seawater lagoon and pier. Beauty treatments available at the Thalassotherapy Spa. Local attractions include Kourium Ancient Theatre, Archaeological Museum, Folkloric Museum, Kollosi Castle, seasonal festivals such as wine festival in September, European Culture Festival during November & December.

Information & Reservations
UK 0870 606 1296
INT. +44 870 606 1296

Paphos Amathus Beach Hotel

Poseidon Ave
62381 Kato
Paphos
Cyprus

✈ Paphos Int. 14km

tel +357 6 264 222
fax +357 6 264 222

pamathus@logos.cy.net
www.pamathus.com

Member of:
The Leading Hotels of the World

The blue of the sea and the blue of the sky is reflected throughout this hotel, with light, airy rooms and beautiful views across the pool and out to the sea. With a design inspired by local monastic architecture, the low-rise building maintains an intimate air, while the commanding columns, marble floors and a lofty atrium bring a sense of space and light.

All rooms and suites have a private balcony or verandah, most overlooking the pool and sea. Ensuite marble bathrooms come as standard, while 19 junior suites have a lounge area and two magnificent suites have separate living rooms.

Service with a smile is the motto of this hotel, where a welcome gift of a fine local red wine and a selection of fruit awaits you. Invitations to a cocktail reception appear weekly, offered with the compliments of the management.

The hotel's extensive health and leisure centre is second to none with a well-equipped gym and professional instructors on hand to offer advice and support. Additional facilities include sauna, steambath, solarium, hydromassage and body massage. The hotel also has an indoor heated swimming pool, a squash court and three floodlit tennis courts.

95

 CY£40-77 (252)

 CY£61-87 (19)

 CY£15-40

☕ included

Honeymoon specials
Upgrade of room when available. Candlelit dinner for two with special menu. White flowers and pink champagne on arrival. Vouchers of CY£50 per couple to be used in the health and recreation centre for the use of sauna, jacuzzi or steambath.

Sightseeing and leisure
At the hotel there is tennis, squash, gym, t-shirt painting, pottery painting, plus therapies such as body wraps, massages and aromatherapy. Nearby, enjoy archeological sites, Akamas peninsula, local markets and villages, shops, boutiques and a quaint fishing harbour.

Czech Republic

The Czech Republic welcomed few tourists until 1989 when its borders finally opened to the outside world.

Today, some 17 million visitors a year appreciate the beauty and mystery of this unspoilt land which adjoins Austria, Germany, Poland and the Slovak Republic.

Most come to view the incredible architecture of the capital, Prague. Buildings from Gothic to Cubist dot the winding lanes and in the new town – Nove Mesto – a youthful vibrancy buzzes through the tiny cafes and individualistic shops. This is also Prague's entertainment and cultural hub – home to excellent centres of music, theatre and art.

Outside of Prague the 79,000 square kilometres of the Republic is relatively undiscovered by tourism, but should not be ignored. As well as many historical cities and castles, highlights include taking the waters in the Victorian spa town of Karlovy Vary or the picturesque train ride to the sleepy village of Krivoklat. In winter, ski the peaks of the Krkonose Mountains. And in summer months, cool off in the glacial lakes of the Sumava or the mysterious caves of Punkevni. But all year-round, don't miss the chance to sit back and watch the world go by with a glass of the world famous Czech beer.

flying time
To: Prague
London: 2 1/2 hrs
NY: 9 hrs

climate
Warm, showery summers and cold snowy winters. July is the hottest month and Dec-Feb see temperatures drop below freezing.

when to go
Prague can be visited year-round but it can get crowded in summer. More rural areas are best visited in summer unless you want to take advantage of the ski areas in the Krkonose Mountains, which should be visited Dec-Feb.

currency
Czech crown

language
Czech, although German and English are widely spoken.

getting around
Prague is a walking city but trams and a good metro system offer respite to the weary traveller.

Hotel Hoffmeister

Information & Reservations
UK 0870 606 1296
INT. +44 870 606 1296

Pod Bruskou 7
Klarov 11800, Prague 1
Czech Republic

✈ Prague 19km

tel +420 2 510 17 111
fax +420 2 510 17 120

www.hoffmeister.cz
hotel@hoffmeister.cz

Tour operators:
UK & US Utell

98

Member of:
Relais & Châteaux

Malà Strana is known as the 'romantic sector' of Prague and nestled in the midst of its 17th-century buildings, at the foot of old castle steps, lies Hotel Hoffmeister. A traditionally fronted building, the hotel is within easy reach of all of Prague's most important cultural sights and the main shopping areas.

The 32 rooms and seven suites are ornately decorated in a variety of colour schemes and all offer high standards of comfort and refinement. Each has climate control, satellite TV and mini bar.

The hotel offers two opportunities for diners; its full service restaurant 'ADA' excels at both Czech and international cuisine and the Cafe Ria is perfect for light meals or dining *al fresco* during Prague's warm summer days. Finally, don't miss the chance to sample a fine bottle of Moravian wine from the extensive local and international cellar held by the hotel's Bar Lily.

The walls of the public areas are lined with the work of artist – and the father of the hotel's owner – Adolf Hoffmeister. His caricatures of cultural icons like Salvador Dali and John Steinbeck adorn the walls and provide the perfect backdrop to your stay in Prague, which is renowned for its art, not to mention beauty, culture and history.

 US$145-230* (32)

 US$205-395* (7)

 US$50-100

 US$10

Honeymoon specials

A three-night stay in the honeymoon suite with special breakfast room service, Sekt and flowers on arrival, one candlelit gala dinner with live music in hotel restaurant (drinks excluded), plus private guided tour of Prague. Price US$1,200.

* Plus tax of 5%.

Sightseeing and leisure

Prague is the cultural centre of the Czech Republic with many theatres, operas, concerts and galleries within easy reach. The hotel is adjacent to Prague Castle, Charles Bridge, Old Town Square and an old Jewish synagogue. Excellent fitness and leisure centre nearby; arrangements in beauty facilities on request.

Hotel Pariz

Information & Reservations
UK 0870 606 1296
INT. +44 870 606 1296

U Obecniho Domu 1
Prague 1, 11000
Czech Republic

✈ Ruzyne Int. 10 miles

tel +420 2 22 195 666
fax +420 2 24 225 475

booking@hotel-pariz.cz
www.hotel-pariz.cz

Tour operators:
UK Cresta
US Concorde Hotels

Even the approach to the Hotel Pariz marks the property as a special place. Lying at the heart of the historic and awe-inspiring city of Prague, the hotel has been transformed back to its *art noveau* heyday – from its striking exterior right through to its stunning and individual interiors.

Originally built in 1904, the government returned the hotel to its owners, the Brandejs family, who have been in the hotel business for more than 100 years, and in 1998 it was completely restored to its original style.

One of the main features is the elegant stairway with case-iron railing and beautifully hand-painted motifs. An equal classic is the Sarah Bernhardt restaurant with original turn-of-the-century mosaics, lighting and gilded decorations. Or sample the Cafe de Paris, where the 1920s atmosphere is recreated with the help of live jazz bands.

All of the 93 rooms boast all the modern-day comforts you would expect, while the bathrooms even have heated floors as well as massage showers.

The Mucha Suite, at the very top of the hotel tower, is renowned not only for its breathtaking views of the charming old city and Prague castle, but also for its unique ambiance.

99

 US$230-330 (88)
 US$390-1,200 (5)
from US$9
from US$8

Honeymoon specials
Room upgrade to deluxe if available. Free entry to the hotel's relax club with sauna. Complimentary champagne on arrival.

Sightseeing and leisure
On site is a beauty salon and hairdresser, shopping and galleries. You are within walking distance of all major sites of Prague, including the Mucha and Kafka museums, State Opera and Prague Castle.

France

flying time
To: Paris
London: 1 hr
NY: 8 hrs
LA: 12-13 hrs

**climate/
when to go**
July-Aug are the
warmest months and
the liveliest time,
with plenty of special
events. Book well in
advance, and at
Easter too. June-Sept
offer more peace
and nicer weather.
The south is warmer
May-Oct, while the
north coast has
similar weather to
southern England.

currency
French franc

language
French

getting around
There are airports in
all the main areas.
The rail service is
one of the best in
Europe, and there
are a number of
good *autoroutes*.
From Britain, use
the Channel Tunnel
or any of the
innumerable ferry
crossings daily.

From the grandeur of Paris to the warm, rustic pleasures of south-west France; from the windswept rocks of Brittany to the star-studded resorts of the Côte d'Azur, France is a country to set you dreaming.

The coastline is spectacular for much of its length, with some of the best sandy beaches in Europe, perfect for romantic strolls. Inland, there are chateaux galore, many turned into luxurious hotels where you can sleep in a bedchamber made for a lord and his lady. As you'd expect, vineyards grace many of the provinces. Champagne, Bordeaux and Burgundy, with their pretty hill-top villages, count among the most famous wine regions in the world.

While the western half of France undulates softly towards the Channel and the Atlantic, the eastern half is marked by magnificent mountains. In the foothills of the Vosges and Jura ranges you can ski and hike in the mighty Alps which border Switzerland and Italy.

The Alps form the eastern boundary of that earthly paradise, Provence. The most famous slice of the Provencal coast is known by the dreamy title Côte d'Azur. Here there are watersports, wonderful restaurants and glitzy casinos aplenty to be found in the glamour-rich, *tres chic* resorts of St Tropez, Cannes, Nice and Monte Carlo.

Château de Bagnols

Information & Reservations
UK 0870 606 1296
INT. +44 870 606 1296

F-69620
Bagnols-en-Beaujolais
France

✈ Lyons 60km

tel +33 4 74 71 40 00
fax +33 4 74 71 40 49

chateaubagnols@compuserve.com
www.bagnols.com

102

Member of:
Relais & Châteaux

Château de Bagnols is set among vast vineyards, forests and rolling green hills in the heart of Beaujolais country. With its majestic towers, moat and honey-coloured stone, the château is one of France's major historic monuments.

You enter across a drawbridge into the beautiful castle which has been lovingly restored throughout, revealing wall paintings created during the Renaissance. In fact, this period is of enormous significance everywhere in the château. The sweeping stone staircases open onto the Renaissance courtyard and the Grand Salon contains one of France's most elaborately carved period fireplaces. Hundreds of specially commissioned items complement the private collection of antique furnishings. Raynaud, one of the old French manufacturers in Limoges, made the blue-and-white china and the old Irish firm Liddell are responsible for the table linen.

Each of the 20 rooms and suites is unique, with antique beds hung with period fabrics, and the bathrooms are stunningly restored.

And as Lyon is known as the gastronomic capital of France, guests can be sure their stay will be a culinary delight. Fresh local ingredients abound and many of the dishes are enhanced with local wines.

 US$340-610 (12)

 US$535-1,000 (8)

 US$78-88

 US$20-42

Honeymoon specials
Room upgrade depending on availability. Flowers and chocolates, local wine and fruit on arrival.

Sightseeing and leisure
Heated outdoor roman pool, 17 metres in diameter and set in its own cherry orchard. Medieval villages and Lyon with its famous art museum. Vineyard tours can be arranged, as can horseriding, horse carriage riding, tennis, trekking and hot-air ballooning near the château. There are also three golf courses nearby.

Château des Vigiers

nformation & Reservations
UK 0870 606 1296
NT. +44 870 606 1296

4240 Monestier
Dordogne
France

✈ Bordeaux 85km

el +33 553 61 50 00
ax +33 553 61 50 20

eservevigiers@calva.net
www.vigiers.com

Member of:
Small Luxury Hotels of the World

Known locally as 'Little Versailles', this French country house hotel located in the countryside to the east of Bordeaux is a haven for romantics, food-lovers and golfers alike. In all its restored grandeur, Château des Vigiers sits in the heart of a region world-renowned for its wine and delectable gastronomy.

The hotel dates back to 1597 and today it has 25 guest rooms in the main house, all beautifully furnished in French country style, and a further 22 rooms and suites in Les Dépendances, where natural local stone and exposed beams dominate the decor and create a romantic ambiance.

For fine dining, choose from the formal gourmet restaurant or the more casual Club House Brasserie. Be sure to peruse the wine list, dripping with fine wines grown in their own grounds.

And don't forget the golf course, which surrounds the château and weaves its way through vineyards and beautiful rolling countryside. It is a true French gem and internationally acclaimed. Meanwhile, during your romantic visit to this delightful hotel, you can also take in a few laps at the pool, play tennis, cycle, go fishing and even horseriding.

103

FF750-1,580 (36)

FF1,000-1,580* (11)

FF220-395

FF95

Honeymoon specials

Bottle of Saussignac, a local sweet wine produced on the estate, chocolates, flowers and fruit basket on arrival.

Honeymoon suite FF1,980.

Sightseeing and leisure

On site is the 18-hole golf course plus 6-hole academy course, driving range and practice area. There are also other activities such as cycling, fishing, tennis and croquet. Private wine tasting excursions to St-Emilion, Pomerol, Graves and Bergerac. Shopping for antiques. Medieval towns of Ste Foy-la-Grande and Monpazier, among others.

Château Eza

Information & Reservations
UK 0870 606 1296
INT. +44 870 606 1296

Rue de la Pise
06360 Eze Village
Côte d'Azur
France

✈ Nice Int. 20 mins

tel +33 4 93 41 12 24
fax +33 4 93 41 16 64

chateza@webstore.fr
www.slh.com/chatueza

104

Member of:
Small Luxury Hotels of the World

Clinging to the walls of the medieval village of Eze, more than 1,300 feet above the sparkling waters of the Mediterranean Sea, the Château Eza is an enchanting, romantic and secluded hotel.

In a part of the scenic and ultra-stylish Côte d'Azur that few know even exists, the hotel is a glorious castle of stone on a narrow cobblestone street, too small even for modern cars.

To reach this castle hideaway which honeymooners will absolutely love, donkeys await at the bottom of the hill to carry luggage up the walkways to a palace that is fit for royalty – indeed this château was once home to H.R.H. Prince William of Sweden.

The medieval feel extends to the 10 bedrooms, all reached along stone passageways and via ancient stone steps. Each room is totally individual but all have been newly decorated and include modern-day luxuries while some have charming fireplaces, private balconies and breathtaking views.

Voted the second most romantic restaurant in the world, Château Eza offers indoor dining or outdoor terraces above the cliff with spectacular, sweeping views along the coast. The gourmet food on offer is created by Nice native Thierry Bagnis, who searches the local markets to bring only the finest food to the table. Truly a delight.

 FF2,000-3,500 (5)

 FF3,000-4,000 (5)

 FF390-550

 included

Honeymoon specials

Complimentary champagne, fruits and flowers on arrival. Information on other packages available upon request.

Sightseeing and leisure

For sightseeing, Monaco, Monte-Carlo, Nice and Cannes are all within easy reach. Don't forget about the Cannes Film Festival in May. Also, extensive leisure facilities nearby. Monte-Carlo Golf Club 5km away, another 30 courses within an hour's drive of the hotel.

Hôtel de la Cité

Information & Reservations
UK 0870 606 1296
INT. +44 870 606 1296

Place de L'Eglise
11000 Carcassonne
France

✈ Carcassonne 4km

Tel +33 468 71 98 71
Fax +33 468 71 50 15

reservations@hoteldelacite.com
www.hoteldelacite.com

Member of:
The Leading Hotels of the World

Rub shoulders with Europe's elite as well as some of the world's top movie stars at this perfect hideaway in Europe's largest walled city.

Hôtel de la Cité, with its neo-gothic architecture, solid stone walls, oak panelling and stained glass windows, is surrounded by stunning gardens and breathtaking views of the Pyrenees. Standing between two historic landmarks – the Château Comtal and the Saint-Nazaire Basilica – the hotel is a central part of this fascinating southern French town, surrounded by the lush Minervois and Corbieres vineyards.

Carcassonne's impressive medieval citadel and the Canal du Midi have both been listed as UNESCO World Heritage sites, while beyond is the land of Cathar castles.

La Barbacane gourmet restaurant is famed for its menus, which combine the freshest local ingredients and innovative recipes – it also boasts the largest wine cellar in the Aude region.

Rooms and suites are individually decorated with baldaquins, canopies and the finest fabrics woven in local workshops. Junior suites have private garden terraces and the pool lies in a romantic setting, sheltered by sun-baked stone walls and lined by cypresses and colourful flower beds.

105

FF950-2,150 (49)
FF2,300-3,200 (12)
from FF200
FF130

Honeymoon specials
Two-night special includes complimentary upgrade to a junior suite or suite with private terrace, flowers, champagne and *petits fours* in room on arrival, buffet breakfast in Chez Saskia or continental breakfast on your terrace, one candlelight dinner at La Barbacane, plus free parking at the hotel. Rates from FF3,000-4,100 per person.

Sightseeing and leisure
Visit the 12th-century Chateau Comtal, Basilique de Saint Nazaire and the 17th-century Canal du Midi. During the month of July enjoy the Festival de Carcasonne and on the first fortnight in August, Les Medievales.

Hotel du Palais

Information & Reservations
UK 0870 606 1296
INT. +44 870 606 1296

l'Avenue de l'Impératrice
64200 Biarritz
France

✈ Biarritz 3km

tel +33 5 59 41 64 00
fax +33 5 59 41 67 99

reception@hotel-du-palais.com
www.hotel-du-palais.com

Member of:
The Leading Hotels of the World

Biarritz, set in a dramatically beautiful landscape at the foot of the Pyrenees, has for centuries courted the rich and famous. The Hotel du Palais, formerly the summer residence of Napoleon III and Empress Eugenia, dominates the town and is a splendid example of Second Empire architecture, blending sumptuousness with both elegance and restraint. The hotel has been painstakingly restored to combine luxury with period charm.

The bedrooms are especially refined, being individually decorated in light shades, with flowing drapes and period antiques. Most are ocean-facing with calming views of the sandy beaches.

Classic French cuisine and mouth-watering regional specialities are served in the hotel's two stunning restaurants: the palatial La Rotonde and the more intimate Villa Eugénie.

Visitors can explore the rolling hills and the small fishing villages surrounding Biarritz, with their pretty, brightly painted houses and many bustling markets that characterise the Basque region.

Sports facilities are unusually comprehensive. The town's busy casinos and inns also provide a stimulating variety of evening entertainment.

🛏 FF1,250-2,950 (134)

🛏 FF2,600-6,350 (22)

🍽 FF290-395

☕ from FF150

🍾 ⚭ 🏊 ⑤

Honeymoon specials

Flowers, fruit basket and perfume on arrival. Double room with sea view, continental breakfast and dinner (drinks excluded) to be taken overlooking the ocean. The package costs from US$430 per couple per day.

Sightseeing and leisure

Outdoor swimming pool, sauna, fitness club, all watersports, tennis, boutique. Golf courses nearby. Romantic walks to Musée del al Mer. Trips to picturesque villages over the Spanish border and prehistoric caves. Tapas-style gala evenings in a Basque farmhouse. Music festivals year round.

Hotel Martinez

Information & Reservations
UK 0870 606 1296
INT. +44 870 606 1296

3 La Croisette
06406 Cannes
France

✈ Nice 25km

Tel +33 4 92 98 73 00
Fax +33 4 93 39 67 82

martinez@concorde-hotels.com
www.hotel-martinez.com

Tour operators:
UK Elegant Resorts
Cresta Holidays

Member of:
The Leading Hotels of the World
Concorde Hotels

Home to the famous film festival, Cannes is France's answer to Hollywood. Commanding grand views over the city and the bay on the famous Croisette Boulevard is the Hotel Martinez, an Art Deco palace which has kept all of its '20s and '30s glamour and style, with spiral staircases, piano bar and hotel staff in crisp white linen.

The glitz is carried through to the spacious, sun-filled rooms and suites. Wooden walnut furniture, carriage clocks, fireplaces, stylish lamps and bold print fabrics make the Martinez a supremely elegant place to stay, continuing the tradition of Cannes as one of the playgrounds of the rich and famous from around the world.

The hotel's Palme d'Or restaurant has a deservedly high reputation, noted for its 1930s furniture including black lacquered armchairs covered in pearl-grey and maroon and its period silverware and glassware. The cuisine is international with regional Provençal recipes such as *bouillabaisse* also on the menu.

For sun-seekers and stargazers alike, a pier clad with stylish pink parasols and sun-loungers stretches out over the azure waters of the Mediterranean. And for true glitz, a Los Angeles-style palm-fringed pool with a private beach awaits.

107

FF1,100-2,100 (393)
FF2,800-15,000 (24)
FF200-900
FF160

Honeymoon specials

Champagne and flowers on arrival. Room upgrade upon availability.

Sightseeing and leisure

Private beach with a variety of watersports, outdoor pool, exercise room. Bay of Cannes, its shops and restaurants. Nice with its beautiful promenade and museums devoted to the works of Picasso and Matisse. Monaco, Monte-Carlo and Grasse are also nearby.

Information & Reservations
UK 0870 606 1296
INT. +44 870 606 1296

Hotel Royal Monceau

37 Avenue Hoche
75008 Paris
France

✈ Orly 30km

tel +33 1 42 99 88 00
fax +33 1 42 99 89 91

royalmonceau@jetmultimedia.fr
www.royalmonceau.com

Toll free:
UK 00800 426 313 55

108

A prodigy of the 1920s, this noble hotel is situated a stone's throw from the Arc de Triomphe and the fashionable shops along the Champs-Elysées and Faubourg Saint Honoré. Yet it has managed to maintain an unpretentious and tranquil character, home to travellers with the highest expectations, and a romantic secret getaway for honeymooners.

The property is imbued with the spirit of the Roaring Twenties, with antique furniture, chandeliers and breathtaking flowers within a timeless elegance.

Indulge in the renowned French cuisine within a garden of flowers, or savour the delights of Italian cuisine amidst Venetian decor at one of the most celebrated restaurants in Paris.

Relax in the heated indoor swimming pool, enjoy a sauna, a steambath and a massage, or brave the hotel's complete state-of-the-art fitness facilities for some vigourous exercise prior to or after having explored the wonders of Paris, from the Eiffel Tower to the Louvre Museum or beloved Notre Dame.

 FF2,700-3,800 (180)

 FF3,900-19,000 (39)

 FF370-500

 FF160-230

Honeymoon specials

Heavenly Honeymoon Programme includes accommodation in a room category of your choice and an upgrade upon arrival, champagne, chocolates, fruit and flowers in the room, daily breakfast, one bottle of wine for any meal taken in the hotel's restaurants, access to health & beauty centre, embroidered bathrobes, plus a voucher for a one night stay in a Kempinski Hotel on your first wedding anniversary.

Sightseeing and leisure

Les Thermes Health and Beauty Centre with pool, sauna, steambath, gym, weight rooms, squash, hairdressing salon, massages. Paris, 'the city of lights', is on your doorstep. The hotel is very close to the Arc de Triomphe, the Champs-Elysées and 20 minutes walking distance from the Louvre and *bateaux mouches*.

Oustau de Baumanière

Information & Reservations
UK 0870 606 1296
INT. +44 870 606 1296

13520 Les Baux
de Provence
France

✈ Marseille 30km

tel +33 4 90 54 33 07
fax +33 4 90 54 40 46

www.oustaudebaumaniere.com

Member of:
Relais & Châteaux

The Oustau de Baumanière is a 14th-century farmhouse imbued with traditional French charm and set in a beautiful meandering garden right in the heart of the romantic Provence countryside.

Each of the 22 rooms and apartments are unique, elegantly decorated and display a combination of tradition and character with modern comfort.

With all the beauty and facilities the hotel possesses it may be difficult to drag yourself away, but if you do there are a wealth of treasures to explore. Arles, the Baux-de-Provence, the Camargue, Nimes, Avignon, Montpellier and Aix-en-Provence are some of the places that are well worth a visit. There are cathedrals to discover, museums to wander round and festivals to take part in, revolving around a myriad of subjects including music, bullfighting and grape harvesting. And of course there is the awesome natural beauty of the countryside to celebrate.

Back at the hotel, chef Jean-André Charial brings generations of experience to the table and will create a gastronomic delight you'll never forget. Certainly you won't forget the hotel's wine list in a hurry – the cellar is a veritable treasure trove, holding more than 100,000 bottles.

109

 US$209-232 (13)

 US$340-355 (9)

 US$80-120

 US$19

Honeymoon specials
Flowers and fruit in the room on arrival.

Sightseeing and leisure
Tennis and horseriding available. Golf course nearby.
Markets and historic villages in the area are worth a visit.

Germany

flying time
To: Frankfurt
London: 1-2 hrs

**climate/
when to go**
The weather can be unpredictable and it can rain at any time. May-Oct are the best months. July temperatures average 18°C in the lowlands and 20°C for more sheltered southern parts. Ski fans will enjoy the cold conditions from Dec-Mar.

currency
Deutschmark

language
German, although English is widely spoken.

getting around
An excellent network of internal flights, high speed train links and coach services. Good taxi and bus services in cities. Car hire is the best way to tour and see the countryside.

Germany is an intriguing blend of old world romance and modern-day glitz.

The wooded mountains of Bavaria, dotted with fairytale castles, contrast nicely with the cosmopolitan buzz of the cities. Hansel and Gretel houses wait to be discovered in picturesque countryside valleys, where rolling hills are covered with vineyards which give way to magnificent mountains, perfect for walking in summer months and skiing in winter.

The old towns and cities are being transformed by modern, innovative architects. Relish the contrasts – explore the myriad of winding streets filled with ancient burgher houses and vaulted cloisters before bursting out into 1990s splendour and extravagance.

The post-war history of Berlin is as fascinating as that of centuries gone by, while cities like Hamburg and Bonn have developed into Europe's finest, with every form of entertainment on offer from opera to pop concerts and ballet to street performance. Indulge in the luxury of a spa treatment in one of Germany's famous spa towns. Pamper yourself like never before and then enjoy the glitz and glamour of these big name resorts.

The magic of Germany will never cease to amaze. Whatever you want you can find it here, between the glistening waters of the North Sea and the Baltic to the north, and Switzerland and Austria to the south.

Hotel Krone Assmannshausen

Information & Reservations
UK 0870 606 1296
INT. +44 870 606 1296

Rheinuferstrasse 10
65385 Rudesheim
Germany

✈ Frankfurt 60km

tel +49 6722 4030
fax +49 6722 3049

info@kroneas.de
www.kroneas.de

The tiny wine village of Assmannshausen sits at the widening of the narrow Rhine river gorge where the Hotel Krone dominates the scene, its small spires and wooden balconies creating the impression of a mansion from days gone by.

The wisteria-covered terrace and raised restaurant are the perfect spots for dining and watching the busy river life gliding past. Much of the building dates from the turn of the century. The interior is perfectly in keeping with the exterior, with large pieces of lovingly polished furniture set against dark panelled walls. Some of the bedrooms are in the main building while others are located in the adjacent annex.

All rooms and the 11 suites have all been recently redecorated and renovated to the highest standard. Each suite is unique and the epitome of comfort and luxury. Beautifully refurbished in a combination of antiques, silk and marble, each has a luxurious marble bathroom ensuite for you to soak away your cares.

The restaurant boasts top-quality international and regional specialities and an exceptional wine cellar. River steamers dock just a two-minute walk away so arrive by boat and the hotel will send someone to meet you and tend to your luggage.

111

 DM185-320

 DM390-780

 DM86-156

 DM22

Honeymoon specials
Fruit platter and flowers on arrival.

Sightseeing and leisure
There are plenty of sightseeing opportunities around. Take a Rhine cruise, walk in the Niederwald forest, tour a wine cellar and taste local wines, visit the local falconry or take the chairlift or cable car for a bird's-eye view of the area.

Greece

flying time
To: Athens
London: 3 hrs
NY: 10-11 hrs
LA: 13 hrs

**climate/
when to go**
The 'season' opens
with the celebration
of Greek Easter.
Beautiful wildflowers
in the spring are
followed by long, hot
summers; and you
can often swim
until mid-Oct.

currency
Greek drachma.
Traveller's cheques
and cheque cards are
useful, but for travel
on the more remote
islands, you will need
drachma.

language
Greek but most
everyone speaks
some English.

getting around
Car hire is not too
expensive, but take
care on the winding
mountain roads. And
remember to get car
insurance. Many
islands have direct
flights to Athens.

There is nothing quite like Greece and its stunning islands to make the rest of the world seem blurred, hesitant and grey.

In the translucent light, the Aegean is the bluest of seas, Greek houses are the most dazzling white, the harbours and their sunlit boats shimmer brilliantly and there is no scent so heady as Greek mountain herbs and pines on a beautiful summer's day.

The intensity of the Greek present makes a striking contrast with the haunting beauty of its ancient monuments, and nowhere more so than in Athens, where the Parthenon overlooks the exuberant capital. From Athens, it is easy to reach idyllic Delphi, sacred to Apollo, or see a play at the ancient and mysterious theatre of Epidauros.

Also from Athens you can hire a boat and sail to literally hundreds of secluded islands which come in an astonishing variety. Some are lush and forested, some rolling with rows of agricultural crops, others stark, rockbound crags rising out of the Aegean.

Just over a hundred islands are inhabited, and all but a very few have excellent sugary-white beaches, capped by the cleanest, warmest, most transparent seas to be found anywhere in Europe.

For sheer romance, it's an idyllic getaway destination.

Elounda Mare

Information & Reservations
UK 0870 606 1296
INT. +44 870 606 1296

77053 Elounda
Crete
Greece

✈ Heraklion 70km

tel +30 841 41102
fax +30 841 41307

elmare@agn.forthnet.gr
www.relaischateaux.fr/elounda

114

Tour operators:
UK Elegant Resorts
Prestige Holidays

Member of:
Relais & Châteaux

The gorgeous island of Crete, legendary birthplace of ancient Greek myth, was once home to King Minos and his dark labyrinth. The Elounda Mare is a secluded little world that enjoys a privileged position overlooking the coastline of Mirabello Bay and the mountain range of Sitia.

The bungalows of Elounda Mare are the perfect place for newly-married couples seeking serenity, romance and seclusion. Each one follows Cretan tradition, blending whitewashed walls with local beige and grey stone and marble. All rooms are furnished with locally crafted dark wood, Grecian folk art and tapestries in rich colours. Wide windows lead onto private terraces, each fitted with a swimming pool.

Beginning the day with breakfast from a rich buffet, guests can watch the fishing boats haul in the catch of the day – and a few hours later see

 GRD43,000-85,000

 GRD54,000-280,000

 from GRD10,000

 included

Honeymoon specials
Sparkling wine, fruit and flowers in room on arrival.
Room upgrade subject to availability.

it served at the Yacht Club. Crowning the small harbour and sandy beach, the Yacht Club also forms the venue for traditional theme evenings with food, music and dance. The more intimate Old Mill restaurant offers a refined menu with a fine selection of Greek and French wines.

The hotel has a private chapel in the grounds and is happy to take care of any arrangements necessary for a perfect wedding.

Sightseeing and leisure

On site are tennis courts, massage, aromatherapy, sauna and steambath. Sailing, scuba diving, a 9-hole, par-3 golf course and gym are also nearby. For sightseeing, Crete is packed with historic attractions including the archaeological remains at Knossos and the Heraklion museum. As well as these, restaurants, markets and breathtaking scenery abound.

Information & Reservations
UK 0870 606 1296
INT. +44 870 606 1296

Kivotos Clubhotel

Ornos Bay
Mykonos 84600
Greece

✈ Mykonos 3km

tel +30 289 24094
fax +30 289 22844

kivotos1@hol.gr
www.slh.com/kivotosc/

Member of:
Small Luxury Hotels of the World

116

Kivotos Clubhotel is a luxurious resort overlooking the magnificent Bay of Ornos. Though new, the Kivotos revels in old-fashioned traditions of service and hospitality, treating all its guests as VIPs. A welcome glass of champagne and a fruit basket await guests on their arrival, compliments of the house. The comfortable rooms benefit from sea views as well as a whole batch of modern amenities including video and colour television. Every guest will feel pampered and at home.

As well as barbecues around the pool, three restaurants offer a variety of delicious food: the gourmet restaurant 'La Medusse', with Greek and French cuisine, the 'Mare' with authentic south Italian food, and the seaside Mediterranean restaurant 'Le Pirate'. Picnics can also be taken on excursions to Delos and other local beaches.

For a truly romantic experience, honeymooners may wish to avail themselves of the hotel's yacht, the Prince de Neufchatel. Available for a daily or weekly cruise, the yacht has spacious teak decks (ideal for sunbathing) and elegant suites with private bathrooms. On board, a crew of three tends to passengers' every need, 24 hours a day.

 DR49,000-135,000 (34)

 DR98,000-218,000 (11)

🍽 from DR11,000

☕ from DR7,500

🍾 💍 ⑤

Honeymoon specials

Welcome glass of champagne, fruits and flowers in room on arrival. Room upgrade upon availability.

Sightseeing and leisure

On site there is a sauna, freshwater and seawater pool, squash, fitness centre, massage and jacuzzi. Nearby/on request: hairdresser, manicure and pedicure, beautician. The area surrounding Kivotos is full of ancient history and archaeological sites to explore. There are also museums, beaches, churches, and a cosmopolitan nightlife.

Information & Reservations
UK 0870 606 1296
INT. +44 870 606 1296

Santa Marina Hotel

Ornos Bay, GR-846 00
Mykonos
Greece

✈ Mykonos 4km

tel +30 289 23220
fax +30 289 23412

info@santa-marina.gr
www. santa-marina.gr
www.luxurycollection.com

Member of:
The Luxury Collection

Mykonos, a glittering jewel in the Aegean Sea, is home to Santa Marina, which sits on a hillside overlooking Ornos Bay. A 20-acre complex of whiter than white dwellings, it is an ideal place to soak up the sun and relax.

The traditional Cycladic architecture, amidst the green lawns and azure sea, blends with the natural and romantic environment of the resort.

Each of the 90 rooms, suites and villas has its own atmosphere and style, all being decorated in beautiful colours and soft furnishings. Fling the windows open or step onto the private terrace to let in the island breeze and enjoy the sea view.

For guests who want a little more than a dip in the sparkling Mediterranean, a variety of sports are available such as waterskiing, scuba diving, tennis and a fully equipped health club. For those who wish to pamper themselves, the Clarins Beauty Center offers treatments and massage by professional beauticians.

Two restaurants: one poolside, and Daniele's restaurant overlooking a charming cove, offer a fine variety of international cuisine – Italian, Oriental and also deliciously fresh seafood.

117

 DR50,000-115,000 (64)

 DR65,000-180,000 (26)

🍽 DR6,000-30,000

☕ included

Honeymoon specials
Complimentary fruit and wine on arrival. Room upgrade when available.

Sightseeing and leisure
Clarins Beauty Center for treatments and massage, gym, sauna, jacuzzi, steambath, tennis, private beach, waterskiing and swimming pool on site. The island of Delos, religious centre for the ancient Greeks, is nearby and takes half an hour by boat. There are also shops, bars, restaurants and clubs nearby.

St Nicolas Bay

Information & Reservations
UK 0870 606 1296
INT. +44 870 606 1296

PO Box 47
PO Box-GR 72100 Aghios
Nikolaos, Crete
Greece

✈ Heraklion 70km

tel +30 841 25041
fax +30 841 24556

stnicolas@otenet.gr

Tour operators:
UK Prestige
US Classic

118

Member of:
Johansens
Grand Heritage Hotels

Encircled by emerald green gardens, this five-star deluxe bungalow hotel is a haven of tranquillity between sea and sun, just two kilometres from the lively town of Aghios Nikolaos.

Nestling among olive, lemon and orange trees, each of the open-plan bungalows and suites are elegant and decorated to a very high standard. Junior and bungalow suites all have private pools, sun terraces and stunning sea views.

Many choices await you for dining. 'Labyrinthos' and the 'Club House' restaurants offer informal buffet breakfast and dinners; the beachfront 'Blue Bay' offers *à la carte* lunch; and for those romantic evenings, visit the poolside 'Minotaure' or the beachfront 'Kafenion' for dining under the stars. Seafood is a speciality of both establishments. Pre or post-dining, relax in the air-conditioned comfort of the hotel's two cocktail bars or simply explore the spacious, cool public areas.

Just a short walk away from the swimming pool you come to the hotel's secluded sun-drenched bay. Sunbeds and umbrellas are provided or if you prefer to keep active, diving, canoeing, waterskiing and windsurfing are available. A short walk also brings you to the town of Aghios Nikolaos with cafes, shops and nightlife to keep you entertained.

 DR35,000-77,000 (57)

 DR50,000-200,000 (46)

 from DR8,000

 included

Honeymoon specials
Champagne, flowers and basket of fruit on arrival. Complimentary room service breakfast any time. Upgrade to superior room subject to availability. Honeymooners also have complimentary use of the health club services such as steambath, sauna and jacuzzi. Complimentary photos.

Sightseeing and leisure
At the hotel's private beach there is a watersports centre with qualified instructors for waterskiing, windsurfing, sailing, scuba diving school. Luxurious cabin cruiser to hire for private excursions. Indoor and outdoor pools, fitness centre, gym, steambath, jacuzzi and massage. Local attractions include Byzantine churches and monasteries, the museum of Minoan Civilisation, Palace of Knossos and Phaistos.

The Tsitouras Collection

Information & Reservations
UK 0870 606 1296
INT. +44 870 606 1296

Firostefani
GR 847 00
Santorini
Greece

✈ Santorini 6km

tel +301 3622326
fax +301 3636738

www.tsitouras.gr
tsitoura@otenet.gr

Originally part of a large mansion complex built in the 19th century, the beautiful Tsitouras Collection perches atop a 1,000ft cliff on the island of Santorini, commanding unparalleled views of the Aegean Sea. Comprising five traditional houses in the Cycladic style, restored and lavishly furnished by its art-loving owner, the Tsitouras Collection is a stunning example of nature and human endeavour working in harmony to create something unique.

Beautiful objects of antiquity grace every wall and corner, and the cool, sculptural interiors with their elegant domes and skylights are offset by warm colours. Each house has distinctive character and romantic associations. The dream-like House of Portraits sits at the heart of the complex, its walls lined with gorgeous gilt-framed oil paintings and engravings including a portrait of Lord Byron. The House of the Winds takes its name from the Tower of the Winds in Athens, its airy comfort combining perfectly with the classic architecture.

A favourite with honeymooners due to its seclusion, The House of Nureyev balances as daintily as a dancer at the apex of the Tsitouras Collection. And The House of Porcelain with its authentic Napoleonic bed and House of the Sea with its hidden nooks complete this romantic hideaway.

119

Honeymoon specials
Complimentary champagne, flowers and fruit basket on arrival.

Sightseeing and leisure
Beauty salon and hairdresser nearby. Boat cruises, wine tasting, the lovely, ancient buildings of Santorini. The Tsitouras Collection also offers a free mini-bar.

 US$365-550

 no restaurant at hotel

 included

Italy

120

The Italians have no false modesty: 'Ours is the most beautiful country in the world', they tell you. And who can argue?

From the snowy northern Alps to the lacy almond groves of Sicily in the south, from the long, liquid sapphire lakes of Como, Garda and Lugano to the sublime and glitzy Amalfi Coast, playground of Roman Emperors, Italy is sensuous, sumptuous and blessed.

Mountains fall sheer into the sea, lakes glimmer amid vineyards and castles, and each hill wears a cape of olive groves and a medieval town on top like a hat. Nowhere else will you find such a concentration of art. The country is roughly the size of Britain but contains half of the greatest art in the entire world. The Uffizi Gallery in Florence alone houses more work by Michelangelo than anywhere else in Italy, along with important works by Botticelli, among others.

Italy was the first country in Europe to recover after the Dark Ages, and the Italians used this headstart to build dream cities such as Venice, Siena, Naples and Rome. They softened the wild contours of the land with villas and beautifully structured, romantic gardens.

Best of all, the Italians learned to cultivate pleasure to a unique degree. Thanks to all the wine cellars and vineyards, well-preserved castles and farmhouses, there are characterful hotels aplenty. Elegance, grace and passion fill every detail here, from designer clothes to the tomato-rich sauces of a hearty Tuscan stew. Beauty is more than skin deep in Italy; it is a way of life.

Information & Reservations
UK 0870 606 1296
INT. +44 870 606 1296

Albergo Pietrasanta

Palazzo Barsanti Bonetti
Via Garibaldi 35
55045 Pietrasanta (Lucca)
Italy

✈ Pisa 25km
✈ Florence 90km

tel +39 05 84 79 37 26
fax +39 05 84 79 37 28

a.pietrasanta@versilia.toscana.it
www.albergopietrasanta.com

122

Tour operators:
UK Elegant Resorts

Member of:
The Charming Hotels
Hospitality in Historical Houses

This intimate, exclusive hotel occupies Palazzo Barsanti Bonetti, a 17th-century building that is one of the most important in this very historical centre of Pietrasanta. Its secluded and private atmosphere is home-like which makes staying at the Albergo Pietrasanta a unique and unforgettable experience.

All rooms are equipped with individual air conditioning units, satellite television, mini-bar and are decorated with a magnificent array of original frescoes.

Pietrasanta is only a few miles away from the famous Forte dei Marni beach and the major sites of historical and artistic interests in Tuscany, providing the perfect destination for that sleek cultural break in the sunshine.

Take time to explore the charming area, visiting the many monuments and cathedrals before heading for the seaside to relax on the beach.

 ITL300,000-480,000 (8)

 ITL500,000-650,000 (10)

 ITL50,000-80,000

☕ included

Honeymoon specials

Welcome drink, Tuscany wine and local biscuits, roses in the room on arrival, breakfast in the room or in the conservatory until 2pm. Room upgrade subject to availability. Candlelit dinner. If stay is longer than seven nights, one night will be free of charge.

Sightseeing and leisure

On-site facilities include gym and bicycles. Nearby is a swimming pool, tennis, golf and watersports. Situated in northern Tuscany, you can take excursions to typical Tuscan villages nearby, boat trips to the romantic area of Cinqueterre, Pisa and Lucca.

Information & Reservations
UK 0870 606 1296
INT. +44 870 606 1296

Brufani Palace

12 Piazza Italia
06100 Perugia
Italy

✈ S Egidio 15km

tel +39 07 55 73 25 41
fax +39 07 55 72 02 10

brufani@tin.it
www.sinahotels.com

The Brufani Palace dates back to the late 19th century and is situated on Colle Landone in the historical centre of Perugia, one of the region's most majestic sites. From the balcony on the edge of the square where the hotel stands, you feel like you're in a Renaissance painting, with your view of the Umbrian hills and valleys sweeping below and the ancient towns of Todi and Assisi clearly visible.

With more than a century of experience, Brufani has mastered the art of hospitality. All the rooms and suites are elegantly decorated and furnished with antiques, and over the years visitors have included royal families from around the world, politicians and stars, including Prince Albert of Monaco and the Queen Mother.

The verdant Umbrian countryside is just waiting to be explored, and don't forget to sample the extravagant regional favourite – truffles. The hotel serves delectable local dishes based on truffles, served with a wide range of world-renowned wines from a well-stocked cellar.

Another must is a wander through historical Perugia, with its maze of medieval churches, alleys and stairways, all perfectly preserved to the extent that you really will feel you have stepped back in time.

123

 ITL490,000* (90)

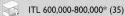 ITL 600,000-800,000* (35)

 ITL100,000-200,000*

 ITL40,000*

Honeymoon specials
Complimentary fruit basket and bottle of Italian wine in room on arrival.

* Rates are inclusive of service; 10% VAT to be added.

Sightseeing and leisure
For history lovers there is plenty to see. Try the National Gallery and the Archaelogical Museum and visit the medieval towns of Todi, Assisi and Gubbio. The Umbria Jazz Festival is in July. There is also a relaxation and solarium centre on site.

Excelsior Palace Hotel

Information & Reservations
UK   0870 606 1296
INT. +44 870 606 1296

Via San Michele di Pagana, 8
16035 Rapallo-Portofino
Coast
Italy

✈ Genoa 32km

tel +39 01 85 23 06 66
fax +39 01 85 23 02 14

excelsior@thi.it
www.thi.it

124

Situated on the cliffs of the Bay of Rapallo overlooking the sapphire sea of the Portofino coast, the elegant Excelsior Palace has come back to life again after a 20-year closure. During the '50s and '60s the Excelsior was frequented by leading names of the cultural and theatrical worlds before its deterioration and eventual closure in 1974.

The hotel has now been totally rebuilt, both inside and out, and expanded from four floors to seven, all to the highest standards of luxurious living. All rooms and suites offer inspirational views and their elegance and comfort will satisfy the most demanding guest with the dominant colours of coral, blue and sand. The Beach Club terraces overlooking the sea and the pool will literally take your breath away. During warm nights enjoy dinner on the terrace, where top Italian chefs present a range of the most typical Ligurian dishes as well as freshly caught fish from the sea below.

There are plenty of opportunities to explore the area with excursions around the Riviera by boat or helicopter or even to go further afield to Genoa.

 ITL370,000-620,000 (108)

 ITL600,000-1,800,000 (17)

 ITL85,000*

 included

Honeymoon specials
Room upgrade: all rooms with sea view and balcony. Complimentary bottle of Italian Spumante and complimentary 30-minute massage.

* Halfboard per person.

Sightseeing and leisure
Beach club. Health and fitness club with beauty farm for massages, facials and body treatments. Excursions by boat to Portofino, San Fruttuoso, Cinque Terre and Genoa. An 18-hole golf course, tennis, diving, waterskiing, windsurfing, horseracing, miniature golf, trekking, discos and museums are all nearby.

Information & Reservations
UK 0870 606 1296
INT. +44 870 606 1296

Piazza Tasso 34
80067 Sorrento
Italy

✈ Naples 60km

tel +39 08 18 07 10 44
fax +39 08 18 77 12 06.

exvitt@exvitt.it
www.exvitt.it

Tour operators:
UK Abercrombie & Kent

Grand Hotel
Excelsior Vittoria

The Excelsior Vittoria is a supremely elegant 19th-century building perched high above the town of Sorrento on the dramatically beautiful Amalfi coast. The hotel was built in 1834 on the site of a Roman villa and in the impeccable gardens and orange grove where archaeological treasures have been found, some of the original columns can still be seen.

Centuries-old frescoes, handsome vaults and mouldings, and antique furnishings characterise the elegance and refinement of this beautifully maintained hotel, which has been owned by the Fiorentino family for more than 160 years. Most rooms have antique iron beds, spacious marble bathrooms and splendid, sweeping views over the Bay of Naples.

Guests can dine *al fresco* against the impressive backdrop of Mount Vesuvius or enjoy traditional Italian and Neopolitan dishes under the majestic painted ceilings of the Vittoria dining room. This grand banqueting room, and the adjoining reception area, hold up to 350 guests and provide a splendid and romantic venue for a wedding party.

Visitors can sip cocktails on the terrace as the sun fades into the horizon, enjoy a moment of meditation in the reading room, take a dip in the hotel pool or enjoy a long, meandering cruise along one of the world's most famous coastlines.

 ITL488,000-695,000 (106)

 ITL882,000-2,942,000 (13)

🍴 ITL75,000

☕ ITL20,000

Honeymoon specials
Complimentary flowers and Italian Spumante on arrival.

Sightseeing and leisure
A private lift links the hotel to the lively port of Sorrento. The archaeological treasures of Naples. Pompeii and the natural beauty of the surrounding area and islands -- Capri, Positano, Ravello, Amalfi, Ischia -- are within easy reach. There is a coiffeur in the hotel.

Information & Reservations
UK 0870 606 1296
INT. +44 870 606 1296

Grand Hotel Fasano

Via Zanardelli 190
Gardone Riviera
Lake Garda
Italy

✈ Verona 45km

tel +39 03 65 29 02 20
fax +39 03 65 29 02 21

info@grand-hotel-fasano.it
www.grand-hotel-fasano.it

The Grand Hotel Fasano stands majestically on the shores of Lake Garda, surrounded by a private park. The hotel was originally built as the royal hunting suite of the Austrian Imperial House and today this tradition merges beautifully with the ultimate in modern comfort.

Start your day on the lakeside terrace with a delicious buffet breakfast and watch the world come alive in the exquisite morning light reflected off the water. The terrace will probably become the focus of your stay here, and you have the option to also eat dinner overlooking the lake. If you'd rather be inside, the restaurants provide impressive gourmet cuisine with a choice of international or specialist Italian dishes on offer. And of course the service is impeccable. You will probably venture back out on the terrace, however, to enjoy unforgettable evenings under the stars. All bedrooms are furnished with style and have either a balcony or terrace overlooking the lake.

Take an excursion by hydrofoil or on one of the old-style steam boats – definitely the best way to get your bearings and discover the striking Italian countryside. Or you could go for a stroll through the beautiful rolling hills surrounding the hotel and take in the fresh lake air.

Honeymoon specials
On request.

Sightseeing and leisure
Sailing, waterskiing and windsurfing are all available and there are three golf courses nearby. Beautiful and historic Verona, the setting for *Romeo and Juliet*, is close by and waiting to be explored.

🛏 US$157-240 (89)

🍽 US$50-100

☕ US$15

Information & Reservations
UK 0870 606 1296
INT. +44 870 606 1296

Grand Hotel Villa Igiea

43 Salita Belmonte
90142 Palermo
Italy

✈ Palermo 25km

tel +39 091 543744
fax +39 091 547654

villa-igiea@thi.it
www.thi.it

Overlooking the bay of Palermo and sloping right down to the seafront, the elegant Villa Igiea, probably one of the best-known hotels in Sicily, was designed at the turn of the century by Ernesto Basile.

The hotel's 'golden book' is full of illustrious names like Kaiser Willhelm of Prussia, Edward VII, Juan Carlos and screen stars Burt Lancaster and Claudia Cardinale. It has also played its part in the darker side of Sicily's history as boss Masino Spador was arrested here.

The rooms and suites are all beautifully decorated with art nouveau furnishings and set in the splendid terraced gardens where the heady scent of jasmine abounds. Visitors can while away the hours in the comfortable reading room or soaking up the sun beside the seawater swimming pool. There is also a tennis court and fitness room.

In the evening, relax and enjoy the melodic sounds of piano music in the American bar. And as you would expect in this part of the world, guests have the chance to sample magnificent regional Mediterranean cuisine in the restaurant, with meals being served on the romantic terrace in summer to ensure you get the chance to really enjoy the view.

127

🛏 ITL280,000-450,000 (114)

🛏 ITL720,000-920,000 (6)

🍴 ITL70,000-200,000

☕ ITL30,000-60,000

🍷 ♿ ◎

Honeymoon specials
Room upgrade, Italian Spumante, flowers.

Sightseeing and leisure
The historical sites of Palermo, including San Giorgio dei Genovesi, Caravaggio's, the stunning cathedral.

Information & Reservations
UK 0870 606 1296
INT. +44 870 606 1296

Hotel Gabbia D'Oro

4A Corso Porta Borsari
37121 Verona
Italy

✈ Verona 18km

tel +39 045 80 03 060
fax +39 045 59 02 93

gabbiadoro@easynet.it

128

The Hotel Gabbia D'Oro, an 18th-century palazzo located in the heart of Verona, is an elegant hotel which oozes romance. Its grand style reflects the rich heritage of the original building, and it contains many original grandiose frescoes, the beamed ceiling, and in the bar area much of the original, ornate carved panelling.

The welcome here is certainly warm and the hotel is small and discreet, with the management determined to ensure your privacy is observed in every way. Just off the reception area is a cosy lounge with high, beamed ceilings, ancient stone walls, fine antiques and Persian carpets. Or you can relax in the intimate bar next door or soak up the sun in the charming L'Orangerie courtyard. Only hotel guests are allowed into the bar and restaurant, reinforcing that 'home away from home' feeling.

All rooms are individually decorated and abound with antique furniture – in some cases they have narrow balconies with wrought-iron detailing which overlook either the street or the courtyard below. A wander around beautiful, historic Verona – Romeo and Juliet's city – is a delight, with many historic sites to be experienced.

 ITL280,000-600,000 (27)

 ITL420,000-1,400,000 (19)

 no restaurant at hotel

 included*

Honeymoon specials
Complimentary champagne. Room upgrade if available.

There is a breakfast supplement during Opera season.

Sightseeing and leisure
Visit Juliet's house, the delightful shopping square Piazza delle Erbe, the Castelvecchio and many beautiful churches. Verona is also an intensive wine production area, so enjoy tasting. Visit Venice for the day or drive to the Italian Lakes. There are also several golf courses nearby.

Information & Reservations
UK 0870 606 1296
INT. +44 870 606 1296

Hotel Londra Palace

Riva Degli Schiavoni 4171
30122 Venezia
Italy

✈ Marco Polo 12km

tel +39 041 520 0533
fax +39 041 522 5032

info@hotelondra.it
www.hotelondra.it

Member of:
Charming Hotels
Small Luxury Hotels of the World
JDB Associates

In this most romantic of cities, the enchanting Londra Palace shines out as a jewel among hotels. Recently refurbished to lavish standards by Italy's Rocco Magnoli – best-known for creating the signature boutiques of top designer Gianni Versace – the 100 windows of the newly-cleaned facade of glistening white Istria stone look out imposingly over the island of San Giorgio.

Just yards away is St Mark's Square and all the glitz, glamour and culture of Venice, with its bustling squares, curved bridges over vivid green canals, fascinating art galleries and museums, and fabulous shopping opportunities.

The hotel exudes elegance. A magical glow lights up the waterfront terrace of the charming Do Leoni Restaurant, where you can enjoy a romantic dinner. Inside, rooms are furnished with authentic 19th-century Bierdermeier pieces, fine original paintings, antiques and sumptuous fabrics. Silks and brocades complement the neo-classical style.

Plush red sofas and multi-coloured mosaic floors dazzle but the general theme is soft and muted. Pale walls, white Corinthian columns, gold-speckled glass and opulent pink marble bathrooms, each with their own jacuzzi, create a chic atmosphere; the perfect spot for romance to flourish.

129

 US$244-410* (33)

 US$345-573* (20)

US$47-63

included

Honeymoon specials
Fruit basket and champagne on arrival plus complimentary guidebook, illustrated Venetian cookbook and entrance to Venice Casino.

Rates subject to 10% VAT.

Sightseeing and leisure
Rialto market, St Mark's Square, Ducal Palace, Accademia Museum, Guggenheim Museum, islands of San Giorgio, Murano, Burano and Torcello.

Hotel Lungarno

Information & Reservations
UK 0870 606 1296
INT. +44 870 606 1296

Borgo San Jacopo 14
50125 Florence
Italy

✈ Florence 8km

tel +39 05 52 72 61
fax +39 05 52 68 437

www.lungarnohotels.com
lungarnohotels@lungarnohotels.
com

Tour operators:
UK Abercrombie & Kent

Member of:
Small Luxury Hotels of the World

130

In one of the world's most romantic cities, a room with a view makes all the difference and the superb Hotel Lungarno can offer not only stunning vistas across the Arno River but attention to detail that makes any holiday to Florence truly romantic and memorable.

Recently restored, this dream of a hotel has some 69 rooms and suites, many with unforgettable views. Windows act like picture frames as you lie in bed and gaze out across the river towards the impressive Ponte Vecchio bridge.

Choose between the stunning cream and navy suite with its floor to ceiling windows overlooking the river and two storey accommodation, and the deluxe duplex from which to admire Florence's most famous bridge or try out the unique Tower room which resembles a romantic medieval castle.

The hotel boasts more than 500 original artworks while the decor is a wonderful mix of old and new. Bottieino Fiorito marble tops in the bathrooms, fresh flowers everywhere and cream *voile* floating from the windows.

Amble through French windows on to a terrace overlooking the river once more or sample some of the best food in the city at the hotel's excellent fish restaurant.

ITL590,000-630,000 (57)

ITL800,000-1,100,000 (12)

ITL70,000-120,000

included

Honeymoon specials
Italian Spumante and complimentary upgrade to suite upon availability.

Sightseeing and leisure
Situated in the centre of Florence, you are close to all the historic sights, markets and the famous Ufizzi museum. The Chianti countryside is just 20 minutes away.

Hotel
Splendido & Splendido Mare

Information & Reservations
UK 0870 606 1296
INT. +44 870 606 1296

Salita Baratta
16-16034 Portofino
Splendido Mare: Via Roma 2
16-16034 Portofino
Genoa
Italy

✈ Cristoforo Colombo 35km

tel +39 0185 26 78 01
fax +39 0185 26 78 06

reservations@splendido.net
www.orient-express.com

Member of:
The Leading Hotels of the World

The dramatic landscape of the Italian Riviera is home to the wild, rugged Portofino regional park, encompassing rocky spurs and promontories, fragrant olive groves and picturesque ruins. Flagstone paths wind through perfumed woods of cypress and pine, climbing to the crest of the jagged hill to reveal views of breathtaking beauty.

At the heart of this earthly paradise lie two delightful pink-washed hotels – the refined, sophisticated and grand Hotel Splendido, with its secluded walkways and undulating palms, and its charming extension Splendido Mare nearer the bay, where the tiny harbour bobs with fishing boats and cruisers and beyond stretches the majestic Mediterranean.

The Splendido was originally a Benedictine monastery, and in 1901 this ancient villa was restored to more than its former glory. Now it can justifiably claim to be one of the world's finest hotels, with a host of romantic associations. Join legendary lovers such as Bogart and Bacall and Elizabeth Taylor and Richard Burton, and experience its quiet, glamorous charm, or enjoy the buzz of social life at the Splendido Mare.

131

US$760-971 (44)

US$1,200-1,685 (25)

US$68

US$37

Honeymoon specials

Champagne and flowers on arrival. Upgrade if available. Breakfast, lunch and candlelight dinner included in special package.

Sightseeing and leisure

Beauty salon, sauna and gym in hotel. Open air heated pool, tennis, private speedboat for excursions. Horse riding and golf are available in nearby Rapallo. Exploring beautiful Portofino. Other local attractions are the fishing village of San Fruttuoso with its ancient Benedictine abbey, the pretty Cinque Terre villages and the historical town of Genoa.

Information & Reservations
UK 0870 606 1296
INT. +44 870 606 1296

Romantik Hotel le Silve

Loc Armenzano
Assisi
Italy

✈ Rome or Florence 180km

tel +39 07 58 01 90 00
fax +39 07 58 01 90 05

hotellesilve@tin.it
www.lesilve.it

132

Umbria is one of Italy's most picturesque regions and from its position deep in the countryside, Romantik Hotel Le Silve offers stunning views. It also offers the ultimate in seclusion. Tucked at the base of the mountains, the woodlands surrounding the hotel are inhabited only by horses and deer.

The 10th-century inn is an intimate hideaway with only 19 rooms and each is furnished with a mix of wood, stone tapestry and antiques. All have incredible views over the countryside and/or the hotel pool and many offer terraces complete with a rocking chair to let you while the time away.

Handmade pasta and freshly baked bread are the specialities of the hotel's rural restaurant and dining *al fresco* is always an option on those warm and inviting Italian evenings.

Le Silve prides itself on offering a simple and relaxing holiday for honeymooners. You can take a romantic walk or horseback ride through the fields. Or take a drive to wander around the incredible basilica in nearby Assisi. The city of Rome is also an easy day trip away meaning every stay offers you the perfect combination of urban sophistication and quaint countryside charm.

Honeymoon specials
Fruit, chocolates and a bottle of wine in room on arrival.

Sightseeing and leisure
Situated close to beautiful Assisi with its centuries-old churches and squares. Horseriding and walks through the surrounding countryside. Local festivals. There is mini-golf nearby.

 from ITL300,000 (19)

 ITL50,000-70,000

 ITL20,000

Romantik Hotel Poseidon

Information & Reservations
UK 0870 606 1296
INT. +44 870 606 1296

148 Via Pasitea
84017 Positano
Italy

✈ Naples 60km

Tel +39 08 98 11 111
Fax +39 08 98 75 833

poseidon@starnet.it
www.starnet.it/poseidon

Tour operators:
UK Italian Expressions

Few swimming pools offer a view like that afforded by the freshwater oasis of the Romantik Hotel Poseidon. Its location high up in the Amalfi hills commands an idyllic view over the so-called 'vertical village': the tiny hillside town of Positano.

The hotel began life as a private home and at first glance still appears to be purely a beautiful villa surrounded by luscious greenery. However, inside you experience all the service and amenities of a first-class establishment. Each of the hotel's 48 rooms and two suites are furnished tastefully with terracotta floors and simple accessories and offer

private terraces with outstanding views of the bay.

The on-site restaurant, La Terraza del Poseidon, offers fine cuisine and on balmy summer nights you can dine on the vast bougainvillea-clad terrace with its splendid views. In 1997 the hotel opened the Laura Elos Beauty Centre offering personalised treatments and a fully equipped gym.

With beautiful, historic sights such as Capri, Amalfi and Pompeii just a few miles away, Positano deserves its title as a 'tiny corner of paradise' and the Romantik Hotel Poseidon is the perfect place from which to enjoy this beautiful unspoilt town.

133

 ITL300,000-430,000 (50)

 ITL560,000-740,000 (3)

 ITL70,000

 included

Honeymoon specials
Complimentary champagne and flowers on arrival.

Sightseeing and leisure
Laura Elos Beauty Center for body and face treatments, massage, Turkish bath, gym and outdoor swimming pool (covered and heated in the winter months). The hotel can arrange excursions to the beautiful areas around Pompeii, Amalfi, Ravello, Naples, Paestum and the island of Capri. All are within easy reach by road or sea transport.

Information & Reservations
UK 0870 606 1296
INT. +44 870 606 1296

Royal Hotel

Corso Imperatrice 80
18038 San Remo
Italy

✈ Nice 65km

tel +39 01 84 53 91
fax +39 01 84 66 14 45

royal@royalhotelsanremo.com
www.royalhotelsanremo.com

134

Member of:
The Leading Hotels of the World

The Royal Hotel is set in a luxuriant, subtropical park overlooking lush, colourful foliage and the stunning beauty of the Mediterranean. And it is perfectly placed for the Promenade Imperatrice, the casino (which dates back to 1905) and the town centre of San Remo, with its luxurious and irresistible boutiques.

San Remo seems like paradise with its wonderful climate, stunning flowers, and a wealth of historical palaces and cultural experiences to enjoy – try visiting Pigna, the medieval village of San Remo. And of course shopping – there is a wonderfully colourful market worth visiting – and a wide range of traditional restaurants in the town.

The hotel has been beautifully renovated and offers style and antique charm combined, and bedrooms are beautifully light and airy with balconies overlooking the azure sea. The on site restaurants will tempt you with a wide range of delicious cuisine, those great views once again, and you will be able to enjoy truly the best of service. Try 'Il Giardino' for summer candlelit dining *al fresco,* and the 'Corallina' Restaurant and Snack-Bar by the pool, which, like the heated sea water pool itself, is open from April-September and provides the perfect alternative to the sandy beach.

 US$188-767 (123)

 US$584-1,039 (17)

 US$49-97

 included

Honeymoon specials

Room upgrade if available. Complimentary Italian sparkling wine and flowers on arrival.

Sightseeing and leisure

Piano bar, fitness room, tennis court, mini golf, bridge room on site, 18-hole golf course nearby. Every Tuesday and Saturday there is an open air market. Also nearby are: The Nobel family's private house, the Russian church, the casino and an olive oil museum. Or take a day tour to Monte Carlo, Nice, Cannes or Portofino.

San Domenico Palace

Information & Reservations
UK 0870 606 1296
INT. +44 870 606 1296

5 Piazza San Domenico
98039 Taormina
Italy

✈ Catania 60km

Tel +39 09 42 23 70 1
Fax +39 09 42 62 55 06

san-domenico@thi.it
www.thi.it

At the luxurious San Domenico Palace, tradition meets state-of-the-art in an impressive fashion. The hotel was first established in 1896 when the existing 15th-century Dominican Monastery was refurbished. With its reputation as the most famous monastery-hotel in the world, it has an enchanting atmosphere with wide, whitewashed passages which, for almost 500 years, only heard the footsteps of monks.

Many original monastic features have been preserved including the cloister, the images of Saints, and the choir stalls. Today you can wonder at these marvels while enjoying the charm of a truly five-star experience. Stand on the elegant terrace with its palm trees and brightly coloured bougainvillaea and take in the sweeping views from the Greek Theatre to the snow-capped peak of Mount Etna located in the historical centre of the town.

In summer, savour a tempting selection of local cuisine while enjoying the view. The gardens provide the perfect setting for that after-dinner promenade with their brilliant year-round colour. All rooms also enjoy a lovely view over the sea and gardens, as the hotel is high above the sea, overlooking the stunning bay of Taormina.

135

 ITL480,000-750,000 (102)

ITL1,030,000-1,300,000 (8)

ITL100,000-250,000

included

Honeymoon specials
Flowers in the room.

Sightseeing and leisure
There are ample historic sites to visit such as the Greek Theatre in Taormina. Or you could take a day excursion to places like Syracuse, Agrigento, Mount Etna or Piazza Armerina. There is also golf and tennis nearby.

Malta

**climate/
when to go**
Feb to June is best
– between the rainy
season and the hot
Mediterranean
summer. Sept and
Oct are also good.

currency
Maltese lira

language
Maltese and English

getting around
The public bus
system is excellent,
though it is a good
idea to hire a car if
you want to explore
the further reaches
of the island. Taxis
are expensive.
There are regular
ferries between
islands.

Malta is a historical jewel. Its streets are crowded with Norman cathedrals and baroque palaces and the country is rich with some of the oldest-known human structures in the world.

The legacy of the various dominations who ruled over the islands throughout the ages are all there to savour. The 3,000 year old city of Mdina, the old capital, is perched on a rocky outcrop and nicknamed 'the Noble City' because of the many aristocratic families who still live there. It is a typical medieval town, situated in the centre of the island, and commands magnificent views.

Nearby, Valletta is a beautifully preserved 16th-century walled city, perfect to enjoy on foot, especially as the streets were laid out to channel the sea breezes in from the harbour, so you can always keep your cool.

Malta and its sister islands of Gozo and Comino are blessed with year-round sunshine and set in sparkling, crystal-clear waters. They offer the opportunity for a wide range of sports, both land and water, including some of the best scuba diving in the Mediterranean.

Combine this with the delicious local cuisine and wine, the bustling open air markets and the local products of delicate lace and multi-coloured glassware and you will have to agree that Malta can truly lay claim to the perfect combination of cultural, artistic and natural treasures.

The Xara Palace

Information & Reservations
UK 0870 606 1296
INT. +44 870 606 1296

Misrah Il-Kunsil
RBT 12 Mdina
Malta

✈ Malta Int. 6km

Tel +356 450560
Fax +356 452612

info@xarapalace.com.mt
www.xarapalace.com.mt

Situated in Malta's ancient capital of Mdina, The Xara Palace captures a sense of history and intimacy. Opened in May 1999, this late 17th century palazzo has been restored with great care to the opulence and charm of former centuries. Creating a secluded atmosphere and offering attention to the individual is the central focus.

There are only 17 individually designed suites, all finished to an incredible standard. Each is filled with antique furniture and original paintings by Maltese masters and international artists. Some even feature a jacuzzi on their terrace or balcony – perfect for relaxing under the stars. The magical atmosphere comes even more alive with *al fresco* dining on warm nights with spectacular views across lamp-lit Mdina from the romantic rooftop restaurant. The finest seasonal produce is provided in mouth-watering northern Italian dishes and richer Mediterranean fare.

If you can drag yourself away from this beautiful hotel, Mdina's understated splendour beckons – once the ancient Norman capital, it is the perfect example of a medieval fortress.

Weddings are easily arranged. Couples can marry here or in the town and follow up their ceremony with an intimate reception at The Xara Palace.

137

US$222-355 (17)

US$11-40

US$14

Honeymoon specials

15% off room rates with room upgrade. Complimentary champagne on arrival. Room service for one evening with dinner served in your suite. No charge for room service.

Sightseeing and leisure

Beauty salon available three kilometres away. Private guided tours of the area. The 18-hole Malta Golf Club is eight kilometres away.

Portugal & Madeira

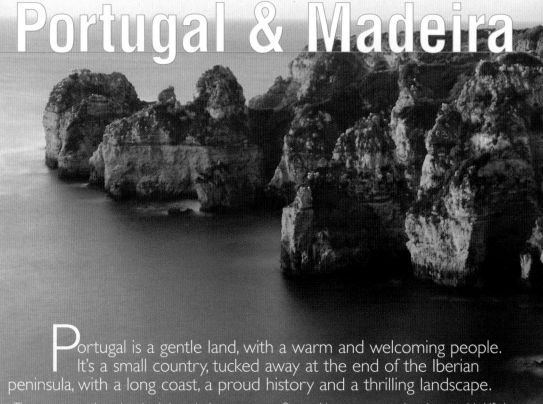

138

Portugal is a gentle land, with a warm and welcoming people. It's a small country, tucked away at the end of the Iberian peninsula, with a long coast, a proud history and a thrilling landscape.

The remote northern interior is hauntingly beautiful. Lisbon, the capital, has all the verve and excitement of a modern metropolis, with a charming medieval mantle of churches, forts and staggeringly beautiful palaces.

The Algarve in the south is famed for glorious beaches, little fishing villages and fabulous golf courses that regularly attract world-wide praise.

And washed by the waters of the Atlantic, the tiny, steep-sided island of Madeira is a miniature paradise. For those who love nature, the dramatic, lush terrain and exuberant flora of this little island provide a romantic and uplifting honeymoon setting.

Portugal is not an expensive place to visit. Life is simple, but standards are high, and good value can be relied upon, especially where food is concerned. Fresh seafood and salads, fine olive oil, garlic – then more garlic – are the hallmarks of Portuguese cuisine. Simply prepared, and in abundant quantities, the food is an ideal match for the country's crisp, white wines.

The whole region is incredibly picturesque. A little exploration away from the tourist trail reveals isolated beaches, hillside settlements, lush valleys with trickling streams and lots and lots of fragrant eucalyptus and pine-studded mountains.

Information & Reservations
UK 0870 606 1296
INT. +44 870 606 1296

Hotel Quinta do Lago

Quinta do Lago
8135-024 Almancil
Algarve
Portugal

✈ Faro Int. 22km

tel +351 289 350350
fax +351 289 396393

reservations@quintadolagohotel.com
www.quintadolagohotel.com

Tour operators:
UK Elegant Resorts

140

Member of:
The Leading Hotels of the World
Orient Express Hotels Group

This luxurious hotel is situated on the dramatic Algarve coastline beside a tidal estuary in the exclusive Quinta do Lago estate, with its undulating hills, pinewoods and championship golf courses.

All rooms are spacious and furnished in light, natural wood and pastel shades. Most rooms enjoy views across the gardens to the Atlantic Ocean beyond. All have either balconies or terraces.

Guests can enjoy cocktails in the Laguna Bar before dining in one of two restaurants offering traditional Portuguese cuisine and Venetian specialities, or al fresco on the poolside terrace where fish, shellfish and meat are barbecued daily.

A romantic wooden footbridge over the Ria Formosa Estuary links the hotel to the pretty beaches and a wealth of sports activities.

The hotel is ideally placed for exploring the spectacular Algarve countryside or perhaps cruising along the still, clean waters of the River Guadiana, and ending the day with typical Portuguese dancing.

The 17th-century baroque church of São Lourenço, decorated with astonishingly beautiful tiles, or *azulejos*, provides a romantic setting for a wedding. Buffets and cocktail parties for up to 200 can be arranged in the elegant São Lourenço room or on the extensive hotel lawns.

 ESC35,000-82,000 (132)

ESC87,000-152,000 (9)

 from ESC7,500

 included

Honeymoon specials
Complimentary champagne and flowers on arrival.

Sightseeing and leisure
Swimming pools, floodlit tennis courts, health club. Bike hire, clay pigeon shooting, deep sea fishing and all watersports available close by. Three championship golf courses on the estate. Romantic walks around the Ria Formosa Estuary and bird sanctuary. Excursions to the towns of Silves, Faro and Olhão. Jeep safaris. Visits to local Portuguese potteries.

Lapa Palace

Information & Reservations
UK 0870 606 1296
INT. +44 870 606 1296

Rua do Pau de Bandeira
No 4
1249-021 Lisbon
Portugal

✈ Lisbon 10km

Tel +351 21 394 9494
Fax +351 21 395 0665

reservations@hotelapa.com
www.orient-expresshotels.com

Tour operators:
UK Elegant Resorts

Member of:
The Leading Hotels of the World
The Orient Express Hotels Group

Lisbon is one of Europe's most sophisticated and architecturally beautiful capitals. Set on a hill, close to the majestic River Tagus, travellers will find the ornate elegance of the Lapa Palace the perfect base for exploration.

Marble stucco, carved wood and richly patterned tiles reveal a stately beauty few modern resorts can hope to offer – yet the hotel was only opened in 1992. The six public rooms are lavishly decorated, as are the 108 guest rooms, which include poolside accommodation, and the luxurious suites. Each is individually decorated and features decor ranging from 18th-century classical designs through to Art Deco chic.

The beauty continues throughout and Lapa Palace boasts stunning gardens to wander round. The Ristorante Hotel Cipriani is equally well-appointed and features Venetian and international cuisine served in bright, airy surroundings.

Also close to the hotel are Lisbon's most famous sights. The Torre de Belém, Castelo Sao Jorge and the ornate Jerónimos monastery. However, to truly get a sense of this quietly beautiful town, you need only walk for a short while down some of its quaint streets, or soak up the peace and tranquillity in one of its characterful, palm-fringed squares.

141

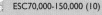 ESC50,000-65,000 (98)

 ESC70,000-150,000 (10)

🍽 ESC8,000

☕ ESC2,800

Honeymoon specials

Three or seven nights in deluxe accommodation, daily American breakfast, fruit, flowers and Porto wine on arrival, welcome cocktail, champagne, one *à la carte* lunch or dinner in the restaurant (excl. drinks), one candlelight dinner in room (excl. drinks), day's sightseeing tour in limo, use of health club, transfers. From ESC81,600 per room per night.

Sightseeing and leisure

Indoor heated pool, health club with Scottish bath, Turkish bath, sauna, solarium, outdoor pool on site. Nearby is the historic and beautiful city of Lisbon, Belém Tower, Jerónimos, Expo '98 facilities now known as Nations Park. Golf on five championship courses can also be arranged.

Information & Reservations
UK   0870 606 1296
INT. +44 870 606 1296

Monte do Casal Country House Hotel

Estoi
8000-661 Faro
Algarve
Portugal

✈ Faro 8km

tel +289 991 503
fax +289 991 341

montecasal@mail.telepac.pt
www.montedocasal.pt

142

Monte do Casal is a small, exclusive hotel geared up for perfect relaxation in a tranquil setting.
The beautiful 18th-century country house has panoramic views across the countryside to the sea and is surrounded by bougainvillaea, almond, olive and fruit trees. The heated swimming pool is set in stunning gardens full of colourful and exquisitely scented flowers and shrubs.

In the summer, dine inside the beautiful old coach house or on the terrace under the palm trees. In cooler weather open log fires warm the lounge, bar and restaurant. The bar and restaurant have been converted from an old coach house with traditional, charming eucalyptus pole and cane ceilings. No matter what the time of year, the superb French cuisine on offer will delight your tastebuds.

The golden beaches of Faro, which stretch as far as the eye can see, are easily reachable from the hotel and for nature lovers, the Ria Formosa Natural Park has many rare species of birds, plants and wildlife. If shopping is on your agenda, visit the market in Estoi where you can barter to buy everything from traditional cataplana copper pans to superb leather goods.

 ESC19,000-35,000 (8)

 ESC24,500-46,000 (5)

 approx ESC6,800

 included

Honeymoon specials
Complimentary champagne and room upgrade if possible.

Sightseeing and leisure
Heated swimming pool. Tennis. Golfing packages for nearby golf courses. Markets in nearby Estoi which also has many historic sights (including the Palace of Estoi) and festivals. The beaches of Faro are only 15 minutes away.

Reid's Palace

Information & Reservations
UK 0870 606 1296
INT. +44 870 606 1296

Estrada Monumental 139
9000-098 Funchal
Madeira

✈ Santa Cruz 22km

Tel +351 291 71 71 71
Fax +351 291 71 71 77

UK toll free: 0800 092 1723

www.reidspalace.orient-
express.com
reidshtl@mail.telepac.pt

Member of:
The Leading Hotels of the World
Orient Express Hotel Group

Madeira's grandest deluxe hotel sits on the outskirts of Funchal, perched on a clifftop overlooking the bay, where hanging vines nestle alongside displays of geraniums, hibiscus and salvias. This is the perfect hideaway for those in search of peace and relaxation whilst enjoying a magnificent subtropical climate.

Built in 1891, this Mediterranean-style hotel, which combines old world charm with luxurious facilities, has always been a favourite of royalty and celebrities. Edward VIII, Sir Winston Churchill and Fulgencio Baptista are among those who have passed through its doors. All rooms are spacious, light and airy, and some, such as those in the Garden Wing and main building, have deluxe marble bathrooms.

There are five restaurants including the turn of the century main dining room, Les Faunes (seasonal), where guests can savour fine French cuisine while enjoying panoramic views of the harbour. The Trattoria Villa Cliff, set against an open-air backdrop, and Brisa do Mar (seasonal) provide a romantic setting for *al fresco* dining.

Activities abound at Reid's – from watersports, tennis, and a health centre with saunas, massage and reflexology – there's something to suit every taste.

143

ESC48,500-115,000 (130)

ESC110,000-548,000 (32)

ESC8,200

included

Honeymoon specials

Heavenly Honeymoon package: 7 nights in standard room with upgrade to Junior Suite if available, honeymoon present, champagne breakfast, daily buffet breakfast in the Garden Restaurant, bottle of Madeira wine, one afternoon tea, one dinner at Trattoria Villa Cliff and one candlelit dinner in Les Faunes/Brisa do Mar (excl. drinks), day tour of the island with lunch and sunset cruise. Price: ESC176,000-194,000pp.

Sightseeing and leisure

Health centre on site with sauna, massage and reflexologist.
Historic town of Funchal and old churches to explore.
Levada walks and mountain-hiking 6,000ft above sea level.
Madeira Night once a week in hotel and sunset cruise.
Golf at nearby Palheiro and Santo da Serra courses
(30% discount for Reid's guests).

Spain

**climate/
when to go**
Carnival in Feb is celebrated with gusto, followed in spring by elaborate Easter Week parades and the first bullfights of the season. Summers are dry, hot and crowded but great for fiestas. Autumns are mellow and warm.

currency
Spanish peseta

language
Spanish, although it is easy to get by with English on the coasts and in tourist areas.

getting around
By air to all the main cities. There is an efficient, reasonably priced network of public transport, from city buses to underground services. Taxis, too, are everywhere.

Romance and Spain have gone hand in hand since the Middle Ages, when Moorish poets introduced the concept of Romantic love and chivalry to Europe.

Spain easily lends herself to dreamy ideals: her land and cities are sweepingly grand and poetic, from the high drama of the Pyrenees and Old Castile down to the charasmatic horse parades, sunbaked hills and beaches of Andalucía. The ancestral mix of Latin temperament and Moorish imagination shows itself vividly in the fanciful architecture, and in the driving rhythms of the famed *flamenco* dance.

For anyone on a honeymoon, it would be hard to beat a romantic stroll through the royal pavilions and rambling gardens of the Alhambra Palace in Granada. Or try Córdoba with its spectacular Great Mosque. But for fun, the most famous of all *plazas de toros* are in Seville and Ronda, where you can pick oranges off the trees in the centre of the city.

Talking of fun, the country is also one of the hippest to be found in Europe. Barcelona has drive and energy, as do Andalucía's cosmopolitan resorts which bristle with designer boutiques and beautiful people lolling under parasols on the sun-drenched beaches

And after the requisite *siesta*, the Spaniards really get going. Nothing starts before 10pm, but then, two days can be crammed into one in the fabulous, thumping nightclubs and bars across the country. Like the *tapas*, Spain is a wonderful mix. It blends old and new, glamour and rustic charm, hot days and cool nights.

Special Hotels Reader Reply Service

To receive brochures and information on the hotels of your choice, please tick those you are interested in, complete the coupon below and drop this page into any postbox – **at no cost to you**. (Please note that a free postal service is only available on postage within the UK – overseas readers will need to affix a stamp for the relevant postal amount.)

- ❏ Aitutaki Lagoon Resort
- ❏ Al Bustan Palace Hotel
- ❏ Albergo Pietrasanta
- ❏ Arlberg Hospiz Hotel
- ❏ Ballylickey Manor House
- ❏ Baron Resort
- ❏ Baros Holiday Resort
- ❏ Bay, The
- ❏ Beaufort, The
- ❏ Begawan Giri
- ❏ Benguerra Lodge
- ❏ Blue Waters Inn
- ❏ Bora Bora Lagoon Resort
- ❏ Brufani Palace
- ❏ Cambridge Beaches
- ❏ Casa No.7
- ❏ Charleston Place
- ❏ Château de Bagnols
- ❏ Château de Feuilles
- ❏ Château des Vigiers
- ❏ Château Eza
- ❏ Chewton Glen
- ❏ Ciragan Palace Istanbul
- ❏ Colony Club Hotel
- ❏ Couples Ocho Rios & Negril
- ❏ Damai Lovina Villas
- ❏ Dan Eilat
- ❏ Datai Langkawi, The
- ❏ Dusit Laguna
- ❏ Eilat Princess Hotel
- ❏ Elounda Mare Hotel
- ❏ Excelsior Palace Hotel

- ❏ Four Seasons Hotel Limassol
- ❏ Fulbari Resort
- ❏ Full Moon Beach
- ❏ Funzi Keys, The
- ❏ Furama Resort Danang
- ❏ Galley Bay
- ❏ Glitter Bay
- ❏ Grand Hotel Excelsior Vittoria
- ❏ Grand Hotel Fasano
- ❏ Grand Hotel Villa Igiea
- ❏ Grand Hotel Zermatterhof
- ❏ Half Moon Beach Club
- ❏ Hermitage, The
- ❏ Hide Safari Camp, The
- ❏ Horizons & Cottages
- ❏ Hotel Alfonso XIII
- ❏ Hotel Casa Del Mar
- ❏ Hôtel de la Cité
- ❏ Hotel du Palais
- ❏ Hotel Gabbia D'Oro
- ❏ Hotel Guanahani
- ❏ Hotel Hoffmeister
- ❏ Hotel Im Palais Schwarzenberg
- ❏ Hotel La Bobadilla
- ❏ Hotel L'Archipel
- ❏ Hotel Londra Palace
- ❏ Hotel Lungarno
- ❏ Hotel Makanda by the Sea
- ❏ Hotel Martinez
- ❏ Hotel Monasterio
- ❏ Hotel Pariz
- ❏ Hôtel Plaza Athénée

- ❏ Hotel Puente Romano
- ❏ Hotel Punta Islita
- ❏ Hotel Quinta do Lago
- ❏ Hotel Royal Monceau
- ❏ Hotel Schloss Monchstein
- ❏ Hotel Splendido and Spl. Mare
- ❏ Hotel Tugu Bali
- ❏ Hotel Villa del Sol
- ❏ Hoteldorf Gruner Baum
- ❏ Huka Lodge
- ❏ Jerusalem Hotel
- ❏ Jewels of Zimbabwe
- ❏ Kempinski Hotel Estepona
- ❏ Kinasi, Ma'fia Island
- ❏ Kivotos Clubhotel
- ❏ Krone Assmannshausen
- ❏ La Digue Island Lodge
- ❏ La Mamounia
- ❏ La Samanna
- ❏ Laguna Beach
- ❏ Lapa Palace
- ❏ Lapa Rios
- ❏ Las Brisas Acapulco
- ❏ Las Dunas Beach Hotel & Spa
- ❏ Le Meridien Fisherman's Cove
- ❏ Le Meridien La Cocoteraie
- ❏ Le Meridien Limassol
- ❏ Le Prince Maurice
- ❏ Le Royal Meridien Baan Taling
- ❏ Lemuria Resort of Praslin
- ❏ Litchfield Plantation
- ❏ Little Palm Island

- ❏ Longueville Manor
- ❏ Mago Estate Hotel
- ❏ Mahaweli Reach
- ❏ Marbella Club
- ❏ Mas de Torrent
- ❏ Matahari Beach Resort & Spa
- ❏ Mauna Lani Bay
- ❏ Migration Camp
- ❏ Mombasa Serena Beach
- ❏ Montanus Hotel
- ❏ Monte Do Casal Hotel
- ❏ Montpelier Plantation
- ❏ Mwagusi Safari Camp
- ❏ Nakatchafushi
- ❏ Nepal Experience, The
- ❏ Nusa Dua Beach Hotel
- ❏ Nusa Lembongan Resort
- ❏ Ottley's Plantation Inn
- ❏ Oustau de Baumanière
- ❏ Palace Hotel Gstaad
- ❏ Palm Island
- ❏ Palmetto Beach Hotel
- ❏ Paphos Amathus Beach
- ❏ Paradise Beach Resort
- ❏ Paradise Cove Hotel
- ❏ Park Hotel Delta
- ❏ Pelangi Beach Resort
- ❏ Penang Mutiara Beach Resort
- ❏ Reid's Palace
- ❏ Residence, The
- ❏ Romantik Hotel le Silve
- ❏ Romantik Hotel Poseidon

- ❏ Royal Hotel
- ❏ Royal Pavilion
- ❏ Saman Villas
- ❏ San Domenico Palace
- ❏ Santa Marina Hotel
- ❏ Secret Harbour Resort
- ❏ Selous Safari Company Ltd
- ❏ Shutters on the Beach
- ❏ Siboney Beach Club
- ❏ Sofitel Coralia Motu Bora Bora
- ❏ Soneva Fushi
- ❏ St James's Club
- ❏ St Nicolas Bay
- ❏ Sunset Marquis Hotel & Villas
- ❏ Suvretta House
- ❏ Swept Away
- ❏ Taplow House Hotel
- ❏ Tongsai Bay, The
- ❏ Tsitouras Collection, The
- ❏ Thurnhers Alpenhof
- ❏ Trident Villas & Hotel
- ❏ Turtle Island Resort
- ❏ Victoria Falls Hotel
- ❏ Vomo Island Resort
- ❏ Wake di Ume & Waka Nusa
- ❏ Waterloo House
- ❏ Windsor Court Hotel
- ❏ Xara Palace, The
- ❏ Zanzibar Serena Inn

Name ....

Address ....

....

Town/City .... County/State ....

Postcode/Zip .... Country ....

Today's date .... – .... – ....
(day) (month) (year)

Date of wedding .... – .... – ....
(day) (month) (year)

How long engaged to date? ....
(months)

Age ....

Special Hotels – Honeymoon Destinations 2000

Reader Reply Service

FREEPOST

2 Ridgeway Road

Farnham

Surrey GU9 8NW

Information & Reservations
UK 0870 606 1296
INT. +44 870 606 1296

Casa No.7

Calle Virgencs 7
41004 Seville
Spain

✈ Seville 20 mins

tel +34 95 422 1581
fax +34 95 421 4527

146

Hidden away in a quaint, quiet street in the heart of Seville, Casa No.7 is the perfect intimate hideaway in one of the most exuberant cities in Europe. Part-Scot owner Gonzalo del Rio opened this stylish, small (only six rooms) hotel in January 1999 and has made it his mission to ensure guests feel they are staying in a private home.

The lounge and reading room, with their deep, comfy armchairs, provide a haven from the bustling streets and are the perfect place to enjoy a pre-dinner sherry, which will probably be from the family sherry business, González-Byass.

Bedrooms are spacious and elegant with personal touches designed especially to make you feel at home, like photos of famous forebears, magazines and a shelf of good books.

Breakfast is served in the beautiful, formal dining room by a white-gloved butler, and for dinner you can choose from the amazing selection of restaurants right on your doorstep. And the personal service means you are sure to get the very best advice on how to see Seville and the area

 PTS22,000* (6)

 no restaurant at hotel

 included

Honeymoon specials
A welcome bottle of sherry on arrival.

* Plus 7% VAT. Also, Easter week and February-April prices are PTS45,000 + 7% VAT.

Sightseeing and leisure
Take a horse-drawn carriage -- or *caballo* -- on a tour of some of Seville's intoxicating sights. You are perfectly situated for visiting the Giralda and Cathedral, both just five minutes walk away, and there are a wide variety of restaurants and tapas bars to enjoy.

Hotel Alfonso XIII

nformation & Reservations
UK 0870 606 1296
NT. +44 870 606 1296

San Fernando, 2
-1004 Seville
Spain

✈ San Pablo 14km

el +34 95 422 28 50
ax +34 95 421 60 33

ww.luxurycollection.com/
lfonsoXIII

A heady mix of Latin charms and Arabian allusions are brought together in perfect harmony at the stunning Hotel Alfonso XIII, built for the 1929 Ibero American Exhibition and named after the famous king who commissioned it.

Arches, arabesques, tiles and mosaics, combined with the scent of orange blossoms, the Alfonso XIII is a place like no other. Modern day comforts are not forgotten in this historic hotel which underwent a refurbishment just a few years ago.

Its past guest list reads like a 'who's who' in Europe and the US, with royalty mixing with movie stars and literary geniuses. Royalty from Britain and Holland to Ethiopia and Nepal have graced these rooms, while you can stay in rooms and suites previously used by such names as Arthur Miller, Fidel Castro, or even Lenny Kravitz.

Your wish is their command at this stylish hotel which is located in the heart of one of Europe's most magical cities on the banks of the Guadalquivir river. The mix of history and modern amenities is as true of the city as it is of the hotel. This is one of the most thriving cities where the buzz of success is inescapable and just as intriguing as its ancient past.

PTS55,500-75,700* (100)

PTS109,000-132,000* (18)

from PTS6,900*

PTS3,000*

Honeymoon specials

Champagne and strawberries in the room on arrival. Late check-out and suite upgrade subject to availability.

* Prices subject to 7% tax.

Sightseeing and leisure

Nearby attractions include the Reales Alcázares, the Cathedral and the Giralda, the Santa Cruz quarter, the Torre del Oro and the Plaza de Espana. The hotel's outdoor swimming pool is open between May and mid-October. Shopping gallery and beauty parlour on site.

Hotel La Bobadilla

Information & Reservations
UK 0870 606 1296
INT. +44 870 606 1296

Finca La Bobadilla
Apdo 144
18300 Loja, Grenada
Spain

✈ Malaga 75km

tel +34 958 321861
fax +34 958 321810

info@la-bobadilla.com
www.la-bobadilla.com

148

Member of:
The Leading Hotels of the World

At the heart of a 1,000-acre estate in the depths of the rolling countryside of Andalusia, this gem of a hotel offers quiet sophistication befitting its magnificent location.

The hotel is almost a recreation of a Moorish village with a labyrinth of quaint pathways, flowering courtyards, vaulted passageways and a soaring marble colonnade. Beyond the main buildings, the countryside rolls on with flower-filled hills and valleys fragrant with the scents of wild herbs, olive groves and almond orchards.

Inside this sumptuous hotel you have the choice of 60 individually decorated rooms and suites where the local architecture is combined with modern-day luxuries. Sink into a huge circular bath with views across the countryside, curl up in front of the open log fires or enjoy the comfort of the four-poster beds.

Work out in the fully equipped gym before plunging into the indoor pool. Enjoy a luxurious massage or beauty treatment before a game of tennis. And after all of that, indulge in fine cuisine at La Finca restaurant, or try some Spanish specialities in the excellent El Cortijo restaurant.

 PTS34,400-51,800 (51)

 PTS58,400-111,000 (9)

 PTS6,300-17.800

included

Honeymoon specials
Basket of seasonal fruits and half bottle of sherry.

Sightseeing and leisure
Day visits to Ronda, Cordoba and Seville. Closer to home are the delights of Antequera and Archidona. Included in the price of the room: tennis, horseriding, archery, pool, jacuzzi, fitness centre, Turkish steambath, Finnish sauna, French bowls, table tennis, children's playground, cycling and lovely walks. Available at extra charge: massages, beauty parlour, hairdresser, boutique, moto-boogies (quads), clay pigeon shooting (if licensed).

Information & Reservations
UK 0870 606 1296
INT. +44 870 606 1296

Hotel Puente Romano

Carretera de Cadiz
Km 177 - 29600 Marbella
Spain

✈ Malaga Int. 55km

Tel +34 952 82 09 00
Fax +34 952 77 57 66

comerci@lapuenteromano.com
www.puenteromano.com

Member of:
The Leading Hotels of the World

Marbella is probably the most elegant and exclusive resort on the Costa del Sol. Located in the heart of the Golden Mile, between Marbella and Puerto Banus, Hotel Puente Romano nestles along the Mediterranean coast, at the foot of the Sierra Blanca mountains.

The hotel comprises a series of low-rise horizontal buildings constructed in traditional Andalucian style and offering secluded and spacious demi-suite rooms with terraces or balconies overlooking waterfalls and acres of lush subtropical gardens. Here, hotel staff strike the balance between privacy and impeccable service.

Puente Romano's three restaurants, El Puente, Roberto Italian and the Beach Club – each different in style – offer a wealth of gastronomic delights. You can select from spectacular buffets and a comprehensive range of authentic dishes featuring local fish and seafood. If you decide to venture out for an evening, Marbella and Puerto Banus offer much in the way of fun.

Weddings can also be celebrated in the hotel with receptions for up to 240 guests catered for in one of its top restaurants.

149

 PTS29,600-49,500 (228)

 PTS34,000-300,000 (77)

 PTS7,500-11,000

 PTS2,900

Honeymoon specials
Cava on arrival. Packages available to readers on request.

Sightseeing and leisure
Puente Romano tennis & fitness centre with 10 tennis courts, four paddle courts, sauna, massage, Turkish baths, three swimming pools, beach club on site and our own golf club, the Marbella Club Golf Resort. Within easy reach of the hotel are some beautiful locations, such as Puerto Banus, Marbella Old Town, Plaza de los Naranjos, Chapel of Santiago, Museum of Spanish Contemporary Engravings.

Kempinksi Resort
Hotel Estepona

Information & Reservations
UK 0870 606 1296
INT. +44 870 606 1296

Playa El Padron
Carretera de Cadiz
s/n Km 159
29680 Estepona, Malaga
Spain

✈ Malaga 75km
✈ Gibraltar 45km

tel +34 95 280 9500
fax +34 95 280 9550

agp.reservation@kempinski.com
www.kempinski-spain.com

150

The 1km stretch of beach between Marbella and Estepona offer some of the most fashionable surroundings in Europe. Now, with the 1999 opening of the Kempinski Resort Hotel, the area welcomes one of its most exclusive resorts yet.

Framed by subtropical gardens, this five-star Moorish-influenced hotel offers many levels of luxurious accommodation. But no matter whether you choose one of the comfortable deluxe rooms or a palatial private suite, you'll be rewarded with a view of the azure Mediterranean Sea, just a short walk away through the swaying palms.

Two on-site restaurants regale your senses with the tastes and smells of Spain and international cuisine, while a beach bar provides snacks and drinks for a spot of more casual dining.

For the perfect romantic evening choose one of the hotel's special candlelit dinners for two in the privacy of your room or terrace.

When day breaks again, take the short stroll on to the golden sands; swim in the hotel's vast freeform pools; work out in the gym or spoil yourself with a visit to the on-site sauna, Turkish baths or beauty parlour. Further afield, tee times to many of the area's championship golf courses can easily be arranged at reception.

 PTS28,500-50,000 (131)

 PTS46,500-300,000 (17)

 from PTS7,000

 PTS2,700

Honeymoon specials
Half-bottle of champagne and flowers on arrival.
Upgrade to honeymoon suite if available.

Sightseeing and leisure
Wellness and beauty centre, medico resort, watersports centre, tennis court plus more than 30 golf courses in the area. Flamenco shows nearby in Marbella, Casino Nueva Andalucia, the caves of Nerja, natural parks.

Las Dunas
Beach Hotel & Spa

nformation & Reservations

JK 0870 606 1296

NT. +44 870 606 1296

La Boladilla Baja
Ctra. Cadiz Km 163.5
Estepona 29689, Malaga
Spain

✈ Malaga 77km

el +34 95 279 4345
ax +34 95 279 4825
www.lasdunas.com
asdunas@las-dunas

our operators:
JK The Air Travel Group
Design Holidays
JS EC Tours

Member of:
The Leading Hotels of the World

The Las Dunas Beach Hotel & Spa, a five-star, Grand Luxe property, is situated directly on the beach in the heart of the Andalucian coastline, between Marbella and its neighbouring village, Estepona. It is one of the most romantic and luxurious hotels on the 'Costa de Marbella'.

The 73-room, flamingo-coloured beach hotel has been constructed in Andalucian style with a Moorish influence, to compliment the traditional buildings in the region and to reflect the area's cultural heritage. The property is surrounded by lush, subtropical, landscaped gardens and fountains, creating the feel of a Spanish hacienda, offering magnificent views over the Mediterranean Sea to Gibraltar and North Africa.

The hotel offers luxurious accommodation and excellent personal service. The Michelin-starred Maitre Cuisiner, Heinz Winkler, was awarded with the 'Grand Prix de l'Art de la Cuisine 1997' by the Academie Internationale de la Gastronomie, and supervises the cuisine at Lido Restaurant. At the new lifestyle venue, Piano Bar & Bistro Felix, Euro-Asiatic flavours prevail, whilst the Beach Club features Andalucian delights.

151

PTS27,000-50,000 (34)

PTS47,000-230,000 (39)

from PTS8,900

from PTS3,100

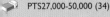

Honeymoon specials

Buffet breakfast for two, candlelit dinner, champagne, flowers and fruit on arrival, two bathrobes personalised with your name, entrance to Spa, including sauna and jacuzzi. Room upgrade subject to availability. Package costs PTS55,000 (not including room rates).

Sightseeing and leisure

Regena Sol Kur Clinic offers traditional and alternative medicine, Spa including 'Dr Schulte's World of Beauty', 40 golf courses along the coast. Pueblos Blancos, inland hilltop villages with ancient Moorish fortresses and whitewashed cottages. Marbella flea market and Puerto Banus, luxury boat anchorage, art galleries.

Marbella Club

Information & Reservations
UK 0870 606 1296
INT. +44 870 606 1296

Bulevar Principe Alfonso
von Hohenlohe
s/n - 29600
Marbella
Spain

✈ Malaga Int. 62km

tel +34 5 282 2211
fax +34 5 282 9884

www.marbellaclub.com

Tour operators:
UK Elegant Resorts

152

Member of:
The Leading Hotels of the World

Formerly the residence of Prince Alfonso von Hohenlohe, an Austrian aristocrat, and now an exclusive club resort and hideaway of the rich and famous, the Marbella Club occupies a prime location along the Golden Mile – Spain's fashionable south coast resort.

A luxurious complex of rooms, suites and villas built in typical Andalucian style, it is surrounded by subtropical gardens. There is a wide range of sports facilities, both on site and nearby, including tennis and a gym at the Puente Romano Tennis & Fitness Club, swimming and golf at top courses and the newly opened Marbella Club Golf Resort.

The hotel's restaurant serves a range of international dishes featuring seafood and local fish. In summer, hundreds of candles placed in the trees light up the terrace to create the perfect scenario for romantic *al fresco* dining. A rich buffet lunch is served in the Beach Club beside the sea.

In the evenings, guests can relax to the sounds of live piano music in the bar or venture into Puerto Banus and Marbella town to sample the nightlife.

The exclusive Beach Club is a popular venue for wedding receptions of up to 250, as guests can enjoy cocktails against a backdrop of incredibly romantic sunsets and breathtaking scenery.

 PTS27,000-70,000 (84)

 PTS48,000-310,000 (46)

 from PTS8,000

PTS2,600-3,000

Honeymoon specials
Cava and flowers in room on arrival. Welcome surprise. Room upgrade subject to availability.

Sightseeing and leisure
Swimming and watersports, tennis, fitness centre and sauna on site. The newly opened Marbella Club Golf Resort, plus golf on some of the other top courses in the area at reduced rates. Nearby, visit the towns and cities of Seville, Granada, Cordoba, Gibraltar and Puerto Banus.

Mas de Torrent

Information & Reservations
UK 0870 606 1296
INT. +44 870 606 1296

E-17123 Torrent
Girona
Catalonia
Spain

✈ Girona 35km
✈ Barcelona 120km

Tel +34 97 230 3292
Fax +34 97 230 3293

mtorrent@intercom.es
www.mastorrent.com

Member of:
Relais & Châteaux

The charmingly situated Mas de Torrent lies at the heart of Catalonia, just an hour and a half from the bright lights of Barcelona and 15 minutes from the main beaches of the Costa Brava. Within easy reach also are dozens of historical towns and sites ripe for exploring, such as the medieval town of Pals and the Roman remains at Emp'ries.

The hotel itself is a delight, and the proud owners have spared no attention to detail. As you enter the main reception area you are greeted with the aroma of fresh flowers, and maybe even a roaring log fire depending on the season. The decor is simple and rustic, yet elegant, with antique furniture and a warm, tranquil atmosphere. The hotel was once an 18th-century Catalan *masia*, a typical farmhouse that has been lovingly restored and equipped with every amenity. It still retains its original charm, however, and the hotel restaurant, with its terrace and local antique lacework, is recommended for its delicious seasonal cooking.

In the main building there are 10 bedrooms and clustered round the pool are 20 luxurious bungalows, each with their own private garden.

If you are a golf fan, there are six courses in the area, all with impeccable greens and, in the case of Mas Nou, boasting awe-inspiring coastal views.

153

from PTS32,000 (25)

from PTS39,000 (5)

from PTS5,500

PTS2,100-2,600

Honeymoon specials
Complimentary Cava and fruit basket on arrival.

Sightseeing and leisure
Apart from the golf, which really is well served in this region, tennis, scuba diving, horseriding and hot-air balloon and light aircraft rides are all popular and easy to arrange, and the local beaches are busy and fun. Be sure to visit the lovely historical town of Girona, and Figueres for the Museum Dali.

Switzerland

flying time
To: Geneva or Zurich
London: 1¼ hrs
NY: 8-9 hrs

climate
Winters are cold, with a lot of snow at high altitude. Summers are warm; the Ticino area has a Mediterranean climate.

when to go
July-Aug is high season. Prices are highest and pistes busiest at Christmas and New Year, half-term and Easter.

currency
Swiss franc

language
German in some areas, French in others, Italian in Ticino. Most people speak some English.

getting around
The Swiss railway system is efficient and the stunning views on the mountain lines are an added delight.

Dazzling white, icing-sugar snow, a fresh cold wind, the scent of pine trees. Only the 'whoosh' of skis breaks the silence...

Dramatic and beautiful, this small country, only a sixth the size of Britain, boasts mountain peaks that rise 15,000 feet and serene, glassy lakes that plunge to unfathomable depths.

Switzerland's loveliest cities hug the lakesides, among them sophisticated and elegant Geneva on the shore of Lac Leman. In winter, the old town's cosy wood-panelled restaurants serve up kirsch-laced cheese fondues. In summer, tables are moved into the streets, and windsurfers and sleek yachts take to the water. Steamers carry visitors out of the harbour, past lakeshore villages, to Lausanne and Montreux.

Geneva is a gateway to both the French and the Swiss Alps, and within a few hours' drive are dozens of mountain resorts offering sports and walking holidays in summer, and some of Europe's best skiing in winter. In fact, Switzerland has more than its fair share of glamorous ski resorts, such as chic, traffic-free Zermatt and Gstaad, favourites of Europe's wealthiest families and film stars.

On the Italian border you find a real gem – the Ticino region. The resorts here could be mistaken for holiday spots on the Mediterranean, by virtue of their sunny weather and long summer season, palm trees and purple bougainvillaea. Only the blue water here is Lakes Maggiore and Lugano, not the sea. Life goes on simply in the rugged mountains, but on the manicured lakefront promenades of Lugano, Locarno and Ascona, the scene is rich, upmarket and positively glitzy.

Information & Reservations
UK 0870 606 1296
INT. +44 870 606 1296

Grand Hotel Zermatterhof

Bahnhofstrasse
3920 Zermatt
Switzerland

✈ Geneva 3 hrs

tel +41 27 966 6600
fax +41 27 966 6699

zermatterhof@zermatt.ch
www.zermatt.ch/zermatterhof

Tour operators:
UK Elegant Resorts
Cadogan Holidays

156

Closed May, Oct-Nov

Member of:
Preferred Hotels

Nestled under the towering slopes of the mighty Matterhorn lies the town of Zermatt, home to the five-star Grand Hotel Zermatterhof.

The hotel was opened in 1879, yet recent renovations have seen this historical building updated with the ultimate in modern convenience. Eighty-six rooms are available including those with canopied beds or beamed ceilings. Two-thirds of the rooms offer majestic mountain views and all offer the elegance and charm that has thrilled hundreds of guests including kings, princes, heads of state and celebrities alike.

The comfort of the hotel is hard to leave but with three excellent restaurants, excursions aren't really necessary. Every taste and dining occasion is catered for.

If you do venture outside, you certainly won't be disappointed. The resort is known for its year-round ski season, yet in summer the area around the hotel is lush and green. Nightlife and shopping are also excellent in the region, which has become a luxury playground for guests from around the world. Whether it's outside exploits or indoor luxury you're after, the Zermatterhof can oblige.

 SFr430-800 (62)

 SFr650-1,790 (24)

 SFr65-150

 SFr35

Honeymoon specials
Flowers, fruit, Swiss chocolates and champagne in room on arrival. Horse carriage transfer, deluxe dinner, free room service, room upgrade to a suite when possible. Also breakfast buffet and free use of sports facilities. Package price from SFr1,380-3,450.

Sightseeing and leisure
Indoor pool, whirlpool, sauna, steambath, massage, fitness room, putting green plus driving net set up in summer. Excursions to the Matterhorn, various mountain railways, hiking, paragliding and, of course, skiing almost all year-round.

Park Hotel Delta

Information & Reservations
UK 0870 606 1296
INT. +44 870 606 1296

Via Delta 137-141
Ascona 6612
Switzerland

✈ Lugano-Agno 35km
✈ Milan 100km

Tel +41 91 785 77 85
Fax +41 91 785 77 35

hotel@delta-ascona.ch
www.delta-ascona.ch

Member of:
Small Luxury Hotels of the World

Surrounded by a 20-acre beautifully landscaped park on the outskirts of Ascona at the top of shimmering Lake Maggiore, the Park Hotel Delta combines Mediterranean ambiance and modern innovation to offer its guests a special experience.

Relax and enjoy is the motto at this exquisite Swiss hotel. Discover some of the lake's many charming islands by boat or take to the hills on the back of the hotel's Harley-Davidson. Or simply stay put and bask in the sheltered grounds or indulge in a sauna followed by a specialist massage, or let yourself be pampered in the Kanebo Beauty Center. Let the hotel bus take you into the village of Ascona or travel by bicycle to explore the surrounding countryside.

Activity-wise, you are spoiled for choice. The Park Hotel Delta offers both indoor and outdoor pools and tennis courts. And golfers have a choice of nearby courses including one of Switzerland's best – the 18-hole Patriziale-Ascona course – while the hotel also offers guests exclusive driving range facilities.

Accommodation ranges from deluxe rooms and lavish suites with terraces overlooking the magnificent park. All are amenity-rich and decorated in Tuscan-style with soothing tones and elegant touches.

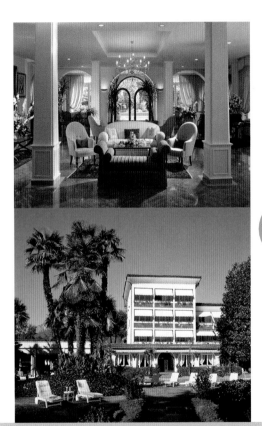

157

 SFR450-700 (36)

 SFR700-1,250 (10)

🍽 included

☕ included

Honeymoon specials
Welcome drink, one bottle of complimentary champagne in the room on arrival, fruits and flowers, plus two exclusive Park Hotel Delta polo shirts.

Sightseeing and leisure
Locarno, Ascona, Lugano, Milano, various valleys and wineries, Madonna del Sasso, Castelli di Bellinzona, Italian markets. Nearby is the 18-hole Patriziale-Ascona golf course plus a driving range at the hotel, eight tennis courts, two swimming pools, Kanebo Beauty Center, kindergarten, animated programme, bicycles and watersports activities.

Palace Hotel Gstaad

Information & Reservations
UK 0870 606 1296
INT. +44 870 606 1296

3780 Gstaad
Switzerland

✈ Geneva 160km

tel +41 33 748 5000
fax +41 33 748 500

palace@gstaad.ch
www.palace.ch

Tour operators:
UK Elegant Resorts

158

Closed April-May; Oct-18 Dec

Member of:
The Leading Hotels of the World

This deluxe hotel, surrounded by pine trees and adorned with castle turrets and towers, is perched atop a hill above the village of Gstaad in the Bernese Alps. Owned and managed by the same family for two generations, the Palace Hotel exudes a friendly and welcoming atmosphere.

The rooms and suites are decorated with soft floral prints, large wooden beams and traditionally carved furniture. Most have private balconies with views extending across snow-capped peaks.

Le Restaurant is a perfect setting in which to enjoy a variety of international cuisine. For more informal dining, there is La Fromagerie, which boasts delicious traditional dishes such as *fondue* and *raclette*, or the canopied terrace set against the backdrop of a superb Alpine panorama. After dinner, guests can dance the night away to the live band, or try out the GreenGo disco, one of Gstaad's most popular night spots.

Or there is the opportunity to be pampered at the hotel's Beautymed Centre, offering a wide variety of treatments provided by Clinique La Prairie of Switzerland. You can also shape up at the health centre or take to the ski slopes. Hot air ballooning, horseriding and even heli-skiing are also all available nearby.

The hotel is happy to make arrangements for weddings, and will organise everything from flowers and orchestras to a horse-drawn carriage or Rolls Royce to convey the bride and groom.

🛏 SFr280-1,160 (76)

🛏 SFr900-2,190 (30)

🍽 from SFr60

☕ included

Honeymoon specials

Complimentary champagne and flowers on arrival. Room upgrade subject to availability.

Sightseeing and leisure

The Beautymed Centre offers a variety of treatments by Clinique La Prairie. Indoor and outdoor swimming pools, tennis, squash, gym, fitness centre with sauna, steambath and massage. Horseriding, year-round skiing. Trips to Church of Saanen and the Lauenen Lake nearby. There are also several festivals throughout the year.

Suvretta House

Information & Reservations
UK 0870 606 1296
INT. +44 870 606 1296

Via Chasellas 1
CH-7500 St Moritz
Switzerland

✈ Milano 175km
✈ Zurich 220km

tel +41 81 836 36 36
fax +41 81 836 37 37

info@suvrettahouse.ch
www.suvrettahouse.ch

Tour operators:
UK Elegant Resorts

Member of:
The Leading Hotels of the World
Swiss Deluxe Hotels

Located in the famous town of St Moritz, this hotel has all the glamour and glitz you would expect to find in one of Europe's top resorts. Set in an inspired location, ringed by tall, fragrant pine trees and larch and with a stunning view of the mountains and lakes of the Upper Engadine, this grand hotel, which was constructed in 1911/12, is still just a stone's throw from the centre of town.

Personal service is the key to the success of this elegant hotel. The staff create a restful, relaxed atmosphere and make sure every visitor will always dream of returning.

Mouth-watering cuisine awaits you at Suvretta House. What could be better than indulging in one of the chef's carefully planned local specialities after a day on the slopes? Along with burning log fires to warm you, hot baths to soothe weary limbs and comfortable rooms with beautiful mountain views, the personal care will astound you and make you feel right at home.

And with a private ski lift and a chair lift it is one of the best places from which to explore the ski slopes in the area. Indeed, Suvretta House is only two kilometres from the skiing areas of Corvatsch and Diavolezza. The Swiss ski school 'Suvretta-Champfèr' has its offices at the hotel and counts up to 120 specialist instructors who offer ski, snowboard as well as cross country lessons.

159

SFr285-720 pppn (210)

SFr570-720 pppn (40)

SFr54-90

included

Honeymoon specials
Complimentary flowers, fruit basket and local wine on arrival.

Sightseeing and leisure
Indoor pool, gym, solarium, massage, beauty treatments, skiing, snowboarding, cross-country skiing, ice-skating rink, curling, tennis, golf driving range and putting green on site. Engadine mountains, horseracing events, polo, dog races, cricket on frozen lake, skating marathons; in summer, hiking, biking, golf and the British Classic Car Meeting.

Turkey

flying time
To: Istanbul, Antalya
London: 3-4¹/₂ hrs
NY: 10¹/₂ hrs

climate/ when to go
Warm throughout the year, Turkey is a popular winter sun destination, especially along the coast. Istanbul is a good destination to visit any time of year.

currency
Turkish lire

language
Turkish but English is widely spoken.

getting around
Internal flights operate regularly between the major cities. There are also good bus and train connections. In Istanbul, explore on foot or travel by taxi. Also use the boats – ferries, water taxis and sea buses.

The place where east meets west, where the familiarity of Europe blends easily with the spice of the Orient, Turkey is a heady mix which is best explored in the ancient, and beautiful, city of Istanbul. Lying on the banks of the Bosphorus, 2000 years of history permeates the air, from the sumptuous Topkapi Palace to the six slender minarets of the famous Blue Mosque and the frenetic alleys of the Bazaar Quarter.

A city dominated by the swath of water that cuts through its heart, exploring the intricacies of the waterway and the city beyond is all part of the mystery and beauty of ancient Istanbul.

Beyond the city lies 5,000 miles of stunning coastline, from the beautiful bay of Izmir, encircled by tall mountains, to Patara with its 11 miles of sandy beach. The vast waters of the Black Sea in the north gives way to the Bosphorus, the Marmara Sea, the Aegean in the west and the Mediterranean in the east.

But Turkey is a destination full of surprises. Amazingly, tulips were first grown in Turkey many, many years ago and St Nicholas (or Father Christmas as he is known today) originated here. Turkish food, also, is exotic and divine and rates among Europe's top cuisines.

The other lasting memory is the warmth of the people of this land. They are kind and giving and believe that a visitor is a 'guest from God' and should be welcomed accordingly.

Ciragan Palace
Hotel Kempinski Istanbul

Information & Reservations
UK 0870 606 1296
INT. +44 870 606 1296

Ciragan Caddesi 84
Besiktas 80700
Istanbul
Turkey

✈ Ataturk 25km

tel +90 212 258 3377
fax +90 212 259 6687

dosm@ciraganpalace.com.tr
www.ciraganpalace.com.tr

In the city where east meets west, this palace is the perfect place to blend the spice and mystique of the east with the glamour and modern-day comfort of the west. Home of the last Ottoman Sultans, the Ciragan Palace is the only hotel in Istanbul located directly on the shores of the striking and mysterious Bosphorus. The property is surrounded by beautifully manicured gardens, terraces and promenades that skirt the shoreline.

Choose between sumptuous suites in the 19th-century marble palace itself, or rooms and suites in the grand hotel in the grounds. Whichever you decide on, rest assured your surroundings will be stunning and the service excellent.

Of course no visit to Istanbul would be complete without a Turkish massage, which can be arranged at the hotel. There are experts on hand to work out any knots you may have developed during your pre-wedding day rush. And for the more active, there is also an indoor and outdoor swimming pool, a sauna and fitness centre, as well as a 9-hole putting green and a solarium at your disposal.

Beyond the magic of this fine hotel, explore the blend of the cultures and the history of three great civilisations from the Romans and Byzantines to the Ottoman Empire before returning to the calm oasis that is the Ciragan Palace.

161

 US$260-550* (284)

 US$750-7,500* (32)

US$42-89

US$26

Honeymoon specials
Local champagne, fruit and chocolate on arrival. Upgrade upon availability.

* Prices exclusive of 17% VAT.

Sightseeing and leisure
Beauty salon on site. Local historic sites include Topkapi Palace, Dolmabahce Palace, Blue Mosque, St Sophia Markets: Grand Bazaar and Egyptian Bazaar.

The UK & Ireland

flying time
To: London,
Manchester,
Glasgow, Edinburgh
NY: 7 hrs
LA: 12-13 hrs

climate
Famously wet. Cold
but not necessarily
icy in winter, warm
but not necessarily
sunny in summer.
You should not rely
on the weather.

when to go
Apr-May for green
landscapes lit by
starbursts of
wildflowers. June
kicks off the tourist
season. Sept-Oct
for gentle warmth
and mellow light,
with fewer tourists.

currency
Pound sterling. In
southern Ireland the
Irish pound or punt.

language
English

getting around
Internal flights to
main cities rarely take
as much as one hour.
Public transport is
efficient – both rail
and buses.

The United Kingdom is an island nation, with a sea which is always near. Whether at the jagged cliffs of Cornwall, the wild coastline of southwest Ireland, the gently sloping, pebbly shores of the English Channel, or the flowering grace of the Jersey shoreline, this is most certainly a place of variety and surprises.

Ancient woods, fertile meadows and bleak moorland crowd the English countryside, as well as glorious man-made features – stately homes with manicured parks, Neolithic standing stones and ruined abbeys.

Scotland is famous for its unspoilt countryside yet offers the metropolitan delights of Edinburgh and Glasgow. Ireland has a wealth of culture and beautiful scenery. Jersey boasts lush green countryside, blonde dunes and an unparalleled mix of English and French sensibilities. But wherever you go, rest assured the people will be invariably courteous and friendly.

The Beaufort

Information & Reservations
UK 0870 606 1296
INT. +44 870 606 1296

33 Beaufort Gardens
Knightsbridge
London SW3 1PP
England

✈ Heathrow 40 miles

Tel +44 (020) 7584 5252
Fax +44 (020) 7589 2834

thebeaufort@nol.co.uk
www.thebeaufort.co.uk

Quietly situated in a classic, tree-lined London square only 100 metres from Harrods, The Beaufort is the perfect stylish base in one of the most exciting cities in the world.

Voted one of the best hotels in the world by Courvoisier in 1995, it is a beautiful, private hotel which prides itself on the tremendous personal attention it provides its guests. The aim is to ensure guests feel at home and as relaxed and comfortable as possible.

On arrival you are greeted at the door and given your own front door key to come and go as you please. In the drawing room there is a well-stocked 24-hour bar where you can help yourself to drinks and relax in one of the large, plump sofas or chairs. The walls of the hotel are decorated with the world's largest collection of English floral watercolours. All of the 28 rooms are differently decorated in warm pastel colours and are full of personal touches like decanters of brandy, Swiss chocolates, fruit, shortbread, and flowers absolutely everywhere.

Enjoy the ultimate in luxury and indulgence – breakfast in bed – hot rolls and croissants with homemade jams and marmalade, all served on fine Wedgewood china.

163

  US$297-429 (28)

  US$486 (7)

  no restaurant in hotel

  included

Honeymoon specials
Complimentary champagne on arrival. Complimentary drinks 24 hours a day. Room upgrade when available.

Sightseeing and leisure
All guests have complimentary use of the Aquilla Health Club nearby. The Victoria and Albert Museum, Science Museum and Natural History museums are all close by, as are the fantastic shops of Knightsbridge.

Chewton Glen

Information & Reservations
UK 0870 606 1296
INT. +44 870 606 1296

New Milton
Hampshire BH25 6QS
England

✈ Heathrow 85 miles
✈ Southampton 22 miles

tel +44 (0) 1425 275 341
fax +44 (0) 1425 272 310

reservations@chewtonglen.com
www.chewtonglen.com

Member of:
Relais & Châteaux

164

Located in 130 acres of wooded and landscaped parkland, in the peace and quiet of the English rolling countryside, Chewton Glen Hotel contains over 250 years of rich heritage.

Its simple 18th-century manor house exterior gives no hint of the luxury within. Each of the beautiful guest rooms is furnished to the highest standards and touches such as overstuffed sofas, roaring log fires and the decanter of fine sherry in the rooms explain why this hotel has been cherished by its many regular guests down the years – including the late Cary Grant.

Many guests come to luxuriate in the facilities and treatments available from the state-of-the-art health spa. Others enjoy the natural beauty of the grounds and proximity to sites such as Stonehenge and the New Forest. Yet all who stay enjoy the chance to dine in the hotel's Marryat restaurant, which currently holds a coveted Michelin Star.

It is no wonder, therefore, that Chewton Glen has a reputation as the primary UK country house hotel. In the last nine years it has won no less than 23 awards. It's currently the only privately owned Five Red Star Hotel in Britain and was recently proclaimed Best Spa in Britain by the UK's Condé Nast *Traveller* magazine.

🛏 £230-550 (53)

🛏 £450-550 (17)

🍽 from £30

☕ £13.50-17.50

🍷 ⊘ 🛎 Ⓢ ✈

Honeymoon specials

Chewton Glen offers special packages; information available upon request.

Sightseeing and leisure

A fully equipped health spa offers over 30 treatments using the finest natural products. There is a 9-hole, par-3 golf course on site, two indoor & outdoor tennis courts with resident professional, croquet lawn, gym, pool and hair salon. Nearby sites include Stonehenge, Wilton House, Exbury Gardens, Lymington, Ringwood & Christchurch markets, New Forest, Salisbury and Winchester Cathedrals.

Taplow House

Information & Reservations
UK 0870 606 1296
INT. +44 870 606 1296

Berry Hill
Taplow
Nr Maidenhead
Berkshire SL6 0DA
England

✈ Heathrow 10 miles

tel +44 (0) 1628 670056
fax +44 (0) 1628 773625

taplow@wrensgroup.com
www.wrensgroup.com

At the end of a grand, sweeping driveway lies the charming and elegant Taplow House, set in six acres of grounds laid out in classic English fashion by the celebrated landscape gardener, Springall.

Rolling green lawns are gently shaded by majestic Burnham beeches and two great tulip trees, one of them planted by Elizabeth I. The house can boast a wealth of historical connections: originally a gift from James I to the first governor of Virginia, it was often visited by Winston Churchill, who came to admire those same magnificent tulip trees.

Indoors is warm and welcoming and the perfect setting for a wedding reception or a relaxed honeymoon. With crystal chandeliers, original oil paintings, and dark oak-panelled bar, Taplow House is the last word in quiet, refined luxury.

Weather permitting, take your evening meal on the Garden Terrace. The Tulip Tree Restaurant offers something for everyone – delicious British and European cuisine from classic to modern.

All the rooms are individually decorated and tastefully arranged to ensure your stay is as comfortable as possible. Each suite is elegant, but the lovely Taplow Suite, with its two bathrooms, beamed Jacobean dressing room and private patio, is especially recommended for honeymooners.

165

£175 (32)

£250 (3)

£25-40

£9-12

Honeymoon specials
Upgrade to superior room if available.

Sightseeing and leisure
The hotel has an on-call aromatherapist. Windsor Castle, Legoland and Cliveden (National Trust property) are among the local sights.

Ballylickey Manor House

Information & Reservations
UK 0870 606 1296
INT. +44 870 606 1296

Ballylickey
Bantry Bay
Co. Cork
Ireland

✈ Cork 82km

tel +353 27 50071
fax +353 27 50124

ballymh@ercom.ie

166 Member of:
Relais & Châteaux

Hidden among the rugged inlets of Ireland's Bantry Bay, this secluded manor house has the ambiance of a beautiful family home cherished and nurtured over the centuries. The main house was originally built some 300 years ago as a shooting lodge by Lord Kenmare. Taken over by the Graves family back in the 1940s, extended and carefully restored, the manor house remains in the family today. It was visited on many occasions by the poet Robert Graves, an uncle of the present owner.

Today, it has been refurbished to become a delightful country house hotel with a perfect compliment of rustic charm and chic elegance. With views of Bantry Bay, the lush and colourful gardens have the Ouvane river running by.

You can choose between elegant main suites in the manor house itself or secluded garden cottages which lie hidden in the park among sheltered lawns and flower gardens. The pool lies in a secluded part of the garden complete with bar and lunch restaurant; while dinner is served in the elegant dining room of the manor house.

Activity-wise, choose from fishing, golf, mountain walks, as well as croquet and horseriding.

🛏 IRL£130-140 (5)

🛏 IRL£170-220 (7)

🍽 IRL£25-34

☕ included

🍾 🚁

Honeymoon specials
Complimentary flowers and half-bottle of Pommery Champagne in room.

Sightseeing and leisure
On site there is a heated outdoor swimming pool and extensive colourful gardens to wander through. Nearby are many famous golf courses, including Bantry Park and Glengariff.

Longueville Manor

Information & Reservations
UK 0870 606 1296
NT. +44 870 606 1296

Longueville Rd
St Saviour JE2 7WF
Jersey

✈ Jersey 8km

tel +44 (0) 1534 725501
fax +44 (0) 1534 731613

longman@itl.net
www.longuevillemanor.com

Member of:
Relais & Châteaux

Set in its own private wooded valley on the pretty island of Jersey, Longueville Manor offers the ultimate in country house living which starts with a warm welcome from Malcolm Lewis and Sue Dufty. They make up the third generation of the Lewis family who have spent the past 40 years perfecting this beautiful manor house.

One of the most prestigious small hotels in Europe, Longueville Manor recently won the ultimate accolade of 'Hotel of the Year' from none other than Egon Ronay.

Over the past eight years the family have renovated the Victorian glass houses along with the Manor's old kitchen gardens. Today, much of the produce is used by the chefs in preparation for sumptuous meals served in the two dining rooms, complemented by renowned wines from around the world.

Each of the bedrooms is named after a rose and has a separate sitting area, complete with books, magazines, fresh flowers and fruit while the bathrooms are luxurious and finished off with thick, oversize towels and robes.

Two suites are available with a private patio – the perfect place to enjoy a sunset cocktail while taking in the views of the Jersey valley beyond.

167

£180-270 (30)

£340-370 (2)

£45-65

included

Honeymoon specials
Champagne and flowers in room on arrival.

Sightseeing and leisure
Close to the hotel you can enjoy beautiful walks, horseriding and watersports. Nearby and worth seeing is Mony Orgueil, probably Jersey's most photographed attraction, dominating the east coast since the 13th century. Situated high above the harbour at Gorey, the castle has spacious grounds and spectacular views.

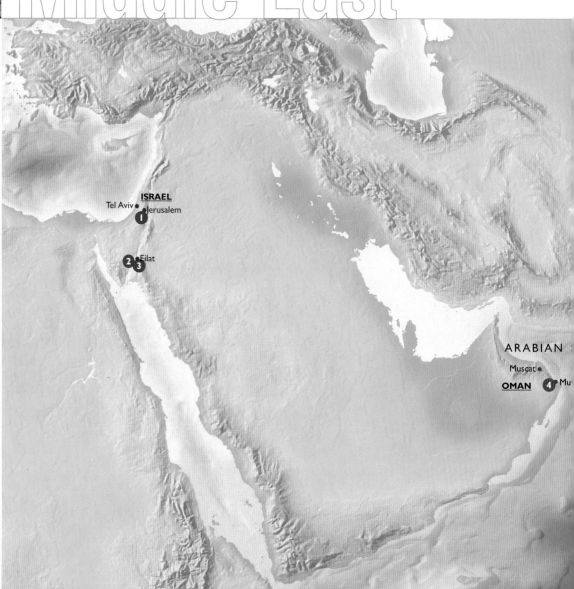

ISRAEL

Tel Aviv • • Jerusalem

Eilat

ARABIAN

Muscat •

OMAN • Mu

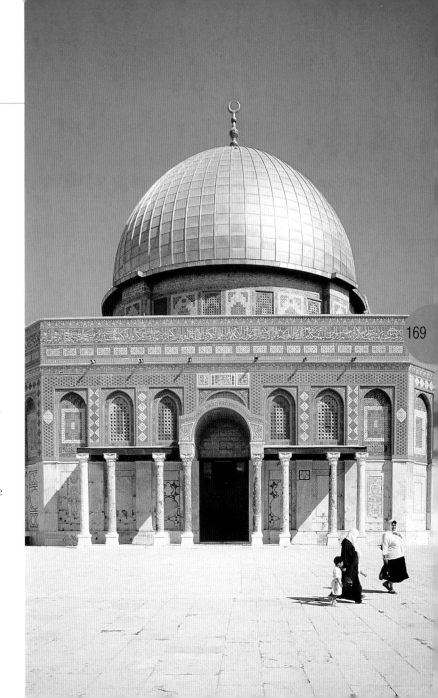

Leave the modern-day Middle East far behind. This is the land of 'The Thousand and One Nights'; a magical mixture of colour, warm hospitality, spectacular archeological sites and history, adventure and surprise.

Romantic Crusader castles perch spectacularly on mountain ranges in the deserts of Syria, while in Yemen's Old City, mosque minarets rise high above the ancient houses. Jordan's one-time capital Petra, built in the third century BC, was forgotten for a thousand years and only rediscovered in the 19th century.

Israel can offer the still but awe-inspiring Dead Sea, diving pleasures in the Red Sea, and the historical and mysterious Jerusalem, perhaps the most fascinating city in the world with a historical legacy like no place else.

As well as the sights, there are beautiful beaches, snake charmers, lively coffee houses, belly dancers, bazaars bursting with carpets, Bedouin rugs, spices and pearls, and a whole range of activities from skiing and camel riding to desert safaris.

For those with a taste for the strange and exotic, the Middle Eastern countries can certainly prove to be a richly rewarding honeymoon destination.

key to hotels

Israel
1 Jerusalem Hotel, Jerusalem
2 Dan Eilat, Eilat
3 Eilat Princess Hotel, Eilat

Oman
4 Al Bustan Palace Hotel, Muttrah

Israel

flying time
To: Tel Aviv
London: 5 hrs
LA: 16-17 hrs
NY: 12 hrs

climate
Summers (Apr-Oct) are hot and dry. Winters are mild with some rain, though it can be chilly in Jerusalem. The warmer south can be uncomfortably hot in mid-summer.

currency
Shekles, but US dollars are readily accepted in hotels, bars and markets.

language
Arabic, Hebrew and English.

when to go
Summer is the main season on the Mediterranean coast but autumn, winter and spring are the popular seasons to visit Eilat and the desert.

The State of Israel is young, celebrating its 50th anniversary in 1998, but the history of the land is palpable.

The landscapes of fertile plains and arid desert seem little changed from descriptions in the Bible. Its surprisingly small area contains a rich variety of scenery and ancient and religious sites. In winter you can ski on the snow-capped slopes of Mt Hermon in the north or take a jeep safari into the southern desert. In summer gaze in wonder at Roman monuments in the morning before taking a swim in the Mediterranean after lunch.

Wherever you are in Israel, you will never be far away from a beach. Along the Mediterranean coast, Tel Aviv, Herzliya and Netanya have long stretches of sand, abundant watersports, and a huge choice of eating places and nightlife, while at the popular Red Sea resort of Eilat you can enjoy year-round sunshine and world-class scuba diving.

Jerusalem must be right at the top of any visitor's sightseeing agenda. The stones of this fascinating city breathe history, and it is as sacred to Muslims and Christians as to Jews. While Jews offer prayers at the Western, or Wailing Wall, along the Via Dolorosa pilgrims follow the alleyways where Jesus is said to have carried the cross to his crucifixion.

Jerusalem Hotel

nformation & Reservations
JK 0870 606 1296
NT. +44 870 606 1296

Antara Ben Shaddad St
PO box 19130
erusalem
srael

✈ Ben Gurion 40km

el +972 2 628 3282
ax +972 2 628 3282

oll free reservations:
JK 0800 3282393
JS I 800 657 9401

aed@jrshotel.com
www.jrshotel.com

Originally built by a feudal lord in the heart of the ancient city of Jerusalem, the Jerusalem Hotel, which is family-owned, has been lavishly refurbished in recent years. The authentic Arab architecture of the last century has been retained and accentuated in the high ceilings, arched windows, cool stone flagging and secluded vine garden. The thick stone walls, cut from creamy Jerusalem stone, have been exposed and pointed with a traditional Arabic plaster.

Each of the 14 rooms is individually and timelessly decorated with antiques and has a beautiful Oriental inspiration. Private balconies overlook the twisting narrow streets and clamorous markets of Jerusalem's Old City, and the ancient, peaceful slopes of The Mount of Olives.

The Eastern influence is continued in the excellent Palestinian cuisine, served to guests at The Vine Restaurant, in the privacy of the pretty garden. Flavourful Bedouin dishes and other local ethnic foods are also a must to try.

From the hotel's location in the heart of the city – only a stone's throw from Damascus Gate – it's easy to wander among historical sites, stroll along the city ramparts at sunset, browse bustling markets, or trek into the nearby Judaen Desert.

171

 US$95-105 (14)

 from US$10-20

☕ included

 🍾💍

Honeymoon specials

Flowers and champagne on arrival. Complimentary night tour to the Windmill Garden, with magnificent views of Jerusalem's Old City walls.

Sightseeing and leisure

Visits to the main markets of the Old City, the Holy Sepulchre, Wailing Wall and Garden Tomb. Hiking trails nearby. Musical and cultural events throughout the year. Beauty salons and health spas available in the area.

Information & Reservations
UK 0870 606 1296
INT. +44 870 606 1296

Dan Eilat

Hotel Area
North Beach
Eilat 88101
Israel

✈ Eilat 2km

tel +972 7 636 2222
fax +972 7 636 2333

daneilat@danhotels.com
www.danhotels.com

172

Located on the sweeping coast of the glorious Red Sea, Eilat is a vacationer's dream. White sands, blue seas and an abundance of marine life lie to the south, while desert and astonishing valleys span the north.

Set on its own stretch of beach within this paradise you'll find the gleaming white walls of the Dan Eilat hotel. With its 378 comfortably furnished rooms it offers every convenience the traveller needs. The restaurants and bars in the property are too numerous to list but all offer high standards of cuisine and attentive service. It's easy to work up an appetite in the hotel's two pools, the extensive fitness gym and on the squash courts.

Outside there is much to explore. The unspoilt desert beckons visitors to its stillness and the nearby Great Rift Valley is one of the world's leading natural phenomena. Diving and snorkelling in the area are excellent and of course, no trip to Eilat would be complete without a trip to the world famous dolphin reef where these beautiful mammals let you enter their world just for a while, but create an experience you will never forget.

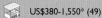 US$240-572* (378)

 US$380-1,550* (49)

 US$25-60

 US$10-15

Honeymoon specials
Room upgrade, champagne and flowers, petits-fours and fruitbasket, T-shirts on arrival.

Prices subject to 15% tax.

Sightseeing and leisure
All manner of sports including squash and tennis. The hotel also has its own gym, Turkish Bath, sauna, spa and jacuzzi. Rich tropical marine life to be explored, coral reefs, underwater observatories and wildlife nature reserve nearby.

Eilat Princess Hotel

Information & Reservations
UK 0870 606 1296
INT. +44 870 606 1296

Taba Beach
PO Box 2323
Eilat 88000
Israel

✈ Eilat 10km

Tel +972 7 636 5500
Fax +972 7 637 6333

princess@isdn.net.il
www.inisrael.com/princess

Tour operators:
UK All main operators

Poised between the desert and the immense Red Sea, the Eilat Princess sits among extensive landscaped gardens at the southern tip of Israel.

The rooms are dressed in cool prints, with king-size beds and balconies that provide sweeping views across the bay to Jordan and Saudi Arabia. Each floor also offers suites with an exotic theme ranging from Thai to Russian, Indian to Chinese. All are romantic and secluded.

Authentic Creole, French, Szechwan and Japanese are among the several varieties of cuisine prepared by award-winning chefs in a variety of settings.

The countless pools and sundecks around the landscaped gardens are connected by a series of bridges with a Venetian inspiration. Whirlpools, waterfalls, waterchutes and underwater grottos are among the park's attractions, and a variety of watersports are available. The semi-private beach offers unparalleled diving and snorkelling, and guests can be pampered at the hotel's spa complex with 12 treatment rooms, beauty parlour and health bar.

For those wishing to hold their reception here, the hotel can provide in-house designers and florists to assist with all preparations.

173

 US$258–522 (420)
 US$440-1,430 (64)
 from US$37
 from US$20

Honeymoon specials

Champagne, flowers and cake on arrival. Room upgrade subject to availability. Free shuttle service to/from hotel. Honeymooners can enjoy a champagne breakfast in their room. 10% discount at the Sansara Health Club.

Sightseeing and leisure

Outdoor jacuzzi, waterslides, tennis courts and Sansara Spa and Fitness Centre with Finnish sauna, gym, private massage and treatment rooms. Trips to underwater observatory, dolphin reef, ostrich farm. Scuba diving, parasailing, windsurfing, snorkelling and waterskiing are available nearby. Desert safaris, trips to Sinai.

Oman

174

This area of the Middle East has long been a hot-bed of political activity. It is also rich in history, oil and archaeological interests. To travel to the Gulf States is to experience a culture unlike any other.

Occupying the southeastern tip of the Arabian Peninsula, boasting 1,700 kilometres of coastline, Oman is a country of contradictions.

The north of the country sees rugged mountains framing swathes of desert, yet the south is lush and green. Picturesque old buildings sit shoulder to shoulder with modern architecture and at the coast, working coconut groves brush alongside white sand beaches that frame the cool blue sea.

Oman has much to offer the active visitor, including diving, rock climbing, sand-skiing and golf. There is a rich archaeological history to explore and exquisite silver and woven bargains to be found in the labyrinthine *souk* in Muscat. And remember, getting lost is half the fun.

Al Bustan Palace Hotel

nformation & Reservations
JK 0870 606 1296
NT. +44 870 606 1296

PO Box 1998
Muttrah
Sultanate of Oman

✈ Seeb Int. 40km

Tel +968 799 666
Fax +968 799 600

albustan@interconti.com
www.interconti.com

Tour operators:
UK Elegant Resorts
Kuoni

Enjoy the grand and exotic and stay at what is reputed to be one of the finest hotels in the world.

The Al Bustan Palace is set in 200 acres of lush gardens, surrounded by a dramatic mountain backdrop, sea and beach. Originally built to host the 1985 Gulf Cooperation Council Summit in Muscat and used to host heads of state, prime ministers and other government ministers, the hotel is now a sumptuous retreat for leisure travellers.

A five-star hotel, it boasts some 250 rooms, including a selection of beautifully decorated junior and grand deluxe suites. All have modern day amenities, from telephone with private voice mail to video cassette recorders, 24-hour room service and valet service.

Indulge in the finest Middle Eastern cuisine and the best gourmet dining in Muscat at the charming Al Marjan Restaurant, or enjoy live Arabic entertainment at the Al Hamra Supper Club. The choice is wide but more local culture is available at the Seblat al Bustan where an authentic Omani dinner with traditional music is hosted once a week.

Make the most of the superb leisure facilities, from the four floodlit clay tennis courts and full time instructor, to the state-of-the-art, fully equipped gym and beauty salon, variety of watersports, diving and deep sea fishing trips or coastal cruises launched from the resort's marina.

175

US$292-333* (198)

US$368-1,860* (50)

US$20-60

US$15-20

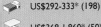

Honeymoon specials

Upgrade to a superior room depending on availabilty, complimentary honeymoon cake, bottle of sparkling wine, flowers and fruit basket on arrival.

* Prices subject to 17% service charge and tax.

Sightseeing and leisure

On site there are tennis courts, gym, sauna, spa, squash courts, beauty and barber salon. All watersports, marina facilities, diving. Nearby, Bait Al Zubair Museum, featuring antique Omani artefacts and jewellery. Muttrah Souq for gold jewellery, silver and pottery. Al Alam Palace, Jalali and Mirini forts.

176

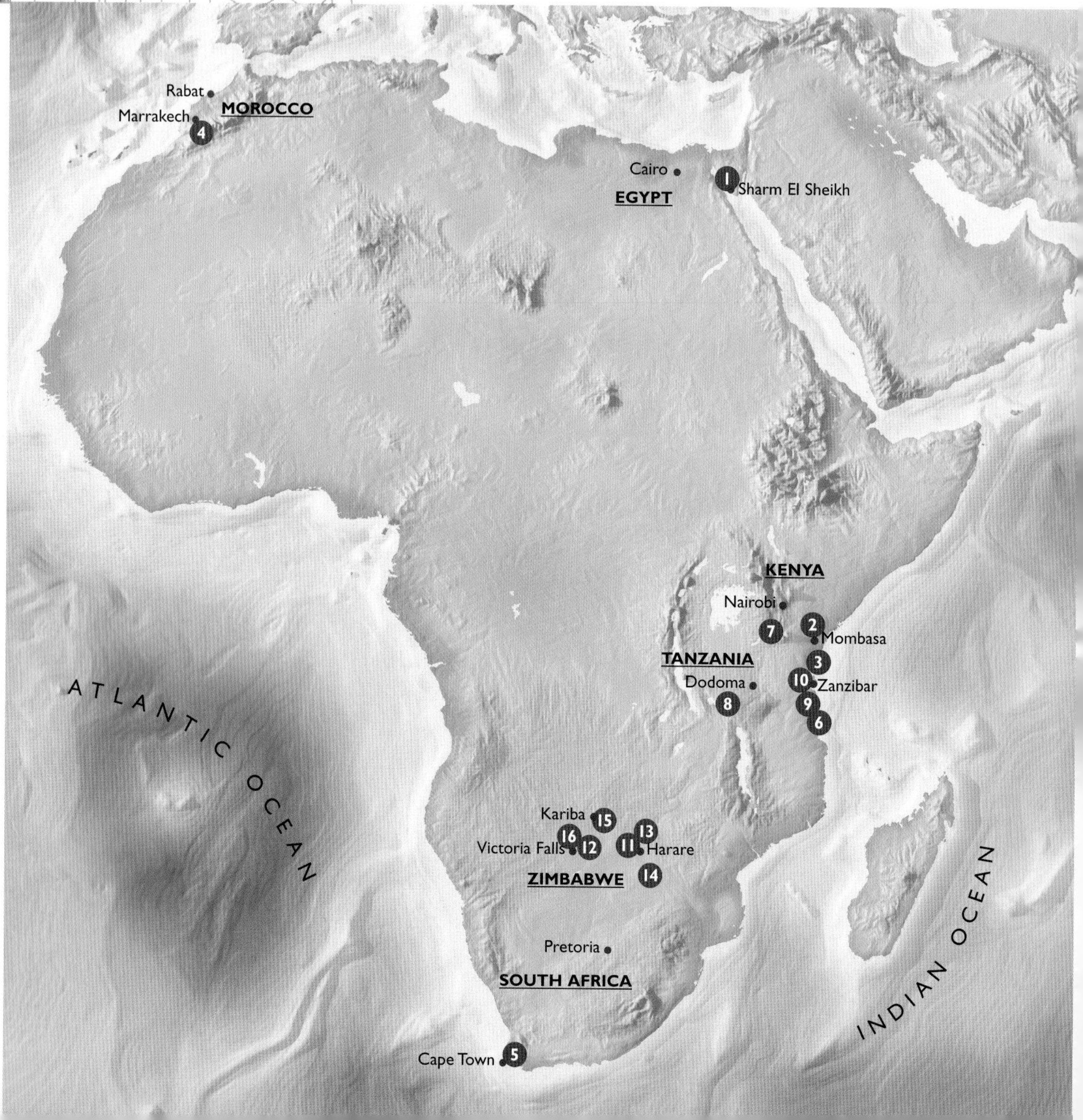

Rabat •
Marrakech • **MOROCCO** (4)

Cairo • (1) Sharm El Sheikh
EGYPT

ATLANTIC OCEAN

KENYA
Nairobi • (2)
(7) (2) Mombasa
TANZANIA (3)
Dodoma • (10) Zanzibar
(8) (9) (6)

Kariba (15)
(16) (12) (13)
Victoria Falls (11) Harare
ZIMBABWE (14)

Pretoria •

SOUTH AFRICA

INDIAN OCEAN

Cape Town (5)

Africa... next to Asia, the largest continent in the world and a heady mixture of peoples, languages, climates and landscapes.

From the stark beauty of the Sahara Desert to the snow-capped peaks of Kilimanjaro, from the mud huts of a Masai village in Kenya to the ancient stone pyramids at Giza in Egypt – no other land provides such contrasts.

There are endless ways to create a memorable honeymoon here. The Swahili countries of Kenya and Tanzania make easy 'beach and bush' locations, combining safari drives through famous African national parks such as The Masai Mara, Serengeti and Ngorongoro Crater, with lazy days spent on their Indian Ocean coastlines and exotic islands.

Zambia offers exciting safaris in the remote parks of Kafue and the South Luangwa, and relaxation on the golden sands of Lake Malawi. Zimbabwe is defined by the path of the Zambezi River, which cascades over the mighty Victoria Falls. In Botswana, the islands and channels of the Okavango Delta, 'Jewel of the Kalahari', are best explored by canoe, or even from the back of an African elephant. Visit, too, the dramatic landscapes of Namibia and the richly coloured desert dunes of Soussesvlei.

South Africa is a land of extremes: from the cosmopolitan cities of Cape Town and Johannesburg to the Kruger National Park, the beautiful Garden Route and its many fabulous beaches, it has something to offer every visitor.

key to hotels

Egypt
1 Baron Resort, Sharm El Sheikh

Kenya
2 Mombasa Serena Beach Hotel, Mombasa
3 The Funzi Keys

Morocco
4 La Mamounia, Marrakech

South Africa
5 The Bay, Cape Town

Tanzania
6 Kinasi, Ma'fia Island
7 Migration Camp, Serengeti
8 Mwagusi Safari Camp, Ruaha National Park
9 The Selous Safari, Dar Es Salaam
10 Zanzibar Serena Inn, Zanzibar

Zimbabwe
11 The Hide Safari Camp, Harare
12 Victoria Falls Hotel, Victoria Falls
13 Imba Matombo, Harare
14 Pamushana, Chiredzi
15 Sanyati, Harare
16 Stanley & Livingstone, Victoria Falls

Egypt

flying time
To: Cairo
London: 5 1/2 hrs
NY: 12 hrs

when to go
The best time to
visit is in the cool
season from Nov-
Mar, though the
coastal area is nice
year-round. Oct is
a good off-season
month when tourist
crowds are low.

currency
Egyptian pound

language
Arabic

getting around
There is a good
system of public
transport. If you
have lots of money
and little time, air
travel is the way to
go. Buses service
virtually every town
and 5,000km of rail
connects just about
every town in the
country. You can hire
service taxis which
carry car loads of
people between
towns.

178

Herodotus, the ancient Greek historian and traveller, once described Egypt as 'the gift of the Nile'. Indeed, for thousands of years it has been the grand playground of emperors and kings.

The Pharaohs, Greeks, Romans, Arabs, Turks and British have all ruled here and modern Egypt is a delightful mixture of traditions.

In the colourful, bustling city of Cairo, always thronged with people, the medieval and contemporary Western world come together – townsfolk in long, flowing robes mingle happily with the Reebok and blue jean-clad, and city traffic competes with ancient donkey-drawn carts.

History lovers will find plenty to savour. Visit the overwhelming Pyramids at Giza and Luxor, built on the site of the famous ancient city of Thebes, with its truly magnificent and awe-inspiring architecture.

For true relaxation take a camel caravan through the vast desert, a lazy cruise down the Nile or a dream dive in the crystal-clear waters of the Red Sea. Here, beautiful white sand beaches abound and the underwater wonders of vibrant corals and exotic fish provide among the best scuba diving in the world.

Baron Resort

Information & Reservations
UK 0870 606 1296
INT. +44 870 606 1296

Ras Nasrani Bay
Sharm El Sheikh
Egypt

✈ Sharm El Sheikh 5km

Reservations:
tel +202 418 3872/419 9206
fax +202 418 4578

resvshrm@baronhotels.com
www.baronhotels.com

The sumptuous Baron Resort at Sharm El Sheikh occupies an outstanding position at the southern tip of the Sinai Peninsula, reached across shimmering desert expanses dotted with verdant oases and towering granite mountains, and overlooking the Red Sea and the magnificent Straits of Tiran.

Renowned for its exquisite coral reefs, the area is a haven for diving enthusiasts, who can explore the colourful underwater gardens and be dazzled by the beautiful marine life on display. There are plenty of other watersports on offer, such as windsurfing and waterskiing, or try the sulphur spring, considered a cure for rheumatism and skin complaints.

The hotel combines a touch of luxury with the warmest of welcomes. Set in 120,000 square metres of green lawns and walkways, and fringed with colourful native flowers and palm trees, there are three pools, including an Olympic-size freshwater pool and a seawater pool complete with jacuzzi, and also a spacious private beach served by numerous restaurants and bars. Order yourself an extravagant cocktail one evening and, if you are lucky, you will have the pleasure of experiencing a famous Sinai sunset, which transforms the whole of Tiran Island opposite to a gorgeous, deep coral-pink hue.

179

US$140-220 (360)
US$500-1,750 (13)
US$25-40
US$10-15

Honeymoon specials
Fruit basket on arrival and upgrade to superior room. Invitation to a weekly reception party.

Sightseeing and leisure
Lying majestically across the Tiran Straits is Tiran Island, and although the island itself is out of bounds, the surrounding reefs are awesome. Explore Gordon Reef to the north, Jackson Reef to the south, or Woodhouse and Thomas reefs in the centre. Sinai mountain and San Catherine mountain, where Moses received the Ten Commandments and through which the holy family travelled en route to Egypt.

Kenya

flying time
To: Nairobi
London: 9 hrs
NY: 17 hrs

when to go
Apr-May sees the
long rains, Jun-Oct is
hot and dry. Nov.
sees the short rains
and Dec-Mar is very
hot and humid.

currency
The Kenyan shilling,
but US dollars are
widely accepted.

language
The official language
is Swahili, though
English is widely
spoken.

getting around
Air Kenya and many
private airlines
connect the national
parks and towns.
There is a daily
railway service
from Nairobi to
Mombasa.

Kenya is one of the oldest and most traditional safari destinations, and seems to perfectly capture the romance of Africa.

The colourful diversity of the wildlife, scenery and people of Kenya, its coastline lapped by the Indian Ocean, has long carried the influence of Arabian traders who found their way to these shores nearly ten thousand years ago. In recent years much of Kenya is perceived to have become over-developed by mass tourism, but there remain many wonderfully unspoilt locations.

The Masai Mara is characterised by huge expanses of rolling savannah grassland and flat-topped acacias. As the name suggests, it is the homeland of the nomadic Masai tribe, who herd their cattle across this land and northern Tanzania, still living in accordance with their age-old traditionsdistinguished by their proud nature and the distinctive red cloth that they wear. In August the Mara provides fresh pasture for the millions of wildebeest follow the seasonal change across the border. This spectacular migration across the Sand River can be viewed from hot air balloon, a trip which most surrounding lodges can arrange.

The confluence of the Arab, Portuguese, Indian and African cultures add a hint of spice to Kenya's exotic coastline. Explore its offshore reefs and islands, so rich with aquatic life.

Mombasa
Serena Beach Hotel

Information & Reservations
UK 0870 606 1296
INT. +44 870 606 1296

PO Box 90352
Mombasa
Kenya

✈ Moi Int. 20km

Tel +254 11 485721/4
Fax +254 11 485453

Tour operators:
UK British Airways Holidays
Kuoni

Member of:
Club Best Hotels of the World

Situated close to Shanzu Beach, just a few miles north of Mombasa, known as Kenya's 'Second City', the Mombasa Serena Beach represents the ultimate escape.

Inspired by the legendary 13th-century Swahili town of Lamu, the resort's 166 rooms and suites lie in flat-roofed Arabesque houses dotted around shady courtyards. Once inside, ethnic designs give a feel for this warm and beautiful country, while in the suites, the muslin canopied beds add a distinctive air of romance.

Traditional African fare as well as international cuisine are available to tempt you at the resort.

Choose from the elegant Fountain restaurant with its outside terrace and gourmet cuisine or visit one of the informal Swahili evenings to capture a true taste of the vibrant local life.

The large swimming pool offers the chance to cool off from the heat of the day or step onto the beautiful talcum-fine sandy beach to enjoy the huge variety of watersports on offer.

Outside the resort, be sure not to miss trips to visit the hippos at nearby Bamburi Nature Trail, to buy jewellery at Bombolulu, or to spend an unforgettable day on safari at the Shimba Hills National Reserve further inland.

181

 US$120-220* (166)

US$320-420*

US$18

US$11

Honeymoon specials
Fruit and flowers in room on arrival. Complimentary canapes and sparkling wine every evening. Room upgrade subject to availability.

Prices subject to 28% taxes and are on halfboard basis.

Sightseeing and leisure
Facilities include hairdressing salon on site, massage and beauty centre nearby. Historical sites of Fort Jesus, Gede Ruins Malindi. Bombolulu workshops and cultural centre, Bamburi nature trail. Mamba village and crocodile farm.

The Funzi Keys

Information & Reservations
UK 0870 606 1296
INT. +44 870 606 1296

PO Box 92062
Mombasa
Kenya

✈ Mombasa 80km

tel +44 (0) 20 8747 0177
fax +44 (0) 20 8995 2055

funzikeys@aboutafrica.co.uk
www.thefunzikeys.com

182

Tour operators:
UK Carrier, Art of Travel,
Casenove & Loyd Safaris Ltd
US African Travel Inc.

A small, undeveloped island off the remote Kenyan east coast is home to the ravishing Funzi Keys, an exclusive community of six lovely stone thatched cottages set along the water's edge, facing west to catch the striking African sunsets.

Light and nature flood in, so that indoors and outdoors seem to merge into one. Rooms are decorated with locally carved wood and shells and even the jacuzzi looks straight onto the sea.

Natural materials, stone floors and rush matting are enhanced by colourful fabrics, and each cottage is blessed with a romantic four-poster bed and private camp fire on the beach.

Everything is designed for your comfort and ease – days are deliberately left unstructured so that you can do exactly as you please, when you please. Listen to the haunting cry of a fish eagle as you dine on the deck of an anchored *dhow* resting serenely

 US$400-500 pppn (6)

 included

 included

 (incl)

Honeymoon specials
Flowers, fruit and chilled white wine on arrival, one champagne breakfast and candlelight dinner served in your suite.

in the calm of the Indian Ocean. Take a trip on the Ramisi River to admire iridescent kingfishers, rare tropical birds, or bathing crocodiles, or be entranced by the dolphins at Funzi Creek.

All of these activities are included in the price of your holiday so it's the ideal opportunity to try something new. If you're feeling lazy, however, a barbecue at sunset or a snooze on the wooden deck beside the pool sounds just the ticket.

Sightseeing and leisure

Snorkelling, sailing, windsurfing, canoeing, *dhow* and boat trips in the bay and Ramisi River, and beach barbecues are all included. Available at extra cost are deep sea fishing, scuba diving, sightseeing and shopping in Mombasa, game viewing in the Shimba Hills National Park, excursions to the Kisite Marine National Park.

Morocco

flying time
To: Marrakech
London: 5 hrs
NY: 12 hrs

when to go
Coastal Morocco is pleasant year-round although winter can bring cool, wet conditions in the north. In the lowlands the cooler months of Oct-April are popular.

currency
Dirham

language
Arabic with Berber dialects, but French, Spanish and English are widely spoken.

getting around
Public transport is pretty good. There is an efficient rail network lining the main towns of the north coast. In Marrakech you can travel easily by bus or collective grand taxi. Hiring a car gives you the option to visit places difficult to reach by public transport.

If exotic is what you're looking for, Morocco is the place for you. This spectacularly diverse land of majestic mountains, green valleys, medieval cities, fertile plains, vast deserts and unspoiled beaches is bursting with a myriad of colours, tastes and scents. Its vibrancy and allure provide an intense and unforgettable experience, an everlasting inspiration for the senses.

Morocco is unique in that it is the African country closest to Europe in geographical and cultural terms, although with its deeply Islamic culture it seems very far from Europe. Many of the cultural influences come from the French-dominated colonial days, while the artistic and architectural influences are closer to geographically nearby Spain.

The beautiful city of Marrakech, low and pink before a great range of mountains, is an entrancing place to be. Famed for its markets and festivals, its beating heart is the huge square in the old city – Djemaa El Fna.

Rows of food stalls fill the air with mouthwatering aromas and at night it turns into a magical realm, where stories are told, fire swallowed and poison snakes charmed. The markets, or *souks*, here are among the best in the country. They are piled high with rugs, woodwork, jewellery, crafts and Moroccan leather, which is said to be the softest in the world.

Information & Reservations
UK 0870 606 1296
INT. +44 870 606 1296

La Mamounia

Avenue Bab Jdid
Marrakech
Morocco

✈ Marrakech 5km

Tel +212 4 44 44 09
Fax +212 4 44 49 40

resa@mamounia.com
www.mamounia.com

Tour operators:
UK Elegant Resorts
US Abercrombie & Kent

La Mamounia, in the heart of Marrakech, stands in a 200-year-old park that was the wedding gift of a Sultan to his son. No ordinary hotel would look at home in such prestigious grounds, but then La Mamounia is no ordinary hotel.

Designed in 1922, the hotel is a fascinating mixture of Moroccan architectural tradition and modernist Art Deco. In the entrance lobby a chandelier illuminates a gold, vaulted ceiling. At ground level, marquetry-panelled arm chairs and Moroccan rugs rest on geometric marble floors. The happy alchemy is continued throughout the public areas, restaurants and bars, even to the

grand casino, through to the suites and rooms, where 1920s blends effortlessly with such details as fine Moroccan tiling and sensuous fabrics.

The hotel has attracted a galaxy of VIPs from the world of stage, screen, fashion, politics and royalty. Winston Churchill painted a picture of the gardens from his hotel window during World War II. More recently Nicole Kidman and Tom Cruise came here for a bit of rest and privacy.

The hotel has a pool, tennis, squash, gym, and a new golf driving range with a resident pro. There is also horseriding nearby. Beyond is the multi-faced, complex and beautiful city of Marrakech.

185

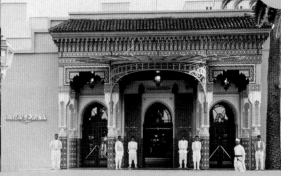

 US$210-485 (171)

US$315-3,150 (60)

US$47-85

US$21

Honeymoon specials

Four-night, three-day package including Moroccan/American buffet breakfast daily, one dinner (excl. drinks) in one of the hotel's restaurants, a bottle of champagne, flowers and fruit on arrival, one horse-driven carriage ride and transfers to/from the airport costs from US$910 per couple in low season in a room overlooking the gardens.

Sightseeing and leisure

On site are a pool, jacuzzi, squash, golf driving range, beauty salon, Hamman, sauna, massage and fitness club. Horseriding and golf nearby. There is a casino in the hotel.

South Africa

flying time
To: Johannesburg
or Cape Town
London: 11 hrs
NY: 15 hrs

**climate/
when to go**
Cape Town is best
visited Sept-Apr.
The rest of the
country experiences
rain in the summer
from Oct-Mar.

currency
South African rand

language
A wide variety
including English,
Afrikaans, Zulu,
Xhosa and South
Sotho.

getting around
South African
Airways' efficient
network of internal
flights connects most
of the major towns,
the national parks
and other attractions.

In this cosmopolitan and sophisticated country, reminders of a fascinating, if turbulent, history abound. And its sheer size and diversity means that there is something here for everyone.

In addition to safaris and its national parks, South Africa offers activities that tend not to be found on the rest of the continent, such as hiking, walking, riding, cycling, wine tasting and scenic train journeys. For wildlife enthusiasts, the Kruger National Park and its surrounding private reserves offer extremely good game viewing and luxuriously appointed lodges. Open-sided vehicles and well trained guides, who are adept at spotting the 'big five' game animals, ensure that your safari is as memorable and exciting as possible.

The famous Garden Route, from Port Elizabeth to Cape Town, follows the coastline. The secluded bays and beaches, waterfalls and forests along the way make this a very dramatic drive, and its final destination is one of the most romantically situated cities in the world. Table Mountain provides a magnificent backdrop to the fine beaches of Cape Town, its acres of vineyards and gardens, and the waterfront is an ideal spot to sample the fine cuisine on offer.

There is so much more to experience in South Africa – the verdant hills and valleys of the Waterberg, the stark landscapes of the Kalahari Desert, and the Indian Ocean coastline around Durban. For those who wish to end their trip in a tropical paradise, Benguerra Island off the coast of Mozambique, can provide a marvellous romantic finale to your African honeymoon.

The Bay

Information & Reservations
UK 0870 606 1296
INT. +44 870 606 1296

Victoria Road
Camps Bay
Cape Town
South Africa

✈ Cape Town Int. 21km

Tel +27 21 438 4444
Fax +27 21 438 4455

res@thebay.co.za
www.slh.com

Tour operators:
UK Carrier Int.
US African Travel

Member of:
Small Luxury Hotels of the World

The Cape Town area was described by Sir Francis Drake as 'the fairest cape in the whole circumference of the earth'. And The Bay provides the perfect base to explore its awesome wonder. Just 10 minutes from Cape Town's centre, it overlooks the stunning Camps Bay Beach and prides itself on first-rate personal service and a great international reputation.

The superb beachfront location gives visitors the perfect chance to soak up the sun on the sand or take in the atmosphere of this vibrant area at 'Sandy B', the new beach-style bar. Every room offers a spectacular view either of the shimmering Atlantic Ocean, majestic Table Mountain, or the craggy Twelve Apostles. All have their own private entrance lobby and en suite bathroom.

The Tides restaurant, which is attached to the hotel, gives you that incredible view of the sweep of Camps Bay Beach and serves outstanding fresh fish and an impressive array of South African wines. The poolside Espresso Bar is great for casual al fresco dining.

The Bay is situated within easy reach of the Cape's most celebrated scenic attractions; including a number of lush golf courses, beaches, the winelands, Victoria & Alfred Waterfront, Table Mountain and Kirstenbosch Botanical Gardens.

187

 US$200-350 (74)

 US$450-680 (4)

 US$4-15

 US$7-11

Honeymoon specials

If your wedding is held in The Bay's Rotunda banqueting centre then the first night's stay is complimentary. Strawberries on arrival in summer months. Room upgrade subject to availability.

Sightseeing and leisure

Swimming pool and beauty salon in hotel, health club and gym nearby. Also close by are squash and tennis courts, golf and watersports. Excursions to Table Mountain, Cape Point, Camps Bay Beach, Kirstenbosch Botanical Gardens, Robben Island. Also, Stellenbosch and Franschoek Winelands and local craft markets.

Tanzania

flying time
To: Tabora
London: 11 hrs
NY: 17 hrs

when to go
April and May are
the months of the
long rains, June-Oct
is hot and dry, Nov
brings the short
rains, and Dec-Mar is
very hot and humid.

currency
The Tanzanian shilling,
though US dollars
are widely accepted.

language
The official language
is Swahili, though
English is widely
spoken.

getting around
Specialist transfer
operators and
internal airlines
connect major
towns, national parks
and airports.

From Mount Kilimanjaro, across the plains of the Serengeti, and to the crystal waters of its Indian Ocean islands, Tanzania is one of Africa's most beautiful countries.

With some of the most unspoilt beaches in Africa it is ideally suited to a honeymoon. On top of that, there is the opportunity to safari in the national parks, as well as freshwater lagoons and verdant forests that reach to the white coral sands and azure waters of the Indian Ocean. On the mainland there are idyllic resorts, and offshore islands such as Zanzibar, Ma'fia and Mnemba offering some of the best diving, watersports and big-game fishing in the Indian Ocean.

Few things can compare with the joys of watching the spectacles of nature unfurl before you – the migration of the wildebeest, a solitary leopard languidly sleeping in the branches of an acacia, or a cheetah racing across the sun-bleached savannah. You can start your day in this country with a dawn balloon ride over the plains, and end watching the sun set while taking cocktails on your verandah. Whether you choose to stay in a beautifully appointed hotel or to sleep under canvas, the sounds of the African night will envelop you.

The southern parks of Selous and Ruaha offer an insight into the Africa of old. Vast and remote, these parks remain the preserve of some of the most discerning safari operators, who offer game walks for guests seeking a chaperone into the heart of the bush.

Africa Archipelago

CONTACT
Africa Archipelago
55 Fulham High Street
London SW6 3JJ
England

tel +44 (020) 7471 8780
fax +44 (020) 7384 9549
worldarc@compuserve.com
www.africaarchipelago.com

Through many years of experience we know that choosing the right honeymoon requires meticulous planning and detailed up-to-date knowledge. We specialise in tailormaking honeymoons to east and southern Africa, as well as to some of the more exotic islands in the Indian Ocean.

We have taken care to select some of the most untouched and romantic destinations in Africa. Most of the accommodation we recommend is in small, exclusive camps, lodges and island hideaways, all of which offer the best in personalised service.

The African dream is one of the most evocative. Just imagine waking to the sound of the Indian Ocean lapping the coral sands of your private island, or gazing down on migrating wildebeest on your verandah as the African sun sets over the Zambezi.

This vast continent has a huge range of landscapes, wildlife and activities, as well as a beautiful coastline and islands, and it is very important to us that we arrange exactly the right honeymoon for our clients.

Please contact us in London, where we can arrange a personal presentation, or over the internet where we have many pages devoted to honeymoon ideas, and let us arrange the Africa honeymoon of your dreams.

Information & Reservations
UK 0870 606 1296
INT. +44 870 606 1296

Kinasi, Ma'fia Island

Ma'fia Island
Tanzania

✈ Dar es Salaam 130km

Contacts:
Africa Archipelago
Tel +44 (0) 20 7471 8780
Fax +44 (0) 20 7384 9549
worldarc@compuserve.com
www.africaarchipelago.com

PO Box 18033
Dar es Salaam, Tanzania
Tel +255 51 843 501
Fax +255 51 843 495

Ma'fia Island, with its studded islets, sand banks and beaches lapped by crystal clear waters, lies a short distance off the great Rufji Delta and was once a regular stop for Arab and Persian *dhows* plying the coastal waters from Mozambique.

Kinasi, a small, luxury lodge which was once a private home, is in an idyllic spot to the south of the island in the beautiful Chole Bay. Now there are 12 luxury palm-topped bungalows spread throughout acres of coconut plantation. Each room is decorated with traditional, brightly coloured African fabrics, with furniture designed by Kinasi's own carpenters, hand-blown glassware and works

of art to create a stylish but personal feel. They also have large verandahs and en suite bathrooms.

Staff in traditional dress are very friendly and serve top-notch local dishes featuring fresh seafood, tropical fruit and vegetables. If you can tear yourself away from the table, activities centre on the sea. The diving here is among the best in the world. Isolated islets and coves provide great places to swim and picnic in private.

The terrace overlooking the Bay is a prime spot for wedding ceremonies with a romantic feel, and receptions for up to 30 guests can be arranged in the grounds or on the island atolls.

 US$130-150pppn (12)

▢ included

☕ included

incl

Honeymoon specials

Champagne and flowers in the room on arrival. Private dinners and personal valet. Entertainment by the local choir and drummers. Laundry included. Honeymoon suite available.

Sightseeing and leisure

Diving, snorkelling, sailing, fishing, excursions by road and sea, volleyball, badminton, tennis and swimming pool. Visits to local villages can be arranged, also to Persian ruins and other archaeological sites, coastal forest and traditional boat-building yards. Guided tours to coconut plantations. Birdwatching on the tidal flats and mangroves. Romantic picnics in coves and channels around the island.

Migration Camp

Information & Reservations
UK 0870 606 1296
INT. +44 870 606 1296

Serengeti
Tanzania

✈ Lobo Bush airstrip 30min

UK contact:
tel +44 (0) 1453 890885
mobile +44 (0) 7714 088822
fax +44 (0) 1453 890885
juliet.halcyon@virgin.net

res@halcyontz.com
www.halcyonhotels.co.za

192

This cosy, beautifully constructed tented camp is situated in the lush Northern Central Serengeti, overlooking the Grumeti River. Big game-watching is the principal pursuit here as the Serengeti migration masses around the site for several months on its way to and from the Southern Plains, and specially tailored safaris give you the chance to get thrillingly close to nature here.

Guided walks, within the vicinity of the property, are available on request, but you can also view game from the comfort of a Landrover, complete with guide. Marvel at lions, leopards, cheetahs and buffalo in their glorious natural habitat.

The 20 individual *en suite* tents with private balconies are set amidst verdant scenery and are oriented westwards to receive the full benefit of the northern Serengeti sunsets. All are tastefully furnished in warm colours with log furniture, and the honeymoon suite even boasts a romantic outside bath.

Enjoy the comfortable lounge, with its cultural and wildlife library, and the refreshing swimming pool, where you can soak up the sun and relax, readying yourself for the arduous task of another candlelit dinner beneath the stars, or in a real bush setting around the camp fire.

US$195* pppn (20)

US$195* pppn (1)

included

included

Honeymoon specials
Complimentary champagne and flowers on arrival.

Fullboard but excludes gratuities, drinks and $25 for park fees.

Sightseeing and leisure
Game drives in the Serengeti, balloon and walking safaris. There are leisure facilities in Arusha Town.

Mwagusi Safari Camp

Information & Reservations
UK 0870 606 1296
INT. +44 870 606 1296

Ruaha National Park
Tanzania

✈ Msembe airstrip 20mins
✈ Iringa 3hrs

UK contact:
Tel +44 (0) 20 8846 9363
Fax +44 (0) 20 8846 9363

tropicafrica.uk@virgin.net
www.ruaha.org

Tour operators:
UK Africa Archipelago
Tim Best Travel
US African Portfolio
Nature Encounters

Ruaha is one of the largest and wildest national parks in the world and one of the finest in Africa. Indeed, Ruaha remains as Africa once was generations ago, yet with all the comforts that today's traveller expects.

Mwagusi Safari Camp is a well-appointed tented camp, owner-run by Chris Fox who was born and bred in the region. With over 30 years experience in the Ruaha, Chris and his enthusiastic team are your hosts.

The camp, built in keeping with traditional African style, is nestled into the banks of a sand river and ideally situated in the middle of the park where the wildlife is most concentrated.

From the minute you touch down at the local airstrip, the adventure begins. Experience a variety of wildlife in this unique overlap of eastern and southern African ecosystems, which supports a vast wilderness of flora and fauna. Within 45 minutes drive from camp, more than 80 species of animal and over 480 species of bird can be seen.

Absorb and marvel at the sights, sounds and smells of the African bush, heightened by the experience of viewing from open four-wheel drive vehicles, or on foot accompanied by an armed guide, or from the peaceful seclusion of your private verandah.

193

Honeymoon specials
Fruit basket on arrival. Airstrip transfers and laundry are included.

Sightseeing and leisure
Experience the African bush on walks and game drives from open four-wheel drive vehicles.

 US$275 (8 tents)
 included
 included
 incl

Ras Kutani/
The Selous Safari Camp

Information & Reservations
UK 0870 606 1296
INT. +44 870 606 1296

Dar es Salaam
Tanzania

✈ Ras Kutani airstrip 2km

Contact:
Selous Safari Co Ltd
PO Box 1192
Dar es Salaam
tel +255 51 128 485
fax +255 51 112 794

selous@twiga.com
www.specialhotels.com

194

Closed mid-April to end May

Tour operator:
UK Africa Archipelago, TTI Ltd

Hidden in tropical forest and flanked on one side by a freshwater lagoon, Ras Kutani lies beside the Indian Ocean on a crescent of deserted beach, white sands and gentle surf, cooled by trade winds.

Traditional bamboo and thatch cottages perfectly harmonise with this serene and idyllic setting. Located on a hill overlooking the ocean, alongside the lagoon or directly facing the beach, each cottage offers complete privacy. All have king-size beds, and spacious verandahs with hammocks for those lazy afternoons.

A selection of fine wines from around the world complements exotic menus which often feature the area's abundant seafood.

A stay at Ras Kutani can also be combined with a visit to the Selous Game Reserve, the largest in Africa where guests can enjoy the truly authentic experience of sleeping under canvas. The Selous Safari Camp offers first-class accommodation 'in the bush' and are owner and managers of both Ras Kutani, The Selous Safari Camp and Mbuyu Aviation, and provide all transfers and charter flights, effecting a professional approach for a truly authentic 'beach and bush' honeymoon.

 US$360 (12)

 US$720 (1)

 included

 included

Honeymoon specials
Sparkling wine with the first dinner. Room upgrade subject to availability. Daily bouquet of flowers in the room. Airport transfers and laundry are included.

Sightseeing and leisure
Full range of watersports including laser sailing, surfing, windsurfing, big game fishing and snorkelling. Island trips and picnics. Safaris to Selous Game Reserve. Game drives, boat and walking safaris led by professional guides. Indian Ocean 'Jolly' flights over islands, coral reef systems and coastline. The capital of Tanzania, Dar es Salaam, is just 10 minutes away by light aircraft.

Zanzibar Serena Inn

Information & Reservations
UK   0870 606 1296
INT. +44 870 606 1296

PO Box 4151
Zanzibar

✈ Zanzibar Int. 8km

Tel +255 54 233587/233567
Fax +255 54 233019 or
    +255 811 333170

serena@zanzinet.com
www.zanzibar.net/serena

Tour operators:
UK Africa Archipelago

Member of:
Small Luxury Hotels of the World

In the legendary Stone Town of Zanzibar, an island whose very name evokes East Africa's exotic past, stands the stunning Zanzibar Serena Inn. Here the ambiance is elegant, romantic and welcoming.

Set in two historic seafront buildings that have been masterfully restored to their former character, the Inn stands proud overlooking the azure waters of the Indian Ocean. From all rooms and suites you can gaze out over the water from terraces and balconies, while inside the interiors echo rich Arabian influences and indigenous East African roots. Each room is air conditioned and decorated to the highest standard.

If you can tear yourself away from the comfort of your room, dining is a feast of variety. The speciality, as one would imagine, is local seafood. But the preparation and use of local spices and flavours is truly inspiring and will linger in the memory long after you've departed.

For those wishing to marry at the Inn, you are spoiled for choice. There is the Serena Terrace, which overlooks the enticing sea; the Sunken Garden, tropical and romantic; Mangapwani, Serena's beach recluse; and the Old Fort, promising an unforgettable Zanzibari ceremony with traditional customs and true romance.

195

US$290-400* (48)

US$500-600* (3)

US$40 (average)

included

Honeymoon specials

Fruits and nuts in room on arrival. A poolside table will be set if you reserve a table for dinner in the à la carte restaurant. The hotel has a special honeymoon room in the historic 'Chinese Doctor's House' with a balcony overlooking the sea. Couples booking this room get all VIP courtesies plus flowers and a gift on their last night.
* Prices quoted are on B&B basis.

Sightseeing and leisure

On site there are facilities for massages, manicures and pedicures. Nearby are salons and beauty parlours and Henna painting artists are available. At the beachside Mangapwani, there is a seafood buffet during the day and all watersports, including deep sea diving, sailing and dolphin safaris. Nearby are markets, the Jozani Forest, Stone Town, spice gardens and tours of old palacial ruins.

Zimbabwe

flying time
To: Harare
London: 10 hrs
NY: 16 hrs

when to go
Dec-Mar is wet.
The hottest dry
time of the year
is Sept-Nov.

currency
The Zimbabwe
dollar. Credit cards
are accepted at
many hotels.

language
English

getting around
Air Zimbabwe
connects major
towns and national
parks. There is a
train service
between Harare
and Bulawayo.

Zimbabwe is thought to have been the site of King Solomon's mines because it is so rich in mineral wealth and good farmland. With its beautiful and varied scenery, it is surely one of Africa's most loved countries.

The country is also home to the spectacular Victoria Falls, one of the natural wonders of the world. Its many national parks are considered some of the best on the continent, with the greatest variety of means to take an adventurous safari – day or night drives, walking safaris, boat game drives, whitewater rafting, canoeing, kayaking, or floating on a houseboat.

You will find a massive variety of game, all in beautiful, unspoilt surroundings, which is an ideal introduction to the many wonders of Africa. The Zambezi River that marks the boundary with Zambia is a must on any visit to Zimbabwe; especially at the Victoria Falls. Here, many thousands of tons of water cascade down the escarpment sending spray up to 500 metres in the air, giving the falls the name 'the smoke that thunders'.

The adventurous may raft through the rapids or bungee-jump from the bridge at the top. There are also some excellent canoe trips on the Upper

Zambezi involving fly-camping on its riverine forest islands. Hwange National Park, the largest reserve in Zimbabwe, is famous for its huge population of over 25,000 elephants. Also home to all the major African predators and plains game, including black rhino and wild dog, Hwange is a superb park in which to be captivated by the magic of life in the bush.

Lake Kariba is one of the world's largest man-made lakes – guests can watch the wildlife that comes to the water's edge from luxurious lodges on the shoreline, from islands on the lake, or even from a houseboat. Lake Kariba and the bordering Matusadona National Park have prolific birdlife and compelling scenery. Here you can experience the best sunsets in the world as the sinking orb transforms the lake into a pool of molten copper and gold while taking in the haunting cry of the fish eagle as it gracefully circles its prey.

The Matopos National Park, just south of Bulawayo, is the last resting place of Prime Minister Cecil Rhodes. Huge balancing boulders piled like strange natural totems seem to defy gravity, and are the most intriguing feature of this area. This is the site chosen by the San bushmen for their curious rock paintings, still miraculously preserved in well-camouflaged caves.

The Hide Safari Camp

Information & Reservations
UK 0870 606 1296
INT. +44 870 606 1296

27/29 James Martin Drive
PO Box ST 274
Southerton
Harare
Zimbabwe

✈ Hwange 46km

tel +263 4 660 554
fax +263 4 621 216

Tour operators:
UK Africa Archipelago,
Grenadier, Art of Travel
US Fun Safaris

198

Zimbabwe's largest National Park, Hwange, comprises 14,650 square kilometres of untamed wilderness inhabited by some of the most prolific game herds in Africa. Containing over 100 species of animals and 400 species of birds, it is also one of the few remaining sanctuaries in Africa where herds of elephant may be seen roaming the plains. The Hide Safari Camp offers the perfect way to experience the wonders of this African treasure.

Specially constructed hides near the water holes are a photographer's paradise, as herds of elephant, buffalo, giraffe and wildebeest are just some of the animals to be seen. Game-viewing excursions, by foot or in comfortable overland vehicles, are also available. Whether guests go in search of big game or just want to trek up the 'fossil rivers' of Kennedy Plans, safaris can be tailormade to suit individual requirements.

Accommodation is in East African-style canvas tents, comfortably furnished with *en suite* shower and other facilities. Each has a large porch area where guests can relax and view the game at their leisure. Although The Hide is right in the heart of the African bush, the candlelit dinners are served with a great deal of elegance and style around a huge dining table.

Honeymoon specials
Honeymoon tent with complimentary champagne.

Sightseeing and leisure
Game drives or walks with professional guides. A variety of species can be seen, including elephant, buffalo, wildebeest, zebra, giraffe, baboon, lion, leopard and cheetah. Guests can also view game from the underground Hides.

US$295-316 (10)

 included

 included

The Victoria Falls Hotel

Information & Reservations
UK 0870 606 1296
INT. +44 870 606 1296

PO Box 10
Victoria Falls
Zimbabwe

✈ Victoria Falls Int. 22km

Tel +263 13 4751
Fax +263 13 4586

Tour operators:
UK Africa Archipelago
Elegant Resorts
Zimbabwe Sun

An opulent building in the grandest of colonial styles, The Victoria Falls Hotel occupies a prime site in front of one of the most spectacular natural wonders of the world. The hotel was built back in 1904 and has recently been restored to bring back the full glory of the original Edwardian features, creating an atmosphere of elegance and grandeur. Some bedrooms have awe-inspiring views of Victoria Falls, the world's largest sheet of falling water.

The award-winning Livingstone Restaurant offers silver service, *à la carte* and *table d'hôte* menus. The Pavilion Brasserie serves light snacks and buffets, while Jungle Junction is an informal restaurant for barbecues. Traditional afternoon tea is served on the verandah, affording views of the gorge of the Falls and bridge linking Zimbabwe to Zambia. Activities include helicopter rides, game drives and sunset cruises along the Zambezi. A private path leads from the hotel directly to the Falls.

Hotel staff will be delighted to arrange wedding ceremonies in the chapel, in front of the Falls Bridge, or in the beautiful extensive grounds of the hotel. And wedding receptions are fully catered for.

199

 US$186-207pppn (168)

 US$600-828 per suite (14)

 from US$20

 included

Honeymoon specials
Flowers and sparkling wine on arrival. Room upgrade subject to availability.

Sightseeing and leisure
Swimming pool, tennis courts, hairdresser on site. Touring desks and assistants are set up at the hotel for booking excursions and activities, such as whitewater rafting on the rapids of the Zambezi, bungee jumping, game drives, cruises and golf at Elephant Hills which is just 3km from the hotel.

Jewels of Zimbabwe

Information & Reservations
UK 0870 606 1296
INT. +44 870 606 1296

Zimbabwe

Bookings & enquiries:
Lesley Cripps
Manor Barn Cottage
Wylye Road
Hanging Langford
Salisbury SP3 4NW

tel +44 (0) 1722 790023
wildlife@dialstart.net

Imba Matombo
imba@internet.co.zw
www.imbamatombo.co.zw

200

Pamushana
mctsales@africaonline.co.zw
www.malilangwe.co.zw

Sanyati Lodge
sanyati@rcon.co.zw
www.sanyati.com

The Stanley and Livingstone
mctsales@africaonline.co.zw

Imba Matombo

Zimbabwe is one of Africa's most loved countries. Home to the spectacular Victoria Falls, vast game reserves, the Zambezi River and Lake Kariba, one of the world's largest man-made lakes, it is a land of plenty. It is also home to some of Africa's finest lodges, which form the perfect backdrop to a romantic journey. Following is a unique 11-night itinerary taking in the delights of four of the best lodges; a trip that is guaranteed to make your honeymoon as exciting as you can imagine.

Day 1: Arrive in Harare and transfer to the exclusive Relais & Châteaux **Imba Matombo** hotel, situated just outside the city. Perched on a hill with commanding views, Imba's emphasis is on luxury accommodation, excellent cuisine and personal service in an informal, yet intimate, atmosphere. It is an ideal spot to kick off your 'Zim adventure' with true African hospitality.

Day 2: Take an early morning flight to Kariba, followed by a boat journey (approx. 50mins) across Lake Kariba to **Sanyati Lodge**, 11 luxurious rooms of natural stone, timber and thatch with stunning interiors of wrought-iron and layers of cream muslin. Here you'll be afforded magnificent views of the lake while bathing in glass-fronted bathrooms, or of the star-studded sky while taking an open-air shower.

Days 3 & 4: Days to spend as you wish: at Sanyati and enjoying the many game-viewing activities around Lake Kariba.

Day 5: Travel back across the lake to board a short flight to Victoria Falls, where your next port of call is **The Stanley and Livingstone**, situated on a 6,000-acre private estate just minutes from Victoria Falls. Named after a reporter and an intrepid

Sanyati Lodge

Itinerary price:
US$3,600 per person

included

included

Honeymoon specials
The 11-night itinerary costs US$3,600 per person. It includes accommodation, meals, drinks and game drives at Pamushana, The Stanley and Livingstone and Sanyati (please note: at Imba Matombo and Sanyati drinks are not included), all road transfers plus the final nights' stay at Imba Matombo. Excludes private charter to Pamushana.

Stanley and Livingstone

Pamushana

Pamushana

missionary, this is a small hotel of just 10 exquisitely furnished suites that simply oozes character. A raised patio overlooks lush gardens and waterholes.

Days 6 & 7: Spend the days exploring the area.

Day 8: Fly to the Malilangwe Private Wildlife Reserve, where your destination is the intimate, ultra-luxurious **Pamushana**, home to just six villas. Set high on an escarpment overlooking Malilangwe Lake, each villa has a private plunge pool set into a teak game-viewing deck equipped with a telescope

and outdoor shower. Other highlights include a gym, sauna, infinity pool and a 7,500-bottle wine cellar.

Days 9 & 10: Relaxing by the pool at Pamushana – after all, it translates as 'place of sunshine'.

Day 11: Here you have a few options: fly back to Harare and spend a final night at Imba Matombo before your trip home; or meet your private pilot who will take you on a 40-minute flight to a lodge of your choice on one of the secluded beaches of Mozambique. The choice, as they say, is yours.

Sightseeing and leisure

The delights of Harare, game-driving excursions on and around Lake Kariba, tour of Victoria Falls, curio shopping, canoeing, fishing, lunch & sunset cruises on the Zambezi River, bungee jumping, whitewater rafting, golf, elephant rides and game drives.

Elephant safari

Indian Ocean Islands

A thousand miles from anywhere, scattered on the waters between the coasts of India and Africa, dozens of Indian Ocean islands fringed delicately by long stretches of dazzling white beaches make perfect, secluded honeymoon retreats.

Their very remoteness is part of their charm. The Seychelles, the Maldives, the Comores and the larger island-nations of Mauritius and Sri Lanka share the magic of being well and truly away from it all. On any of these isles you find yourself adapting very quickly to a slower pace and tuning into nature.

In the Seychelles you can wonder at giant tortoises, and in the markets of the Comores or Perfume Isles breathe in the heady scents of ylang ylang, jasmine and patchouli.

Yet more natural wonders lie beneath the ocean. For scuba divers this is a magical part of the world and non-divers can explore the underwater marvels with a snorkel, mask and flippers.

When on Mauritius you can walk among the brilliantly-coloured corals on the sea bed wearing a special helmet, and from Mahé in the Seychelles you can stay dry, but still get some glorious close-ups of the reef from an innovative sub-sea viewer.

key to hotels

Benguerra Island
1 Benguerra Lodge

Maldives
2 Baros Holiday Resort, North Malé Atoll
3 Full Moon Beach Resort, North Malé Atoll
4 Laguna Beach, South Malé Atoll
5 Nakatchafushi, North Malé Atoll
6 Soneva Fushi Resort, Kunfunadhoo Island, Baa Atoll

Mauritius
7 Le Prince Maurice, Ile Maurice
8 Paradise Cove Hotel, Ile Maurice
9 The Residence, Belle Mare

Seychelles
10 Chateau de Feuilles, Praslin
11 Hotel L'Archipel, Praslin
12 La Digue Island Lodge
13 Lemuria Resort of Praslin
14 Le Meridien Fisherman's Cove, Mahé

Sri Lanka
15 Mahaweli Reach Hotel, Kandy
16 Saman Villas, Bentota

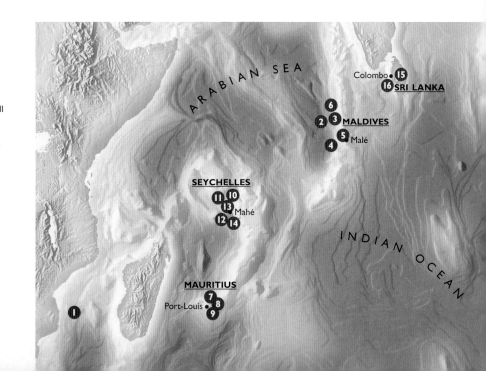

Benguerra Lodge

Information & Reservations
JK 0870 606 1296
NT. +44 870 606 1296

Benguerra Island

✦ Vilanculo 25km across sea

Contact:
PO Box 87416
Houghton 2041
Tel +27 11 483 2734
Fax +27 11 728 3767

Tour operators:
UK Africa Archipelago

Member of:
Classic Safari Camps of Africa

Situated off the coast of Mozambique and accessed by air, the luxurious Benguerra Lodge offers unsurpassed exclusivity in a tranquil and remote setting. The island is encircled by silver beaches, turquoise seas and coral reefs supporting a vast array of jewel-like fish.

The luxury thatched lodge is flanked by secluded chalets merged into a natural milkwood forest bordering Benguerra Bay. Each chalet, built on stilts with reed walls and thatched roofs, has a double room with *en suite* bathroom and a private balcony with views overlooking the ocean.

A mosaic of forest, savannah and wetland ecosystems sustain a diverse abundance of flora and fauna in this idyllic island getaway, which is now a designated nature reserve.

Fresh seafood and exotic Portuguese dishes are served at the lodge where service is attentive and discreet. A well-stocked bar offers a wide range of wines and imported liqueurs.

This is a haven of peace and tranquillity and an ideal base to try out activities such as snorkelling, diving and sailing on a traditional *dhow*. You can drive to a remote part of the island and picnic and sunbathe in seclusion, explore the bird life or simply comb deserted beaches in solitude and serenity.

203

 US$235

🍽 included

☕ included

Honeymoon specials
Complimentary champagne in room on arrival. All meals and accommodation, teas and coffees, daily laundry, snorkel trip with lunch, Landrover trip, island tour and sunset cruise in a *dhow*. Three, four, five and seven-night packages cost from US$851.

Sightseeing and leisure
Visits to mainland markets and local church services. Sailing trips to see flamingos in the wild. Talks with local witchdoctor. Romantic walks along secluded beaches. Birdwatching. Sunset cruises on *dhow*. Deep sea and fly fishing, snorkelling. Fully-equipped diving facility.

Maldives

flying time
London: 13-14 hrs
NY: 19-20 hrs

**climate/
when to go**
Tropical. Always hot
at 25-30°C. High
season is Nov-April
when the weather
is dry and hot.
May-Oct is wetter
with high humidity
and the possibility
of heavy monsoon
showers.

204

currency
Maldivian Rufiyaa,
but prices at resort
hotels are usually
in US dollars.

language
Dhivehi. Many
people speak
some English.

getting around
By *dhoni*, speed
boat, sea plane
or helicopter.

There is a place on this earth where you go to do nothing but chill out – the Maldives. These 1,190 dots of land in the Indian Ocean are the closest you can get to being castaways.

If it is peace, quiet and your own private palm tree that you want, look no further. Hotels here do not have their own garden, they have their own island.

About 80 of the tiny, scattered islands have been developed for tourism, with just one resort hotel apiece. These are car-free zones you can walk around in a matter of minutes. Some are of the 'no news, no shoes' variety, with few facilities and no hot water. Others have mod cons such as air conditioning, pool, tennis courts, spa and a choice of restaurants.

The time-honoured and fun way of getting about this country – 99% of it being sea – is by *dhoni*, a wooden-hulled water-taxi, though nowadays there are speed boats and helicopters for long distances.

The islands are grouped in 26 atolls, each atoll surrounded by coral reef teeming with fish; no wonder more than half the visitors to the Maldives go scuba diving. This is one of the world's very best dive sites and a superb place to take up the sport. All the resort islands have diving schools offering a range of internationally recognised PADI (Professional Association of Diving Instructors) courses.

The sightseeing above water level is certainly no less impressive. Take a *dhoni* trip to a neighbouring island, and a visit to a Maldivian village where the locals might set up a few souvenir stalls. Some resorts even offer deep sea fishing trips and, if you long for the sight of traffic, you can reboard your *dhoni* and head into the country's capital, Malé, to check out the sights.

After dark, entertainment is low key. The country is strictly Muslim and Maldivians do not drink alcohol, though most varieties are available on the individual resort islands. There are new experiences to be had, though. Try your hand at moonlit line-fishing and maybe land a grouper or two.

Baros Holiday Resort

Information & Reservations
UK 0870 606 1296
INT. +44 870 606 1296

/o 39 Orchid Magu
20-02 Malé
Maldives

✈ Malé 16km

el +960 323 080
ax +960 322 678

Tour operators:
UK Kuoni

Situated in the North Malé Atoll, the private island that houses Baros Holiday Resort is as close to perfection as you'll get. Lush ferns and foliage offer shade from the bright sun that lights the resort and around the island stretch white sand beaches along calm azure seas.

Tucked discreetly among the island's thick lush vegetation are 59 deluxe rooms, all with traditional Maldivian thatched roof, and a terrace providing the perfect venue to watch the day drift away. Close to these lie the highlight of the resort – 16 wooden bungalows built on stilts stretching out over the sea which offer the ultimate in romance and seclusion.

Succulent steaks and seafood served with an Asian twist are the specialities of the hotel's four restaurants. After dining relax in the Captain's Bar with its unique nautical design.

The diving and snorkelling here are superb. But you may also like to try windsurfing and catamaran sailing, as both are easily arranged. Also unmissable are excursions to the neighbouring islands – which are uninhabited. Pack a picnic and enjoy your own romantic desert island for the day. As the sun goes down, you'll be collected and taken back to the luxury of Baros where another perfect evening awaits.

205

 US$170-180* (59)

 US$170-200* (18)

 included

included

Honeymoon specials
Fruit basket and a bottle of wine in room on arrival.

* Prices quoted are on half-board basis.

Sightseeing and leisure
Daily entertainment programme. Also, most watersports are available including boating, fishing, diving, windsurfing, catamaran sailing, skiing and canoeing. You can also go island-hopping and take excursions to the capital of Malé.

Full Moon
Beach Resort

Information & Reservations
UK 0870 606 1296
INT. +44 870 606 1296

c/o 39 Orchid Magu
20-02 Malé
Maldives

✈ Malé 6km

tel +960 323 080
fax +960 322 678

Tour operators:
UK Kuoni

206

As your speedboat skims across the crystal clear waters that surround the North Malé Atoll, Full Moon Beach shines like a jewel in the distance in this beautifully deserted island paradise.

With 52 water bungalows and 104 two-storey guesthouses to choose from, the resort is one of the larger in these islands. Each room is spacious and all offer uninterrupted sea views. Furnishings are simple to reflect local style but this traditional look is combined with mod cons, as all rooms are air-conditioned and have telephones and mini-bars.

Dining takes place under the stars at one of the hotel's many restaurants and bars. Choose from elegant dining on steak and seafood, or relax in the casual atmosphere of the on-site pizzeria. None of the restaurants will disappoint.

There's also much to fill your days at the resort. Diving and watersports are obviously on offer but you can also workout in the gym, work on your backhand on the tennis courts or work on your tan as you relax by the swimming pool. All you have to decide is whether to choose a pina colada or fresh coconut water drunk straight from the shell. The choice is all yours.

 US$170-180* (52)

 US$170-200* (104)

 included

 included

Honeymoon specials
Fruit basket and a bottle of wine in room on arrival.

* Prices quoted are on fullboard basis.

Sightseeing and leisure
Swimming pool, children's pool, shopping arcade, gym and tennis courts. The hotel can assist in booking sightseeing trips and excursions to other islands.

Laguna Beach

Information & Reservations
UK 0870 606 1296
INT. +44 870 606 1296

c/o 39 Orchid Magu
20-02 Malé
Maldives

✈ Malé 12km

Tel +960 445 903
Fax +960 443 041

Tour operators:
UK Kuoni

Located on the northern tip of the South Malé Atoll, this first-class resort is set in lush green gardens and surrounded by abundant coral reefs, both just waiting to be explored.

The hotel offers 115 deluxe rooms housed in two-storey or individual bungalows or, choose to stay in one of the 17 stunning, over-the-water suites that stretch out across the colourful reefs. Here your closest neighbours are the fish and stingrays that dance playfully beneath your over-sea verandah.

Italian, Chinese and continental cuisine are on offer in the five hotel restaurants. But for those quiet evenings, you can order room service to allow yourselves the privacy you may well be needing. Either way, the food is outstanding and the service top-notch.

Of course, no trip to the Maldives would be complete without experiencing life under the water. Diving and snorkelling can be arranged by the hotel – as can sailing, windsurfing and fishing.

If you'd prefer not to get your feet wet, the hotel is also happy to arrange excursion island-hopping or visits to the nearby town of Malé. Or why not just stay on site and enjoy all the facilities they have to offer… after all, at Laguna Beach, Heaven really is a place on earth.

207

 US$170-180* (115)

 US$170-200* (17)

🍽 included

☕ included

Honeymoon specials
Fruit basket and a bottle of wine in room on arrival.

Prices quoted are on half-board basis.

Sightseeing and leisure
Health club, gym, sauna, tennis courts, table tennis and billiards. All watersports, including boating and fishing, diving, windsurfing and catamaran sailing. You can also go island-hopping and take excursions to the capital of Malé.

Information & Reservations
UK 0870 606 1296
INT. +44 870 606 1296

Nakatchafushi Tourist Resort

c/o 39 Orchid Magu
20-02 Malé
Maldives

✈ Malé 24km

tel +960 443 847
fax +960 442 665

Tour operators:
UK Kuoni

Situated on the western side of the North Malé Atoll, Nakatchafushi houses 51 round, thatched bungalows set in lush, tropical grounds festooned with flowers and shrubs.

Each of these idyllic self-contained units faces the beach and comes equipped with air conditioning, mini-bar and tea and coffee making facilities. Inside, pastel coloured decor and white marble floors create an air of cooling calm that aids in your quest for relaxation and tranquillity.

The hotel has four restaurants and dining is available late into the evening for the night owls among you – and there is much to do in the evening. Choose to go night fishing, dance till the early hours in the disco, or simply sit back with a cocktail in the over-water bar and watch the fish play the night away in the tropical waters of the lagoon. Staying up late is never a problem at Nakatchafushi as tomorrow you can spend the entire day relaxing on the miles of sugary white sand that line the resort.

If you'd prefer to keep busy, there's a whole world of experiences to explore – both underwater and on land, including sightseeing, diving and sailing. Opportunities and delights never end in this secluded private island hideaway.

Honeymoon specials
Fruit basket and a bottle of wine in room on arrival.

Prices quoted are on half-board basis.

Sightseeing and leisure
Swimming pool and guest gift shop. The hotel can assist in booking sightseeing trips and excursions to other islands.

US$170-200* (51)

included

included

Information & Reservations
UK 0870 606 1296
INT. +44 870 606 1296

Soneva Fushi

Kunfunadhoo Island
Baa Atoll
Maldives

✈ Malé Int. 115km

Contact:
Soneva Pavilion Hotels
Tel +44 (0) 1932 230808
Fax +44 (0) 1932 230809

sonresa@soneva.com.mv
www.soneva-pavilion.com

Member of:
Small Luxury Hotels of the World

Blessed on all sides by a private shallow lagoon encircled by a coral reef, the 100-acre island of Kunfunadhoo is a Robinson Crusoe-style hideaway in the middle of the Indian Ocean. At the edge of the lapping, clear waters, just a few steps up on the beach, are the villas of the Soneva Fushi resort.

All the rooms are naturally styled in soft, light colours to reflect the vibrance and warm ambiance of the island. Villas available range from a standard Rehendi bungalow to the luxurious Presidential Suite with its own pool, dining room and lounge area. Four-poster beds are found in many of the villas. Modern furnishings are tastefully concealed inside natural objects – TV/VCR inside a water hyacinth case – maintaining modern comforts but still providing a true desert island experience.

By day, lunch under a canopy of trees by the beach, or enjoy a quiet desert island picnic on one of the many surrounding islands of the Baa Atoll. By night, the two restaurants serve a range of delightful dishes – both international and 'east meets west' cuisine. For romantics, you may dine by lantern light on the beach or by your villa.

Raison d'Etre at Soneva Fushi health spa is open to ease the mind and soul with a variety of beauty and body treatments.

209

US$155-990 (55)

US$450-1,380 (7)

from US$50

US$17

Honeymoon specials

Champagne on arrival and candlelit romantic dinner (offered all year round). From 8 May to 23 June 2000, honeymooners receive champagne on arrival, candlelit dinner, desert island picnic, plus one free beauty treatment for each person.

Sightseeing and leisure

Health spa incorporating wellness programmes, beauty treatments, yoga, fitness training and massage. A wide variety of watersports, including snorkelling, windsurfing, scuba diving and game fishing. There is also volleyball, table tennis and badminton on site. Visit local fishing village, or embark on excursions to the islands of Mahlos and Eydhafushi.

Mauritius

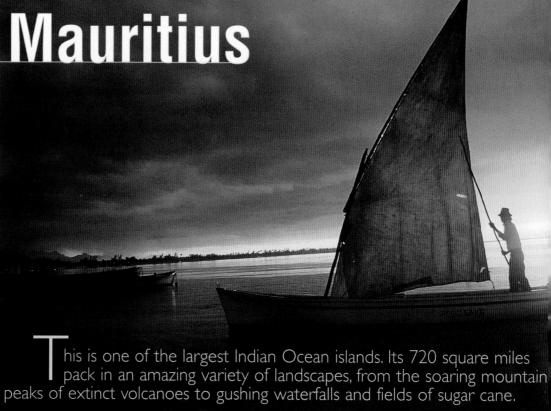

flying time
London: 11-12 hrs
NY: 17-18 hrs

**climate/
when to go**
Any time but do
not expect tropical
weather from
May-Oct. Hindu
festivals, Cavadee
(Jan-Feb) and
Divali (Oct) are
spectacular.

currency
Mauritian rupee

language
The official language
is English. French,
Creole, Hindi and
Chinese are also
spoken.

getting around
Local bus, taxi or
car hire.

210

This is one of the largest Indian Ocean islands. Its 720 square miles pack in an amazing variety of landscapes, from the soaring mountain peaks of extinct volcanoes to gushing waterfalls and fields of sugar cane.

The one million people who live here are a harmonious mix of races and cultures, including African, Indian, Chinese and European. Everyone joins in the festivals that seem to happen almost weekly.

The food is a *pot pourri* too, featuring spicy samosas, Chinese sweet-and-sour dishes, and the delicate but aromatic home-grown flavours of smoked marlin.

In the capital, Port Louis, tower blocks are starting to dwarf the old colonial buildings, though it only takes a walk through the Victorian wrought iron gates of the central market to find yourself in a scene that hardly seems to have changed in a century.

Odorous halls are thronged with housewives eyeing up freshly caught sailfish and the goat that goes into a tasty curry. Grains and pulses overflow from huge sacks in the warren of stalls, where you haggle with vendors over carvings, vanilla pods and spices.

Aside from spending time on the glorious beaches, seek out the dodo (stuffed) in the Mauritius Institute museum; the 85 types of palm trees in the Botanical Gardens at Pamplemousses; and history-brought-to-life at Domaine des Pailles, the island's nearest equivalent to a theme park, where you can see how sugar cane is made into rum – the islanders' favourite tipple.

Le Prince Maurice

Information & Reservations
UK 0870 606 1296
INT. +44 870 606 1296

Choisy Road
Poste de Flacq
Mauritius

✈ SSR Int. 45km

tel +230 415 1083/4
fax +230 415 1082

UK reservations:
tel +44 (0) 1462 713100
fax +44 (0) 1462 713200
ga.tourism@BTInternet.com

The deluxe Prince Maurice enjoys an idyllic location on the east coast of the beautiful and romantic island of Mauritius. Surrounded by luxuriant vegetation and washed by the warm waters of the Indian Ocean, the hotel offers an escape to a world of unparalleled luxury.

Secluded white sand beaches and turquoise waters tempt the sea and sun lover. The all-suite accommodation is situated either on the beach or overlooking the fish reserve, with some elevated on stilts to take advantage of the breathtaking views. Each suite has been designed using natural materials – wood and stone which help to reinforce the impression of calm luxury and refined elegance. The senior suites are especially luxurious, some with their own private terrace, pool and courtyard with an open-air marble bath.

The accent is on fine gastronomy and local flavours at the L'Archipel restaurant or La Barachois – a unique floating restaurant on the fish reserve.

A vast range of sports are also offered, including golf at the 18-hole championship course of Belle Mare Plage, waterskiing, tennis, squash and windsurfing. There is also a gym with jacuzzi, sauna and steam baths. The lagoon also provides a tranquil setting for a spot of fly fishing.

211

Honeymoon specials
Flowers, polo shirts, fruit baskets and a bottle of sparkling wine on arrival.

Sightseeing and leisure
Natural attractions include Pamplemousses Botanical Garden, Seven Coloured Earth of Chamarel, Black River Gorge and the sacred lake of Gran Bassin. A wide range of sports such as golf at Belle Mare Plage and a host of water activities.

 from US$300 pppn (89)
 US$50-70
 included

Paradise Cove Hotel

Information & Reservations
UK 0870 606 1296
INT. +44 870 606 1296

Anse La Raie
Mauritius

✈ SSR Int 60km

UK enquiries:
Tropical Locations
tel +44 (020) 8427 7300
fax +44 (020) 8427 7400

Tour operators:
UK Tropical Locations

212

Located at the northern tip of the island and set in lush gardens around a secluded cove, Paradise Cove is a delightful hotel where the emphasis is on personalised attention. So much so that each guest is welcomed by name and throughout their stay they are treated like visitors in a private home.

Built in traditional Mauritian style, each of the 67 deluxe rooms and suites have been decorated with tropical shades to reflect the ambiance of the island. Fitted with all amenities, they are all sea-facing and have terraces or balconies with direct access to the sugary beach.

The secluded cove is the ideal place to relax. You can while away the hours lounging in hammocks strung from palm trees on the beach or take a picnic hamper to one of the small private beaches dotted around the peninsula. For the more adventurous, there's a tremendous selection of watersports such as deep sea fishing, catamaran sailing, windsurfing and underwater sea walks.

Two restaurants, a beach and poolside bar offer a choice of formal and casual dining with the emphasis on fresh seafood and local cuisine brimming with exotic flavours. Paradise found.

 £123-134* (47)

 £149* (20)

 included

 included

Honeymoon specials

Tropical Locations' special honeymoon package starts at £1,498 per person and includes flights and seven nights accommodation on half board basis. Also, honeymooners receive sparkling wine on arrival, plus candlelight dinner and an upgraded room if available.

* Rates are per person per night half board.

Sightseeing and leisure

Health centre complete with gym, massage and sauna. Tennis, archery and cycling. All watersports are available and include undersea walks, catamaran cruises, deep sea fishing and submarine dives.

The Residence

Information & Reservations
UK 0870 606 1296
INT. +44 870 606 1296

Coastal Road
Belle Mare
Mauritius

✈ Plaisance 48km

Tel +230 401 8888
Fax +230 415 5888

residenc@intnet.mu
www.theresidence.com

Tour operators:
UK Elegant Resorts
Classic Connection

Located on one of the most beautiful beaches in Mauritius, guests at The Residence could forgive themselves for thinking they had gone back in time. With its grand, high-vaulted entrance lobby, columned terraces and freeform pools, the hotel seems to be part of the Roaring Twenties when times were good and the living was easy.

Rooms and suites are positively stunning and decorated in harmonious blends of beige and white, with honey-coloured woods and delicate wrought-iron embellishments.

The best of modern international cuisine is on offer in The Dining Room, prepared with native produce. For something a little more spicy, Creole dishes can be enjoyed in the oceanfront setting of The Plantation. Afternoon tea is a real treat with delicate teas and a selection of pastries and cakes.

There is also a huge choice of watersports, including scuba diving, sailing and snorkelling, and plenty of land-based activities such as tennis. If you prefer to be less active, The Sanctuary, the hotel's ultra-luxurious spa, is just as enticing and treatments here are as good for the soul as they are for the body. The Sanctuary uses renowned La Prairie beauty products and now has nine cabins in which to totally pamper you.

213

RS7,800-14,950 (151)

RS11,210-32,700 (20)

RS1,900

included

Honeymoon specials
Champagne and flowers in room on arrival. Room upgrade when available.

Sightseeing and leisure
The Sanctuary Health and Beauty Centre is on site, plus swimming pool, children's pool, jacuzzi, waterskiing, windsurfing, snorkelling and tennis. Local attractions include Pamplemousses Botanical Garden and the capital of Port Louis with its bustling market.

Seychelles

flying time
London: 10-12 hrs
NY: 18-19 hrs

climate/ when to go
Tropical. Hot and humid Nov-Feb although slightly cooler and drier Mar-Oct. The temperature stays at a constant 20-30°C all year.

currency
Seychelles rupee.

language
Creole although English and French are widely spoken.

getting around
By ferry, plane or helicopter between the islands. By bus, taxi or hire car on Mahé and Praslin.

You cannot return from the Seychelles without having acquired a new skill – sega dancing.

The sexy, hip-wiggling dance is the traditional accompaniment to folk tunes that expresses 200 years of history on these beautiful, far-flung islands.

The Seychelles archipelago is made up of 115 islands, spread over such a vast area that getting between them often involves flights rather than boat trips. An amazing fact is that only a handful are inhabited and 90% of the population live on Mahé. This is where international flights land and most visitors stay.

It is here that you find the country's tiny capital, Victoria, with its echoes of former British rule. The island's main beach, and by far the busiest on the Seychelles, is a long curve of pale sand known as Beau Vallon Bay. This is excellent for watersports and for people-watching, but if you want a beach all to yourself, hire a car for a day and explore the coastline.

A worthwhile day trip takes you on a glass-bottom boat or a submarine to see the coral reef of the Marine National Park, then to Moyenne Island, where you can meet the giant tortoises and bask in the blissfully warm waters of a shallow lagoon.

Mahé and the other main island, Praslin, are both rocky and have huge granite boulders littering their powdery white sands. Both are lush and hilly, with jungly tropical scenery and splashes of pink, purple and scarlet flora highlighted against the emerald green. A walk in Praslin's mysterious Vallée de Mai brings you under the shadow of rare and exotic plants, like the coco de mer palm, which can only be found in this part of the world.

Château de Feuilles

Information & Reservations
UK 0870 606 1296
INT. +44 870 606 1296

Pointe Cabris
Praslin
Seychelles

✈ Praslin 11km

Tel +248 233 316
Fax +248 233 916

reserv@chateau.com.sc
www.chateau.com.sc

Member of:
Relais & Châteaux

Perfectly positioned high above Pointe Cabris on Praslin Island, the Château de Feuilles offers awe-inspiring views of 15 of the most beautiful islands floating like dots of sweet sugar in the middle of the Indian Ocean. It is a stylish and luxurious small resort hotel that nestles comfortably, almost unobtrusively, in the hillside.

This former gentleman's residence, surrounded by outhouses built in exotic wood and covered with latania leaves, is now an exclusive resort with only nine rooms, suites and bungalows. Each is spacious and furnished with rare island wood, and equipped with air conditioning, ceiling fan, a living room corner with desk, mini-bar and mosquito net.

Gaze out across the tropical gardens with flowering bougainvillaea from the secluded terraces or relax in the swimming pool, the panoramic jacuzzi or have a massage. Night-time swimming is particularly fun when you can lie back and admire the thousands of stars and planets against a clear sky.

The cuisine is a homage to sea and sun here. Specialities revolve around local produce from the hotel grounds and seafood caught around the island. Creole dishes, exotic fish and giraffe crab will give you a true taste of Seychelles cuisine.

215

 US$290-370 (5)

 US$370-450 (4)

 from US$45

included

Honeymoon specials
The hotel will provide complimentary car rental (excluding petrol & insurance) if you book direct.

Sightseeing and leisure
Enjoy trips to the extraordinarily beautiful beaches of Praslin and the famous Vallée de Mai National Park. Also, you can go snorkelling, swimming, deep sea fishing or take excursions to the neighbouring islands.

Information & Reservations
UK 0870 606 1296
INT. +44 870 606 1296

Hotel L'Archipel

Route des Cocotiers
Anse Gouvernement
Praslin
Seychelles

✈ Praslin 10km

tel +248 232 242
fax +248 232 072

archipel@seychelles.net
www.larchipel.com

Tour operators:
UK Elegant Resorts

216

Many believe that Praslin, the second largest island in the picturesque group that makes up the Seychelles, is the most beautiful. That's an opinion you may well believe yourself as you drive up the lush wooded avenue to L'Archipel and arrive at your villa overlooking the perfect curved bay of soft sand and sparkling azure sea beyond.

Beamed ceilings and romantic muslin drapes characterise the traditional fittings of the airy rooms here. Each has a lovely sea-facing verandah and some suites also have their own private jacuzzi.

Dining is also an experience here. There is a restaurant in the main building and one beachside, or you may choose to dine on the privacy of your own verandah – but wherever you decide, the food is always superb. Dishes are overseen by the creative influence of the hotel's French-trained chef.

During the day you can explore Praslin's two tiny villages or set out on your own. Closer to home, the hotel's enticing bay offers many water activities, such as snorkelling and windsurfing. But for the ultimate romantic excursion, take a cruise to one of the nearby secluded islets and enjoy your own desert island for a day.

 US$355 (21)

 US$455-595 (3*)

 US$45

 US$20

Honeymoon specials

Basket of fruit, bottle of champagne in room on arrival. Room upgrade subject to availability. One day's car hire (subject to five-day minimum stay).

* Six additional suites will be constructed by Aug 2000.

Sightseeing and leisure

All watersports, from windsurfing to snorkelling, and private cruises to secluded islets. Deep sea fishing, diving and bottom fishing can be arranged at additional cost. Nearby are nature reserves, bird sanctuaries and neighbouring islands. There is a casino a short distance from the hotel.

nformation & Reservations
UK 0870 606 1296
NT. +44 870 606 1296

La Digue Island Lodge

Anse Reunion
La Digue
Seychelles

✈ Mahé 40 miles

el + 248 234 232
ax +248 234 100

lodge@seychelles.ner

La Digue Island Lodge borders on the Anse Reunion beach, nestling in an exotic tropical garden of coconut palms, takamaka trees and a variety of flowering plants: it's the perfect environment for keeping you cool in the tropical sunshine. Even the rooms have roofs of thatched latanier leaves for keeping off the heat.

The island is an untouched tranquil paradise surrounded by an encircling coral reef. The dramatic scenery presents contrasting colours of azure sea, vibrant green vegetation and brilliant white sand interspersed with incredible pink rock formations that so characterise the Seychelles.

The fragrance of vanilla delights your senses as does the exciting array of wild flowers.

A limit on the number of motorised vehicles helps to keep the island unspoilt and a charming way to travel around is by oxcart, though cycling is also popular.

Creole cooking is a speciality of the hotel's restaurant which is built with a cool sandy floor and high pointed thatched roof overlooking the beach with a spectacular view of Praslin islands. Relax and sip a cocktail at the pool bar or dance the night away to the rhythm of sega music in this tropical paradise.

217

US$303-437 (59)

US$437 (9)

US$6-40

US$9-15

Honeymoon specials
Rooms decorated with flowers on the day of arrival. Complimentary fruit basket.

Sightseeing and leisure
Boat excursions, Grand Anse Beach, Source D'Argent Beach, Lunion Estate and Vueve reserve.

Lemuria Resort of Praslin

Information & Reservations
UK 0870 606 1296
INT. +44 870 606 1296

Anse Kerlan
Praslin
Seychelles

✈ Praslin 4km

tel +248 281 281
fax +248 281 000

UK reservations:
tel +44 (0) 1462 713100
fax +44 (0) 1462 713200
aga.tourism@BTInternet.com

The Lemuria Resort is situated in the magnificent landscape of Anse Kerlan providing a vista of outstanding beauty. There are two stunning beaches, surrounded by high ground from which a freshwater stream runs. Luxuriant and rare vegetation abounds and the hotel enjoys a sheltered position, washed by the warm waters of the calm lagoon.

The entire property is designed in complete empathy with its natural surroundings. The main building and three-tiered swimming pools incorporate indigenous granite rocks, and trees remain *in situ* in the interior. The luxury all-suite accommodation with their thatched roofs blend perfectly, scattered over the 90 hectares of land and all facing the Indian Ocean. The restaurants of Lemuria Resort present exquisite cuisine with an international flavour as well as local seafood.

Lemuria Resort's stunning and challenging 18-hole championship golf course makes full use of the diversity of the terrain among dense palm groves, woodland ferns and the Indian Ocean. You will truly be inspired by the magnificence of this dramatic interior and the efforts to preserve it – watch out for the turtles who still come to lay their eggs on the beach.

 US$320 pppn (88)

 US$50-70

 included

Honeymoon specials
T-shirts, basket of fruit and a bottle of champagne on arrival.

Sightseeing and leisure
On site there is a gym, sauna and jacuzzi, tennis courts, snorkelling plus most watersports. You can visit the bird reserve of Cousin Island nearby or a little further away, Aride Island has one of the most beautiful bird parks in the world as well as many botanical treasures. There is also the Vallée de Mai National Park. Lemuria 18-hole Championship Golf Course opens in June 2000.

Le Meridien
Fisherman's Cove

Information & Reservations
UK 0870 606 1296
INT. +44 870 606 1296

PO Box 35
Mahé
Seychelles

✈ Seychelles Int. 15km

el +248 247 247
x +248 247 742

our operators:
K Kuoni
lassic Connection

The Seychelles archipelago is a jewel set in the transparent lagoons of the Indian Ocean. On the island of Mahé, home to rare and exotic birds and lush flora and fauna, Le Meridien Fisherman's Cove is a little paradise in its own right. Situated at the tip of the beautiful beach of Beauvallon, the local architecture of simple stone and slate blends well with the tropical gardens which surround it.

The rooms and cottages all have their own terrace affording ocean views. The cottages have small private gardens where couples can relax in serenity and seclusion. Recently 14 luxurious Junior Suites and four Senior Suites have been added.

The decor is bright and comfortable with wood panelled walls, colourful rugs and bedspreads, cane furniture and pottery lamps. And for the totally tropical touch, all rooms have direct access to the beach.

The hotel has two restaurants. On the menu are Creole specialities of the region with the emphasis on seafood delicacies. Grilled, curried, served with ginger – all are to a high standard and delicious.

In the evening the Blue Marlin Bar, with its sweeping ocean views, is a popular retreat serving cocktails and pre-dinner drinks to the tones of light classical music and jazz.

219

 US$412-640 (62)

 US$612-752 (16)

US$7-50

US$22

Honeymoon specials
Fruit, flowers and wine in room on arrival. One day's free car hire excluding insurance.

Sightseeing and leisure
Swimming pool, scuba diving, snorkelling, tennis, golf, volleyball, billiards, boules, ping-pong, deep sea fishing, sailing, plus other watersports. Bicycle hire. Massage and hairdressing on request. Visits to nature reserves, bird sanctuaries, coral reefs. Trips by chartered boat to neighbouring islands. The capital of Mahé with its restaurants, art galleries and markets.

Sri Lanka

flying time
To: Colombo
London: 11hrs
NY: 18hrs

climate/ when to go
Tropical monsoon, northeast monsoon (Dec-Mar). Southwest monsoon (June-Oct). Dec-Mar is best for the south and west coasts, May-Sept on the north and east.

currency
Sri Lankan rupee

language
Tamil, Sinhala and English

getting around
Plenty of buses and trains. Hiring a car is a popular option.

health
Immunisation against cholera and hepatitis, plus anti-malaria.

Once upon a time Sri Lanka was known as 'Serendib'. From this we have devised the word 'serendipity' – a happy and unexpected accidental discovery.

True to form, the pear-shaped island nation set in the Indian Ocean is both happy and unexpected. Only 240 miles long and 140 miles across at its widest point, it is nevertheless a wonderful mix of extremes.

Dry desert plains are set against jungles, home to leopards and elephants. The fresh mountain tea estates, serene and isolated, soar above the bustling capital of Colombo. A single day can see the sun rise and set over the ruins of majestic civilisations and modern luxury beach resorts to be found along the long stretches of glorious sandy beaches and deep crystal clear waters.

A land of tea and coconuts, monasteries and temples, quiet villages and frenetic festivals, Sri Lanka will provide one unexpected delight after another. Discover it all for yourself.

Mahaweli Reach

Information & Reservations
UK 0870 606 1296
INT. +44 870 606 1296

35 PBA Weerakoon
Mawatha
PO Box 78
Kandy
Sri Lanka

✈ Colombo 125km

Tel +94 74 472727
Fax +94 8 232068

mareach@slt.lk
www.cyberserv.net/mahaweli

Kandy was the ancient capital of Sri Lanka and as such offers many sights to enthral the visitor. Positioned directly on the banks of the river, which is Sri Lanka's longest, Mahaweli is a luxurious resort that actually loops the town and offers a superb base for exploration.

The 113 air-conditioned rooms are comfortably furnished and all have balconies overlooking either the river or the hotel's huge freeform swimming pool. They also contain television and mini-bar.

The on-site restaurant specialises in traditional Sri Lankan cuisine, which is renowned for its rich flavours and original use of spices. Delicious local and international dishes are also served at regular theme nights and barbecues. The hotel also offers nightly entertainment such as dance troupes, live music and romantic river cruises.

The facilities at Mahaweli Reach are superb, with billiards, tennis and river fishing just an example of the activities available. Off site, you can choose from excursions to many of Sri Lanka's awesome attractions. Essential visits during any stay are to the Temple of the Sacred Tooth Relic, the Sigiriya rock fortress, the Esala Perahera with authentic folk dancers and elephant parade, and the endearing Elephant Orphanage – don't miss bathtime at 3pm.

221

US$120-150 (113)

US$200-450 (2)

from US$15

US$7-11

Honeymoon specials

Champagne, cake, chocolates and flowers in room on arrival. Also, souvenir from the hotel and upgrade to a suite depending on availability.
* Please note: minimum stay of three nights to qualify for the above special.

Sightseeing and leisure

The hotel offers swimming, billiards, tennis, boating, fishing and Ayurvedic Health Centre on site. Golf course 40 minutes' drive from hotel. Beauty salon nearby. Local sites include Temple of the Sacred Tooth Relic, Royal Botanical Gardens, Kandyan Arts & Crafts, Elephant Orphanage at Pinnawela, colourful bazaars. The Esala Perahera with folk dancers & elephant parade for a fortnight during July/Aug.

Saman Villas

Information & Reservations
UK 0870 606 1296
INT. +44 870 606 1296

Aturuwella
Bentota
Sri Lanka

✈ Colombo 92km

tel +94 34 75 435
fax +94 34 75 433

samanvil@sri.lanka.net
www.lanka.net/SamanVilla

222

Tour operators:
UK Elegant Resorts
Premier Holidays

Member of:
Small Luxury Hotels of the World

Described as Sri Lanka's most luxurious resort, Saman Villas perches on a rocky headland on the island's west coast by a quiet fishing village. Behind you lie lush avenues of green coconut palms, to each side stretch miles and miles of pure white sand, and in the distance all you see is the beautiful blue and enticing waters of the Indian Ocean.

Twenty-seven suites make up the resort and all are angled to ensure each verandah or balcony offers superb coastal views. Inside, wooden floors, traditional matting and rattan furnishings create an air of simple elegance. They are all spacious, consisting of a living room, sleeping deck, dressing room and sumptuous bathroom with courtyard.

US$120-315* (27)

US$5-20

US$8-12

Honeymoon specials
Champagne, heart-shaped cake and flowers on arrival.
Upgrade to deluxe suite subject to availablity.

* Prices subject to 22.5% service charge and taxes.

The two restaurants are also perfectly positioned with either sea or garden views. Choose from a wide selection of western, eastern and spicy Sri Lankan dishes. And service is impeccable.

Facilities at the hotel are perfect for active types. There is an on-site fitness room for those who want to stay in shape plus a sauna and steambath, while a variety of watersports and archery can be found close by.

Water-babies will also love the infinity-style swimming pool that, from ground level, appears to merge into the azure waters of the Indian Ocean. The pool connects with a large terraced garden which extends along the rest of the seafront from north to south.

Traditional Sri Lankan weddings can be arranged by the hotel and tailored to the couple's religious specifications. Held in traditional costume with singing and music native to the area, it's a colourful way to celebrate your vows.

Sightseeing and leisure

Fitness centre, sauna, massage, steambath, aromatherapy. Swimming, table tennis, badminton, snooker, darts and other indoor games. Library facilities and evening entertainment programmes. Be sure to take tours of parts of the island and go on a river cruise. Nearby are Buddhist temples, a turtle hatchery and coral sanctuary.

Nepal

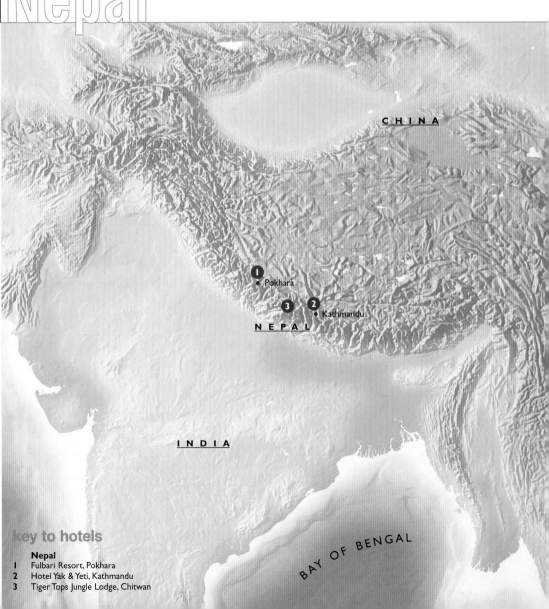

flying time
To: Kathmandu
Europe/UK: 12-14 hrs

climate
Nepal can be visited
throughout the year
but the best months
are mid-Sept to
mid-May. The months
of March and April
provide spectacular
rhododendron
forests in regions
easily reachable from
Kathmandu or
Pokhara. The
monsoon months
of July-Aug can be
hot and humid but
is a time when the
countryside is lush
and green.

currency
Nepalese rupee

language
Nepali is the official
language but English
is widely spoken.

getting around
Information available
from Nepal Tourism
Board:
tel +977 1 256909
fax +977 1 256910
info@ntb.wlink.com.np
www.welcomenepal.
com

224

CHINA

Pokhara

Kathmandu

NEPAL

INDIA

BAY OF BENGAL

key to hotels

Nepal
1   Fulbari Resort, Pokhara
2   Hotel Yak & Yeti, Kathmandu
3   Tiger Tops Jungle Lodge, Chitwan

Astride the great Himalayan frontier is a country ranging from vast lowland jungles at around 200m above sea level, to the highest mountains on earth, which include ten of the world's fourteen 8,000-metre peaks.

From the jungles of the Terai, stronghold of the Royal Bengal tiger and the Greater One-Horned rhinoceros, the land begins to rise. At first it climbs gently through hills chequered with fertile terraces, small villages and ancient cities. Then the slopes steepen and merge into massive walls, where trees cease to exist and snow and ice begin. Even higher, the savage beauty culminates in Sagarmatha, 'Goddess Mother of the World', the highest mountain on earth, Mount Everest.

This is Nepal, home to 22 million people whose customs and languages are as diverse as the terrain itself. Nepal is a land where deities mingle with mortals, and strange legends follow yak caravans down from the mountain passes to become part of the Hindu folklore. Here live the Gurkhas, famed for their courage, the Sherpas, legends in mountaineering, and the Newars, skilled craftsmen who contribute to the rich artistic heritage of the Kathmandu Valley. Kathmandu, capital of the only Hindu monarchy in the world, is a unique blend of religions, temples, palaces and people.

It is in this mystical land of diversity, beauty and excitement, a land unparalleled in the world, that a holiday with a difference awaits.

The Nepal Experience

Nepal

All enquiries:
Tiger Mountain
PO Box 242
Kathmandu, Nepal

tel +977 1 411 225
fax +977 1 414 075

info@tigermountain.com
www.tigermountain.com

226

Chitwan Park

For many, an ideal honeymoon is synonymous with adventure. So for the intrepid couple, Nepal could have just what you're looking for.

Sandwiched between China to the north and India to the south, Nepal seems untouched by time. Here beats the heart of a country steeped in cultural heritage, where tribes and villages await discovery. And to make your pilgrimage trouble-free, Tiger Mountain has put together a wondrous eight-day journey you'll never forget.

Day 1: Arrive in Kathmandu, capital of the only Hindu monarchy in the world, and transfer to the deluxe **Hotel Yak & Yeti**. Resplendent amongst rolling greens draped around a little lake, the Yak & Yeti blends three distinct architectural styles: traditional Nepali, neo-classical and contemporary.

Day 2: Enjoy a tour of Kathmandu City, including the House of the Living Goddess and the oldest Buddhist shrine in the world – Swayambunath. Also visit Patan, the Tibet Handicraft Centre and Bhaktapur, home of medieval art and architecture, also known as the 'city of devotees'.

Day 3: Today you transfer to the airport for the 30-minute flight to the grass airstrip at Meghauly. Transfer through the jungle to the famed **Tiger Tops Jungle Lodge** located in the heart of Royal Chitwan National Park, a 932sqkm area which is one of Asia's most spectacular wildlife sanctuaries.

All double rooms here are attractively furnished and have solar-powered reading lamps and ceiling fans, with solar-heated showers in the ensuite bathrooms.

Day 4: Today is reserved for wildlife fun. Activities

Package price:
US$1645.00 per person

 included

 included

Hotel Yak & Yeti

Honeymoon specials

The itinerary featured here includes: flowers and fruit on arrival; upgrade in all properties (supplementary cost of US$500pp at Yak & Yeti and Fulbari for honeymoon suite), plus special locally made wedding gift.

This programme is meant as a guideline and may be tailored depending on individual requirements.

Tiger Tops Jungle Lodge

Fulbari Resort

Elephant safari

include wildlife viewing from elephant back, nature walks and treks, bird-watching and boat trips. All excursions are escorted by experienced naturalists.

Day 5: Take a five-hour scenic drive to the valley of Pokhara, at the foot of the Annapurna Himalaya. Here, the deluxe **Fulbari Resort** is your home for the next few nights. The resort overlooks the Seti river canyon and offers a 140-km vista of the Annapurna mountain range. The Fulbari offers

deluxe accommodation, all with private balconies overlooking the expansive gardens. And from the resort you can enjoy hikes, mountain flights, pony treks or simply relax in the heated swimming pool.

Day 6: Day at leisure at the Fulbari.

Day 7: Fly to Kathmandu; farewell dinner and stay overnight at the Hotel Yak & Yeti.

Day 8: Your dream adventure comes to a close, and you'll be whisked off for your flight home.

Sightseeing and leisure

Kathmandu Valley, Royal Chitwan National Park, Pokhara, plus wildlife viewing from elephant back, nature walks and treks, bird-watching, Landrover drives, boat trips, elephant camp visits and more. At the Yak & Yeti, there are also pools, tennis courts, health club and a casino which is open around the clock.

Fulbari Resort

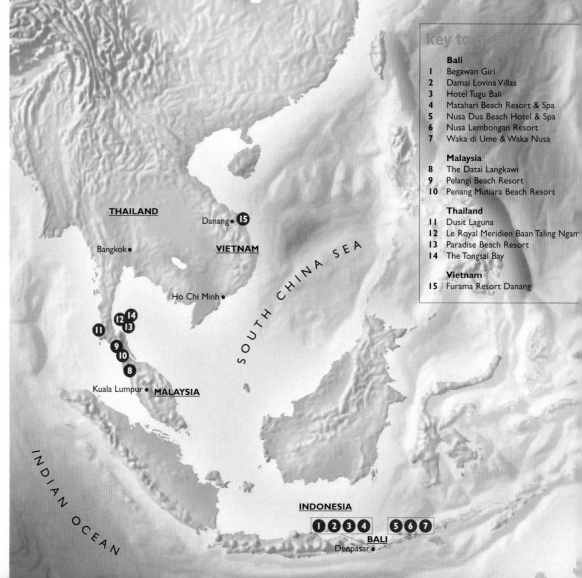

key to hotels

Bali
1	Begawan Giri
2	Damai Lovina Villas
3	Hotel Tugu Bali
4	Matahari Beach Resort & Spa
5	Nusa Dua Beach Hotel & Spa
6	Nusa Lembongan Resort
7	Waka di Ume & Waka Nusa

Malaysia
8	The Datai Langkawi
9	Pelangi Beach Resort
10	Penang Mutiara Beach Resort

Thailand
11	Dusit Laguna
12	Le Royal Meridien Baan Taling Ngam
13	Paradise Beach Resort
14	The Tongsai Bay

Vietnam
15	Furama Resort Danang

THAILAND

Danang • 15

Bangkok •

VIETNAM

SOUTH CHINA SEA

Ho Chi Minh •

12 14
13

11

9
10

8

Kuala Lumpur • MALAYSIA

INDIAN OCEAN

INDONESIA

1 2 3 4   5 6 7

BALI

Denpasar •

From the South China Sea to the Indian Ocean, encompassing stunning coastlines, fertile plains, verdant paddy fields and vast mountain ranges, lie some of the most beautiful lands in existence.

Everywhere in the lush, sticky heat, the earth erupts in a sensual display of rich vegetation and tropical blooms. Blessed with a staggering array of birds, butterflies, monkeys, and other exotic fauna, including sadly dwindling numbers of tigers, leopards, elephants, rhinos and black bears, a visit to southeast Asia will capture your heart and set your spirits soaring.

Not even the skyscrapers of Malaysia's Kuala Lumpur, the seedy red light district of Thailand's Bangkok, the booming industry of Vietnam's Ho Chi Minh City, or the encroaching tourism of the dazzling island of Bali, can erode the mystical beauty and serenity to be discovered at every turn.

Spiritual Bali charms with its Hindu temples and festivals. Vietnam, despite its violent history, possesses a people of immense culture and grace, and the calm, green spaces of Hanoi are a delight. Malaysia buzzes with vibrant good cheer, a harmonious blend of cultures and creeds. Visit the capital's Chinatown for raucous bustle. Thailand is by turn hectic, hospitable and heavenly, with bustling waterways, towering Buddhas, magical ruins and breathtaking rainforests.

229

Bali & Lombok

T his mountainous island of startling beauty is the jewel in Indonesia's crown. Emerald-green rice terraces hug the contours of the hills, reflecting the clouds scudding over the frittering palm fronds.

Everywhere there are tiny shrines, adorned with mossy statues and offerings – incense sticks laid on small rice packets, and gifts of fruit, magnolia, hibiscus and richly scented frangipani flowers. These represent an untiring commitment of time and artistic endeavour; a constant reminder of the Balinese love of beauty coinciding with devotion to religious principles. Indeed, Bali is a prayer to the gods, where heaven and earth are held in balance by daily obeisance. The Balinese know their luck: this is one of the world's most charmed places.

Tourism has come to Bali, but it has been skilfully marshalled. The biggest hotels are clustered on the palm-fringed peninsula of Nusa Dua in the south, away from the more raucous backpacker streets of Kuta, or its quieter twin Sanur. Ubud, set among lush, wooded valleys high up in the hills inland, is the artistic capital which simply oozes character and where you can slake off the day's dust with a coconut-shell scoop of water under open skies. Bali is perfect for honeymooners: poetic and spiritual, yet comfortable and accessible.

The Balinese regard marriage as a sacred union of the physical and the spiritual, blessed by the gods. 'Where is Wayan?' they ask all young couples. Meaning, 'Where is the first born?' You see, families are at the centre of their lives and you will feel you have a special place among them.

flying time
London: 18 hrs
LA: 18 hrs
NY: 24 hrs

climate/ when to go
May-Sep, in the dry season, is ideal. But any time of year is good, although you might need to shelter under a big banana-leaf umbrella during a wet-season downpour in Dec-Feb. The high season for religious ceremonies is Oct-Nov, but there are lots of smaller ceremonies that take place all year.

getting around
By taxi, bus, *bemo* (covered pick-up truck) or *dokar* (horse-drawn trap). It is also easy to hire your own car, jeep, motorbike or bicycle.

231

Begawan Giri

Information & Reservations
UK 0870 606 1296
INT. +44 870 606 1296

PO Box 54
Ubud 80571
Bali

✈ Denpasar 45km

tel +62 361 978 888
fax +62 361 978 889

begawan@indo.net.id
www.begawan.com

232

For those of you who like the idea of relaxing in your own private estate set in lush, tropical gardens, Begawan Giri (translated as 'Wise Man's Mountain') may just be the answer. Here, in the serenity of a hilltop garden fed by Holy springs, five peaceful residences are set amongst lovingly tended gardens and perched high above the Ayung River.

Each of the villas (which can be hired in part or whole) has been individually designed, with an eye to *feng shui*, to ensure the maximum of comfort and peace. Each one is designed to be in harmony with an aspect of nature or the spirit, and all are furnished with antiques, handmade furniture and exquisite fabrics as well as boasting a personal butler, private pool, king-size beds and verandahs.

The emphasis at Begawan is on freedom. If you would like a romantic dinner in your suite, or a picnic by the plunge pool, then you shall be obliged.

 US$475-2,950* (21)

 US$25-85

 from US$15

Honeymoon specials

Sparkling wine, flowers, fruit platter in suite on arrival. Complimentary airport transfer plus outdoor 'his & her' massage and cleansing dip in spring pool.

* Prices quoted are based on two people per suite per night and subject to 21% tax & service charge.

If you fancy a candlelit meal at the Kudus House Restaurant, you can have that too.

For real pampering, Begawan has its own holistic traditional spa. Enjoy a luxurious Balinese massage with aromatic oils or exotic body treatments such as the Javanese Lulur and Balinese Spice. The nearby village of Ubud, with its artists' studios, antique shops, tucked away temples and village markets, is a must to visit.

Sightseeing and leisure

Holistic massage and beauty treatments at The Source, library, water gardens and natural spring pools. The hotel can organise excursions, whitewater rafting, sightseeing and shopping trips as well as traditional dance performances. Bali's cultural centre, the village of Ubud, is close by. Tours of Kintampani Mountain, Bedugal Lake, Besakih Mother Temple.

Damai Lovina Villas

Information & Reservations
UK 0870 606 1296
INT. +44 870 606 1296

Jalan Damai
Lovina
Bali

✈ Denpasar 80km

tel +62 362 41008
fax +62 362 41009

damai@singaraja.wasantara.net.id
www.damai.com

234

Nestled in the gentle hills overlooking the bay of Lovina, among rice paddies, spice plantations and stunning jungle-clad ravines, are the Damai Lovina Villas, Bali's gourmet retreat. Quiet, secluded and very romantic, they make the perfect hideaway. Located only a couple of hours' drive from the airport and the crowds of the south, they are a secret gem offering two of the greatest luxuries of all – beauty and tranquillity.

The eight bungalows are built in traditional Balinese style and have a cool, open-plan opulence. Stylish four-poster beds, antiques, beautifully and meticulously crafted teak furniture, textiles which recreate ancient Indonesian patterns, and striking open-air bathrooms with spas create a warm atmosphere of tropical style and elegance.

A mouth-watering blend of French and tropical cuisine – colourful and varied – is presented simply

 US$168-206 (8 bungalows)

US$38-45

US$6-18

Honeymoon specials

Champagne, a basket of tropical fruit, and a beautiful arrangement of flowers each day. 'Romance at Damai' honeymoon package: details available on request. Traditional Balinese wedding celebration available with Hindu ceremony, Balinese music, private gourmet feast.

and beautifully by the resident French chef, who creates a new set menu each night.

Enjoy the excitement and beauty of a full Balinese wedding ceremony, with a reception for up to 40 guests which can be easily arranged by the hotel's attentive staff on request.

The Damai is light years away from the crowds of the south and to those who have visited, it's a slice of heaven here on earth.

Sightseeing and leisure

Beautician by appointment. Traditional Indonesian massage, diving at Mendangan, swimming in the bay in Lovina and golf in the volcanic crater at Bali Handara Golf Course. Watching dolphins playing at sunrise. Walks in the unspoilt countryside, watching the sun set behind Java's volcanoes. Bedugal Botanical Gardens, the waterfalls of Git-Git, the hot springs of Banjar and spice plantations.

Matahari Beach Resort & Spa

Information & Reservations
UK 0870 606 1296
INT. +44 870 606 1296

PO Box 194
Pemuteran
Bali

✈ Denpasar 3 hrs

tel +62 362 92 312
fax +62 362 92 313

nonpluse@compuserve.com
www.matahari-beach-resort.com

236

Travel past soaring mountains, lush paddy fields and delicate holy temples to the old fishing village of Pemuteran in northwestern Bali to be met with a warm welcome at the Matahari Beach Resort & Spa. Benefiting from spectacular views of the Java Sea and a glorious black sand lava beach, this lovely, unspoilt location provides a very restful retreat.

Both body and soul are catered for here: indulge in the pleasures of the senses with a four-hand synchrone massage and spa treatment and relax to the soothing sounds of splashing water fountains amid shady pavilions and marble terraces. The scen of lotus and frangipani flowers float through the warm air, lending an exotic aura to your holiday.

Bungalows have been constructed in complete harmony with the environment, using local material such as marble, bamboo and sandstone. Shining parquet floors and high, hand-plaited ceilings are

 US$194-424 (32)

 US$20-70

 included

Honeymoon specials

The traditional Balinese honeymoon experience is offered in full and at no extra expense: welcome flowers and cocktail, upgrade according to availability, one Balinese massage per person, excursion to Munduk waterfalls and the Tamblingan Lake including picnic and gamelan music with two musicians. Royal Parwathi Package (costs extra): pre-wedding spa treatments, champagne, private 10-course gala dinner, a night in the Bali Sari (King's bed).

teamed with intricate wood carvings and ornate stone masonry to impart a graceful tone.

Sunken bathtubs give way to private gardens, where you can shower beneath a water-spouting dragon statue. At night, dine on exceptional 'east-meets-west' cuisine while drinking in panoramic garden views and excellent wine from the hotel's unique cellar, while you watch a traditional dance display with Balinese gamelan orchestra.

Sightseeing and leisure

Snorkelling, diving off Menjangan Island and around the Liberty Wreck, Bali's most visited diving site, mountain biking, windsurfing, trekking tours at the Bali Barat National Park, golf at Bali Handara Golf & Country Club, tennis. On site is the exclusive Parwathi Spa offering many treatments including the wonderful 4-hand synchrone massage, gym and beauty salon. Balinese dancing, cookery and wood and stone carving classes.

Hotel Tugu Bali

Information & Reservations
UK 0870 606 1296
INT. +44 870 606 1296

Nr Batu Bolong Temple
North of Kerobokan
Canggu Beach
Bali

✈ Denpasar 8 miles

tel +62 361 731701
fax +62 361 731704

UK contact:
tel +44 (0) 1737 371908
US contact:
tel +888 ART TUGU

238

bali@tuguhotels.com
www.tuguhotels.com

This exquisite hotel, situated near an ancient fishing village on the lush west coast of Bali, is the result of a dedicated quest by its art-loving owner to create a 'museum-boutique' representing the rich heritage and history of Indonesia. The effect is stunning – a haven from the rigours of the world, with something beautiful and unique to discover around every corner.

Interiors are brimming with relics and artefacts. Intricately carved Javanese wooden screens, Balinese stone sculptures, Dutch Colonial stained glass, and even a reconstructed 18th-century Chinese temple, all conjure up an aura of romance.

Not at the expense of comfort however – huge, canopied beds strewn with rose petals, marble floors, silken fabrics and sunken baths fed with water from a nearby spring make for luxurious living, and the courteous, attentive staff add to the delight of this magical, spiritual retreat.

The passion with which this collection was put together is infectious, and it is the perfect setting for lovers. Of the 25 thatched suites and pavilions that rest beside or over lotus ponds and gardens, the Puri Le Mayeur and Walter Spies Pavilion, named in honour of two distinguished artists, are especially appropriate for honeymooners.

Honeymoon specials

Honeymoon Romance package includes: one bottle of champagne; candlelight dinner; daily fresh flowers and fruit; Balinese massage; horse-drawn cart tour.

Sightseeing and leisure

Fantastic on-site spa and massage facilities, spring-fed swimming pool, open-air garden stage for classic cultural performances. Floodlit tennis courts and Nirvana Golf Club nearby. A short walk away is Canggu fishing village, and also available is surfing, mountain biking and horse-drawn cart tours. Island tours are available courtesy of the hotel concierge.

 US$250-450 per couple (25)

 US$20-60

 US$10-20

Nusa Dua
Beach Hotel & Spa

Information & Reservations
UK 0870 606 1296
INT. +44 870 606 1296

PO Box 1028
Denpasar
Bali

✈ Denpasar 12km

Tel +62 361 771 210
Fax +62 361 772 617

ndbhnet@indosat.net.id
www.nusaduahotelandspa.com

Member of:
The Leading Hotels of the World
The Audley Group

Set on Bali's southern shores, the Nusa Dua Beach Hotel & Spa is immersed in the pageantry of one of the world's most vibrant and intriguing cultures. An aquamarine ocean, azure skies stretching into the distance, silver sands, a golden sun and the deep greens of the beach-side palms are the palette with which the Balinese gods painted this fabled isle.

The guest rooms are regal and celebrate the richness of Balinese culture in a sumptuous tapestry of classical decor and unmatched comfort. Personalised rooms offer a rich panoply of the island's arts and crafts, including Balinese ikat and batik textiles and ornately painted wall panels.

Guests can dine in high style in any number of fabulous venues ranging from gourmet Asian cuisine enjoyed *al fresco* to a colourful Italian bistro, or a sizzling beachside barbecue.

Recalling the royal water palaces of Bali's last kings, a particularly beautiful feature of the hotel is the lagoon pool. Here you will find a perfectly tranquil oasis of soothing fountains, frangipani and bougainvillea scented gardens and sparkling water where romance and relaxation go hand in hand – a true taste of paradise to enjoy.

239

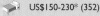 US$150-230* (352)

 US$300-2,800* (28)

 US$35-45

 US$15

Honeymoon specials
Flowers, fruit and chocolates on arrival.

* Prices subject to 11% tax plus 10% service charge.

Sightseeing and leisure
Massage treatments, body scrubs, spa with sauna, lap pool, steam rooms. Jacuzzi, hair and beauty salon and gym. There is an 18-hole golf course five minutes away from the hotel. Budaya Cultural Theatre. Club Tabuh, the hotel disco, presents a variety of evening programmes every week from Thursday till Sunday. Ulu Watu, temple to the sea spirits, is nearby.

Nusa Lembongan Resort

Information & Reservations
UK   0870 606 1296
INT. +44 870 606 1296

PO Box 3846
Denpasar 80001
Bali

✈ Denpasar 26km

tel +62 361 725864
fax +62 361 725866

sales@nusa-lembongan.com
www.nusa-lembongan.com

Tour operators:
Gold Medal Travel

240

A paradise awaits you at Nusa Lembongan, a secluded, tropical island off the eastern coast of Bali. Sapphire-blue seas lap gently at the pristine white beaches, while swaying palms shelter the 12 exclusive villas that make up this charming resort.

Each villa is constructed from natural materials such as wood and thatch, and furnished in a chic, contemporary style. Seven villas overlook the bay and five are set among lush, tropical gardens, each boasting their own private, romantic terrace.

There are also nine private decks set high up on the rocks around the headland which command panoramic views of Sanghiang Bay and the silhouette of Mount Agung – use them for sunbathing, fishing, or a romantic dinner *à deux*.

The waters around the island are known for their colourful marine life and there are a host of watersports available, as well as glass-bottomed boat rides to view the underwater scene. Guided tours take in an ancient underground dwelling, traditional houses and boatyards, and the seaweed farms that fuel this island's economy. Or you can hire a mountain bike and explore the many trails that wind through the lush, mountainous terrain.

  US$200-500 (12 villas)

 US$15-40

 US$10-20

Honeymoon specials

Welcome drink, tropical fruit platter and small honeymoon gift on arrival. Other romantic 'surprises' can be arranged.

Sightseeing and leisure

On site are fabulous spa facilities offering traditional treatments and massages. The reef surrounding the resort is a marine park, with diving, snorkelling, surfing, fishing and glass-bottomed boat rides on offer. Also, there are traditional village crafts, boat building and mountain biking.

Information & Reservations
UK 0870 606 1296
INT. +44 870 606 1296

The Waka Experience

Bali

✈ Denpasar 45km

Waka di Ume
tel +62 361 973178
fax +62 361 973179

Waka Nusa
tel +62 361 723629
fax +62 361 722077

wakaexperience@balinesia.com
www.wakaexperience.com

The Waka Group offers an 'experience' quite different to other hotels. Choose from a selection of small, boutique hotels that offer a true Balinese experience, plus sailing cruises and jungle treks. But honeymooners will take particular delight in Waka di Ume and Waka Nusa.

A very different resort; an oasis of serenity only minutes from Ubud, the island's cultural heart, Waka di Ume comprises 16 individual bungalows. These are scattered down a hillside and flanked by lush rice paddies and from every window you have views across the seemingly endless fields. Relax beside the temple-like pool, or pamper your body with a traditional Balinese massage. Here you are surrounded by the textures and colours of nature; by homespun fabrics; fragrant *alang alang* grass roofing; flowers and foliage.

Waka Nusa is set on the island of Nusa Lembongan, just to the southeast of Bali and reached by a short boat trip on board the WakaLouka catamaran. The bungalows are set apart for privacy in gardens with tropical flowers. The king-size bed is the centrepiece of the rooms, and the architecture is Balinese with *alang alang* grass roof and natural wood details. The perfect setting for an unforgettable honeymoon.

241

 US$115-190*

 from US$15

 US$5-9

Honeymoon specials
Balinese massage, romantic candlelight dinner either in room or at restaurant, champagne breakfast, fruit basket with flowers, flowers throughout the room. Price: US$58 per person.
* Rates are per bungalow per night and subject to 21% tax & service charge. Full board packages at Waka Nusa are available.

Sightseeing and leisure
Sail to Lembongan Island aboard the 23-metre WakaLouka Catamaran for a gorgeous day out or a few days stay. The voyage to the island takes about two hours, and once there, you can go snorkelling, surfing, or visit the local village for shopping. The Waka Tangga 'spiritual trek' through the jungle and up to temples and mountains in central Bali is also recommended as is the Waka Land Rover journey.

Malaysia

flying time
To: Kuala Lumpur
London: 12¹/₂ hrs
NY: 20 hrs
LA: 18-19 hrs

**climate/
when to go**
Tropically hot and
humid all year. Try to
avoid wet seasons,
which affect beaches
and watersports. The
west coast gets most
rain Apr-May and
Oct-Nov; the east,
Nov-Feb. There are
many Chinese, Indian
and Christian festivals,
such as Chinese New
Year (Jan-Feb) and
Deepavali (Oct-Nov).

currency
The Malaysian ringgit,
or 'dollar'.

language
Bahasa Malaysia.
Chinese, Tamil and
English are widely
spoken.

health
Immunisation against
typhoid, tetanus,
polio, hepatitis and,
for some areas,
anti-malaria tablets.

242

The world's tallest structure, the Petronas Twin Towers complex, soars above Malaysia's capital Kuala Lumpur – a symbol of the country's headlong race into the 21st century.

But Malaysia is still a place where you can discover untamed nature at its most tropical. A day's drive from Kuala Lumpur brings you to the Taman Negara National Park, where you can go jungle trekking on the lookout for giant monitor lizards and brilliant butterflies. And on the jungle-clad island of Borneo, which contains the Malaysian states of Sarawak and Sabah, climb south-east Asia's highest mountain, Mount Kinabalu, see orangutans, take a river trip through tropical rainforest and stay in traditional bamboo longhouses with families of the Dayak tribe.

Malaysia has fine, empty beaches for those who like solitude, and newly developing beach resorts like Kuantan and Cherating on the east coast of the peninsula, where a night-time attraction is watching leatherback turtles lay their eggs in the sand.

As a contrast to the sun-baked beaches and steamy jungles, there are the cooler highlands, all within easy reach of Kuala Lumpur. For British civil servants in Malaya in the 19th century, the hill station in the Cameron Highlands, with its fruit orchards and tea plantations, was like a home from home. It still has something of the old colonial atmosphere and today's recreation includes tennis, golf and hill walking.

Go to Melaka and see the legacy of the 17th-century Portuguese churches and pink-brick mansions put up by Dutch traders in the 1600s. Like the rest of Malaysia, Melaka has a mixed population of Malays, Indians and Chinese. Feel the clock being turned back as you walk through the old Chinese quarter, between the old-style shop houses and dragon-roofed temples.

The Datai Langkawi

Information & Reservations
UK 0870 606 1296
INT. +44 870 606 1296

Jalan Teluk Datai
07000 Pulau Langkawi
Kedah Darul Aman
Malaysia

✈ Kuala Lumpur 20km

tel +60 4 959 2500
fax +60 4 959 2600

datai@ghmhotels.com
www.ghmhotels.com

Tour operators:
UK Elegant Resorts
Abercrombie & Kent

Tucked in the middle of an ancient and tropical rainforest and perched on the fringe of a jungle cove on the north-western tip of Langkawi, The Datai has a secluded white beach caressed by the gentle waves of the Andaman Sea.

The Datai's villas are scattered throughout the forest and linked to the main hotel and other facilities by a series of pathways. Each has its own terrace and an elevated dining verandah. Inside, calm tones, soft lighting and warm, red *balau* flooring carry through the atmosphere of lush foliage and jungle to be found outside.

Open-air dining among the tree tops is a rare treat that can be enjoyed every day in the Pavilion, the hotel's authentic Thai restaurant. *Al fresco* dining is available at the Beach Club, while an enticing blend of Malaysian and international cuisine is on offer in the hotel's main dining room.

To soothe body and soul, the Datai has its own spa, situated next to a secluded stream, which offers massage, aromatherapy, and traditional Malaysian body treatments.

If that doesn't appeal, there is an 18-hole golf course right next to the resort, which promises not only a fine game but the most incredible views of the nearby mountains while you play.

243

RM1,045-1,700

RM1,760-6,700

US$25-50

US$15

Honeymoon specials
Fruit, flowers and half-bottle of champagne on arrival.

Sightseeing and leisure
Health club with gym. Snorkelling, windsurfing and sailing. Scuba diving and deep sea fishing can be arranged off site. Lakes, caves and waterfalls to explore. Take a boat ride to Pulau Dayang Bunting, otherwise known as Lake of the Pregnant Maiden. Other attractions include the hot spring Telega Air Hangat, the Gua Cerita, and the black sandy beach of Pantai Pasir Hitam.

Pelangi Beach Resort

Information & Reservations
UK 0870 606 1296
INT. +44 870 606 1296

Pantai Cenang
07000 Langkawi
Kedah
Malaysia

✈ Langkawi Int. 8km

tel +604 955 1001
fax +604 955 1122

pelangi.pbl@meritus-hotels.com

Langkawi is the largest of the cluster of 104 islands that lie between the Andaman Sea and the Straits of Malacca. This tropical paradise is famed for its legends and myths as well as its peaceful beauty.

The Pelangi Beach Resort is an idyllic haven of traditional ethnic wooden chalets set in 30 acres of lush tropical gardens, right on top of a fabulous white, sandy beach. Decoration is typically Malay – beautifully ornate and ceremonious.

Pelangi is the Malay word for 'rainbow' and guests will certainly experience the full gamut of tropical colours and experiences here. The large chalets are all traditionally decorated in fine style and have spacious balconies to relax on, absorb the tropical atmosphere and adjust to the unhurried pace that is Pelangi. Three restaurants offer a choice of western, local and Thai dishes and feature succulent meats and fresh catches from the sea.

The beautiful, verdant island is waiting to be explored. Inland, waterfalls abound in the dense jungle and provide the ideal opportunity for a trek. And the surrounding open seas are dotted by islands and offer you the opportunity to go island-hopping, fishing and barracuda trolling, or indulge in your favourite watersport – from parasailing to windsurfing to catamaran sailing. The choice is yours.

🛏 US$131-176 (328)

🛏 US$222-411 (22)

🍽 US$9-26

☕ US$6-11

🍾 ⊙ 🤿 ⎙

Honeymoon specials
Couples are guaranteed a king-size bed during their stay. Welcome drink, fruit basket and sparkling wine on arrival.

Sightseeing and leisure
Hair and beauty salon on site. Full range of watersports. Shopping arcade. Golf course nearby. There are a vast amount of local attractions to visit, such as Field of Burnt Rice, Mahsuri Mausoleum, Black Sand Beach, Langkawi Craft Complex and the Crocodile Farm.

Penang Mutiara
Beach Resort

Information & Reservations
UK 0870 606 1296
INT. +44 870 606 1296

1 Jalan Teluk Bahang
11050 Penang
Malaysia

✈ Penang 40km

tel +604 885 2828
fax +604 885 2829

pmr@po.jaring.my
www.penang-mutiara.com.my

Member of:
The Leading Hotels of the World

Penang Mutiara Beach Resort is an extraordinary hotel complex with a lively Malaysian personality. Nestling in 18 acres of lush tropical greenery, it lies on what is arguably Penang's finest beachfront – Teluk Bahang, or 'the glowing bay'. Every private balcony of this unique hotel's 438 spacious rooms faces the sea. Natural materials have been used in combination with light colour schemes to give the hotel's interior an airy, contemporary feel, whilst maintaining the elegance that one would expect from a 'Leading Hotel of the World'.

For centuries, travellers and traders were drawn to these sun-drenched shores, and their influence can still be seen in the island's rich cultural heritage and architecture, and experienced in the warm welcome you will undoubtedly receive. It can definitely be tasted in the delicious flavours of the varied and exotic food.

Gracious living is the key to the cuisine at Penang Mutiara. Boasting four restaurants, you are spoilt for choice: Italian, Chinese, Japanese, Malaysian and a wide selection of European cuisine is readily available.

Then there's always the unspoilt panoramic view of the garden and ocean while you sip champagne at the Palmetto Lounge. It's the perfect romantic setting in which to start those first few days of your life together.

245

 US$153-224 (406)

 US$395-1,974 (32)

from US$15

from US$13

Honeymoon specials
Honeymooners receive fruits and flowers on arrival plus king-size bed decorated with flower petals. Room upgrade subject to availability. One bottle of house wine for a seven-night stay.

Sightseeing and leisure
Fitness centre on site: gym, whirlpool, sauna and steambath. Also, salon with beauty facilities. Visits to butterfly farm, botanical garden, Penang Hill Railway, Kek Lok Si Temple, Fort Cornwallis, Snake Temple, international sports arena. Five shopping centres. Many traditional and religious festivals throughout the year.

Thailand

flying time
To: Bangkok
London: 14 hrs
NY: 22-23 hrs
LA: 19 hrs via Seoul

**climate/
when to go**
The best months are
Oct-Feb. A particular
attraction is the
festival of Loy
Krathong, held in Nov,
when thousands of
little candle-lit boats
are floated on the
country's waterways.

currency
Baht, but US dollars
widely accepted.

language
Thai. English is also
widely spoken.

getting around
There is an efficient
rail system; hire cars
are cheap and readily
available. Bangkok is
best negotiated from
the boats and ferries
that ply their trade on
the canals or in a *tuk-
tuk*, a three-wheeled
motor scooter.

Formerly known as Siam, and still referred to by Thais as *Muang Thai* or 'Land of the Free', Thailand is a friendly kingdom where modernity exists alongside a charming and unique 700-year-old culture.

Thailand has managed to preserve its cultural heritage to a unique degree, so has much to offer visitors. Sample the exotic pleasures of Bangkok, the 'Venice of the east', on a cruise through its countless waterways, past glorious illuminated temples and the world-famous floating market. While there, visit The Grand Palace and Temple of the Emerald Buddha, two of the oldest and largest temples in Bangkok built by King Rama I nearly 200 years ago, one of which houses the gigantic gold-plated 'Reclining Buddha'.

Go beyond the cities where there are some enthralling natural environments: dense bamboo forests, fields of delicate orchids, waterfalls and velvet green mangroves, as well as areas of sumptuous cultivated land of coconut and rubber plantations and acres upon acres of rice fields.

For a different scene, North Thailand affords plenty of scope for both cultural sightseeing and escapes into the vast countryside. Chiang Mai is the best base for exploring the region, offering its own sights and numerous hiking and trekking options. Finally, move to the coast and discover glorious beaches, Thailand style, watched over by 40-feet-high Buddha statues.

Whatever the location, the spiritual calm of Buddhism – over half the male population has passed through monkhood – suffuses all aspects of Thai life.

See

amazing
THAILAND 2000
Enchantment for the next thousand years

Contact: Tourism Authority of Thailand, 49 Albemarle Street, London WIX 3FE. England UK. Tel. (44-27) 499-7679 ext. 201 Fax. (44-27) 629-5519
E-mail Address : info@tat.demon.co.uk Internet: www.tourismthailand.org, www.amazingthailand.th

Dusit Laguna

Information & Reservations
UK 0870 606 1296
INT. +44 870 606 1296

390 Srisoontorn Rd
Cherngtalay District
Amphur Talang
Phuket 83110
Thailand

✈ Phuket 22km

tel +66 76 324 320
fax +66 76 324 174

dlp@dusit.com
www.dusitlaguna.com

Member of:
The Leading Hotels of the World

White silvery sands. Beautiful lagoons. The salty tang of sea breezes. Abundant coconut groves. Shimmering, emerald Andaman waters. In the distance a solitary boat sways gently to the rhythm of the waves. Overhead a clear sky of unbelievable blue stretching away to infinity is lit by the everlasting tropical sun. All this and more is to be found at the romantic Dusit Laguna on the exotic island paradise of Phuket.

Classic simplicity and elegance are the hallmarks of the resort's rooms and suites. A king-size bed is crowned with a white, damask canopy. Golden brown interiors are suffused with discreet lamps,

while outside, sunlit balconies overlook the magnificently landscaped gardens.

Exquisite regional and international cuisine can be enjoyed at the hotel's four restaurants and two bars. Immaculately prepared Thai dishes, freshly barbecued seafood, cool refreshing drinks and delicious snacks are all available, accompanied by Thai musicians and the famous Phuket sunset.

The hotel's wedding package, including a Thai Buddhist ceremony, complete with three Buddhist monks, photographer, room upgrade, flowers and garlands, plus champagne breakfast and a candlelit Thai dinner, is available on request.

249

 US$270 (214)

 US$430-750 (12)

US$18-50

US$14

Honeymoon specials

Honeymooners are guaranteed a king-size bed, complimentary fruit and flowers, a honeymoon cake and a bottle of wine on arrival. A splendid Thai wedding ceremony is available.

Sightseeing and leisure

Beauty salon and massage by appointment. Angsana Spa with massages and body treatments. Jungle treks on elephants, Jeep safaris, canoe trips to nearby islands and visits to Wat Chalong, Phuket's largest temple. Mountain biking, sailing, scuba diving, windsurfing, fishing, canoeing, swimming, beach volleyball, tennis, table tennis, fitness room and golf nearby.

Le Royal Meridien
Baan Taling Ngam

Information & Reservations
UK 0870 606 1296
INT. +44 870 606 1296

295 Moo 3
Taling Ngam Beach
Koh Samui
Suratthani 84140
Thailand

✈ Koh Samui 45km

tel +66 77 423 019
fax +66 77 423 220

talingng@samart.co.th
www.meridien-samui.com

UK Elegant Resorts

250

Set among the green trees of a coconut plantation, overlooking one of Koh Samui's most beautiful beaches, Baan Taling Ngam lives up to its translation of 'your home on a beautiful cliff'.

The secluded grounds of the resort hide beautifully deluxe rooms and suites, luxury villas and the premier accommodation, the Royal Villa, or Baan Napa. All have traditional teak interiors and private balconies or patios. If you'd prefer to be closer to the soft sands, take one of the beach suites.

Dining takes place in the clifftop Lom Talay restaurant, which serves exceptional Mediterranean and Thai cuisine, or try the delicious fresh seafood in the seafront Promenade restaurant. You'll certainly have worked up an appetite with all the facilities the hotel offers. Snorkel, dive, windsurf, or waterski in the tranquil waters of the Ang Thong Marine National Park that surrounds the resort. Or you can take a romantic sunset island cruise. Back on dry land, mountain biking or four-wheel drive safaris are easily arranged.

Whatever you choose, the massage, sauna or dip in one of the seven hilltop pools will help you wind down ready for the next perfect day in paradise.

 US$200-3,000 (40)

 US$300-3,000 (37 villas/suites)

 US$20-50

 US$17

Honeymoon specials
Complimentary bottle of white wine, honeymoon cake, rose petal in heart shape at turndown, honeymoon card from the manager, fruit basket and flowers, brass bell. The hotel also offers wedding and other tailormade packages and are available on request.

Sightseeing and leisure
Full range of hair styling and beauty treatments, therapeutic massage on site plus sauna and workout facilities. The hotel also boasts seven outdoor pools, licensed PADI dive school, tennis courts, mountain biking, snorkelling, kayaking plus most other watersports. Nearby, Ang Thong Marine National Park, Chawaeng beach, butterfly farm, Hin Ta Hin Yai.

Paradise Beach Resort

Information & Reservations
UK 0870 606 1296
INT. +44 870 606 1296

18/8 Maenam Beach
Koh Samui 84330
Thailand

✈ Koh Samui 10 mins

tel +66 77 247 227/32
fax +66 77 425 290

paradise@loxinfo.co.th
www.kohsamui.net/paradise/

Tour operators:
UK Kuoni

Member of:
Swiss International Hotels

Nestled on the shores of the central part of Thailand's tranquil Maenam Beach in a luscious tropical garden, this small, personal resort offers you the chance to truly relax and get away from it all in an island Eden.

Endless white beaches welcome sun and sea lovers and watersports enthusiasts. Or guests can relax around the resort's sparkling freshwater swimming pools or take a dip in the jacuzzi.

All rooms have private balcony or verandah and are creatively furnished in bright colours and provide modern comforts such as air conditioning, mini-bar, refrigerator, satellite TV and video.

The Paradise Terrace is a beachfront restaurant where you can feast on fine Thai cuisine and a wide range of fresh fish and local specialities, or try the Roma for a delicious taste of Italy.

And from the comfort of your sunlounger at Paradise Beach you can decide which excursions to take – ranging from a variety of sightseeing tours, diving, deep sea fishing, island hopping and even a romantic moonlight cruise.

251

 US$132-185 (86)

 US$153-206 (19 villas)

 US$13-30

 US$8

Honeymoon specials
Complimentary flowers, fruits and sparkling wine. Welcome drink. Candlelight dinner and room upgrade when available. A Buddhist ceremony with blessing by monks is available.

Sightseeing and leisure
Two freshwater swimming pools, jacuzzi, watersports, diving, deep sea fishing, island hopping and moonlit cruises. Big Buddha, waterfalls, monkey theatre, Angthong National Park.

Information & Reservations
UK 0870 606 1296
INT. +44 870 606 1296

The Tongsai Bay

84 Moo 5
Bophut
Koh Samui
Surat Thani 84320
Thailand

✈ Koh Samui 3km

tel +66 2 254 0056/62
fax +66 2 254 0054/55

info@tongsaibay.co.th
www.tongsaibay.co.th

252

Peace. Quiet. Stunning private bay and beach. Twenty-five acres of colourful tropical gardens. Romantic. Secluded. This is Tongsai Bay.

When the resort was built in 1986, the owner didn't cut down one single tree. The land on the hill was so naturally beautiful that the cottages were built around the existing vegetation and native coconut palms. It could even be said that Mother Nature is the real architect here.

The new Tongsai Grand Villas, which opened in December 1998, are specially created for romance. Muslin curtains frame the beds and every room has an open-air terrace from which to sneak panoramic views of this idyllic tropical hideaway. In these, the air-conditioned bedrooms alone are 54 square metres, with polished teak floor, rattan furniture, celadon lamps and lovely Thai silk curtains.

The huge, open-air Maka-wood terrace provides the *piece de resistance*: open-air bathtubs where you can lie back and soak up the incredible views. There is even a romantic gazebo where you can sleep, and while dozing off, gaze at the moon and stars above (mosquito net included).

Style runs throughout Tongsai where there are three restaurants with some of the best Thai food on the island — and three bars for the discerning palette.

US$256–1,282 (87)

US$26–64

US$14

🍾 ⚭ ⓢ

Honeymoon specials
Welcome drink, bottle of wine, fruit basket and flowers on arrival.

Sightseeing and leisure
On-site facilities include windsurfing, catamaran sailing and other watersports, as well as tennis courts, snooker room, swimming pool and exercise room. You can also have massages on the beach. Nearby are the Hin Lat and Na Muang waterfalls, Samui Hin, one of the highest points on Koh Samui, the unique stone formations of Hin Yai, Big Buddha Temple.

www.SpecialHotels.com

Want to know **more** about some of the

            special hotels featured

                 in this **collection?**

           Why not use our new on-line

          interactive brochure...

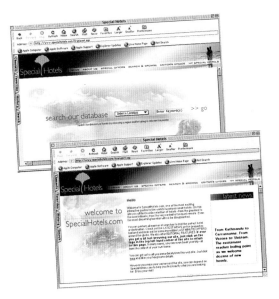

● Guided tour of each hotel with more pictures and detailed information of facilities, colourful travel pieces, itineraries and up-to-the-minute weather reports.

● Instant email link-up and on-line booking facilities.

● Choose your favourite hotels and create a personalised shortlist, and enjoy exclusive benefits by becoming a registered user of www.SpecialHotels.com.

● Read what our writers have to say about their travel experiences. Why not let us know of your experiences by using our 'Feedback' facility?

● www.SpecialHotels.com is the easy route to making your world-class hotel reservation today.

Vietnam

flying time
To: Hanoi, Ho Chi
Minh City
London: 13 hrs
There are six flights
a day to Danang Int.

**climate/
when to go**
The weather is
tropical in the south
and monsoonal in
the north, bringing a
hot, rainy season
from mid-May to
mid-Sept and a
warm, dry season
from mid-October
to mid-March. When
one region is wet or
cold, or steamy hot,
there is always
somewhere else
that is sunny.

currency
Dong

getting around
Flights are relatively
expensive. Slow and
overcrowded buses
run just about
everywhere at rock-
bottom fares. Train
travel can be even
slower but is more
comfortable.
Vietnamese law does
not allow foreigners
to drive.

The name Vietnam was
once synonymous with a
brutal jungle war and the spectacular
failure of American power.

More recently, however, the country has opened up
as a holiday destination with its incredible beauty,
fascinating history and culture and delicious cuisine.
Four great religions and philosophies have shaped
Vietnam – Confucianism, Taoism, Buddhism and
Christianity – resulting in one of the most
fascinating mixes of people and beliefs you could
find anywhere. Vietnamese food also offers an
amazing variety – there are said to be nearly 500
different traditional dishes.
So obviously there is a phenomenal amount to see
and do – or you could simply opt to get away from
it all and relax on a stunning beach.
Ho Chi Minh City (what was Saigon) is truly the
heart and soul of Vietnam. The streets are a myriad
of shops, stalls and vendors, and amidst all this
frenzied activity you will also find the timeless
traditions and beauty of the ancient culture.
The capital, Hanoi, is smaller, quieter and greener
than Ho Chi Minh City and has the feel of a French
provincial city, though with all the development going
on in the country, this is changing fast.
The city of Danang was a strategic air and sea port
during the Indochinese war and nearby, China Beach
was made famous during the war era as American
servicemen went there for their in-country R&R,
attracted by the beautiful sandy beaches.

Furama Resort Danang

Information & Reservations
UK 0870 606 1296
INT. +44 870 606 1296

68 Ho Xuan Huong St
China Beach
Danang City
Vietnam

✈ Danang Int. 7km

tel +84 511 847 333
fax +84 511 847 666

furamadn@hn.vnn.vn
www.furamavietnam.com

Situated on the famous China Beach, the luxury Furama Resort Danang is setting new standards of excellence in Vietnam. Recently voted 'Asia's Best Resort Hotel' by the prestigious American magazine *Epicurean Review*, the magnificent hotel blends French colonial style with traditional Vietnamese architecture.

Designed to blend with the natural environment, the resort is a low-rise development on a site which has been luxuriantly landscaped with indigenous vegetation and trees. You'll get your first glimpse of the sea and beach upon arrival in the main entrance hall. Each of the beautifully designed rooms and suites features a balcony with a private view of either the ocean or the garden and freshwater lagoon. And the beach simply has to be seen to be believed – stretches of white sand that seem to go on forever and are never crowded.

When (or if) you tire of soaking up the sun on your stunning beach, there is a wide variety of sports and leisure facilities. Watersports include a scuba diving school with experienced international instructors, waterskiing, snorkelling, speed boats and trimaran sailing.

And for sustenance during your visit, the resort offers a choice of three restaurants with culinary temptations ranging from exotic Vietnamese flavours to Continental cuisine.

255

 US$140-190 (152)

 US$200-400 (46)

US$5-28

US$8-12

Honeymoon specials

20% room discount for a minimum stay of three consecutive nights; 30% room discount for a minimum stay of five consecutive nights. Plus, free use of health club, sauna, steambath, tennis courts and the huge jacuzzi lagoon.

Sightseeing and leisure

Explore Vietnam's stunning cultural heritage including the ancient seaport of Hoi An, the former imperial capital Hue and the Holy Valley of My Son (classified World Heritage sites by UNESCO). The famous Cham Museum and the mystic grottos of Marble Mountains are within 15 minutes drive of the resort.

South Pacific

flying time
To: Fiji, NZ and
Cook's via
Rarotonga, and Bora
Bora via Tahiti
London: 22-25 hrs
LA: 12-14 hrs
NY: 18-20 hrs

**climate/
when to go**
Tropical and pleasant
all year. Average
annual temperature
is 25°C.

currency
The Fijian dollar;
New Zealand dollar
in NZ & the Cook's;
Central Pacific Franc
(CFP) in Bora Bora.
US dollars welcome
almost everywhere.

language
English is generally
spoken along with
the indigenous South
Pacific languages.

getting around
Frequent inter-island
air services. Often
islands can be
reached by ship or
launch. On the
ground, local taxis
are available in main
centres. In New
Zealand, car hire is
the best option.

key to hotels

Bora Bora
1   Bora Bora Lagoon Resort
2   Sofitel Coralia Motu Bora Bora

Cook Islands
3   Aitutaki Lagoon Resort

Fiji
4   Turtle Island Resort
5   Vomo Island Resort

New Zealand
6   Huka Lodge, Taupo

NORTH PACIFIC OCEAN

FIJI

COOK ISLANDS

BORA BORA

Auckland
NEW ZEALAND

SOUTH PACIFIC OCEAN

Few places in the world can match the romance, magic and allure of the South Pacific islands.

Fiji, the Cook Islands, Bora Bora, Vanuatu, Tongo and New Zealand, to name but a few, are magical places to visit. It is hard to find anywhere more remote than these lonely outposts, but what they lack in ease of access they more than make up for in the sheer beauty and romance of their setting and atmosphere.

The Cook's 15 islands occupy just 93sq miles amidst 850,000sq miles of ocean. Rarotonga, the main island, is spectacular, with mist-capped mountains and dense jungle. Protected by a coral reef, it has palm-fringed beaches and clear waters teeming with fish. Here, and on Aitutaki (said to have one of the finest lagoons in the Pacific), there are picture-postcard beaches.

Like the Cook Islands, the island of Bora Bora is a copywriter's delight. Words flow as easily as the peaceful and unhurried days in this warm and sunny climate to conjure up everyone's idea of the South Pacific. Colourful lagoons, perfect breakers thundering on the distant reef, coral gardens alive with fish, soft breezes in the palms, warm sand drifting through warm

toes: this could be Heaven on earth. So, too, with Fiji, a sophisticated tropical idyll with marvellous beaches, colourful coral reefs and rose-tinted sunsets straight from a picture book.

And for a slightly different journey in the South Pacific, try New Zealand, the land of adventure sports. Both heli-skiing and bungee jumping are a part of everyday life here. But it's also the land of a thousand shades of green, and in the countryside you can discover endless fields, tumbling waterfalls and icy glaciers. And if nothing else, relax beside Lake Taupo, New Zealand's largest lake formed in a volcanic crater.

Information & Reservations
UK 0870 606 1296
INT. +44 870 606 1296

Bora Bora Lagoon Resort

Motu Tooppau
B.P. 175
Vaitape
Bora Bora

✈ Bora Bora 20mins (by boat)

tel +689 60 40 00
fax +689 60 40 01

bblr@mail.pf
www.boraboralagoonresort.orient
-express.com

258

Tour operators:
UK Elegant Resorts
US Islands in the Sun

Member of:
The Leading Hotels of the World

Discovered by Captain Cook in 1769, Bora Bora has been described as the most beautiful island in the world. And set on an atoll in the midst of this paradise's crystal clear lagoon is Bora Bora Lagoon Resort, the ultimate in romantic getaways.

You sleep in a 528 square foot bungalow modelled on a traditional Tahitian home. Thatched roofs and gleaming wood interiors house king-sized beds, separate seating area and individual sundeck. The magnificent over-water bungalows offer private swimming areas and, spectacularly, an illuminated glass coffee table to view – and even feed – the colourful marine life without getting your feet wet.

And dining is always special here. Whether you sample the five-star cuisine at the over-water Otemanu restaurant, informal menus at the Café Fare, buffet or á la carte, or dine al fresco at one of the weekly Tahitian feasts, you won't be disappointed.

During the day you can canoe across the lagoon or swim with turtles at the nearby Lagoonarium. Feed sharks on the nearby reef, take a 4x4 excursion into the main island's lush interior, or simply relax on the talcum-fine sand and enjoy the silence that characterises this magical resort.

 US$520-710 (78)

 US$820 (2)

 US$55-80

 included

Honeymoon specials
Exotic fruit basket, champagne, flowers on bed on arrival.

Sightseeing and leisure
The hotel is located on a private island where the main attraction is the lagoon and most of the activities are focused here, including complimentary snorkelling, sailing and canoeing. Waterskiing, deep sea fishing, scuba diving and shark-feeding are other attractions. Complimentary use of outdoor pool, two flood-lit tennis courts and gym.

Sofitel
Coralia Motu Bora Bora

Information & Reservations
UK 0870 606 1296
INT. +44 870 606 1296

B.P. 516-98730 Nunue
Bora Bora

✈ Bora Bora 20 mins (by boat)

tel +689 60 56 00
fax +689 60 56 66

H8989@accor-hotels.com
Reservation_Tahiti@accor-hotels.com

Situated on its own tiny, palm-clad islet (or 'motu') in the turquoise seas surrounding Bora Bora in French Polynesia, Sofitel Coralia Motu is a new resort that eschews luxury swimming pools and saunas in favour of purity and natural beauty.

Coral gardens teeming with marine life skirt its three private, white beaches, ripe for exploring in your snorkelling gear, while magnificent views of the famous Bora Bora lagoon and Mount Otemanu can be enjoyed above the shimmering waters.

If you crave a little more sophistication, a complimentary five-minute shuttle service will whisk you to the mainland and Motu's nearby sister hotel on Bora Bora whenever you wish, where you can enjoy unlimited access to the Sofitel Marara's swimming pool, tennis courts and many other facilities.

Otherwise, you should find everything your heart desires on this little piece of pure paradise. Thirty thatched bungalows with coconut-matted walls offer all mod cons. Choose from one of 20 built over the water, with wooden decks and glass 'windows' in the floor from which to view the colourful, watery tableau, or from the remaining 10 bungalows set on stilts on the beach or among the trees on the surrounding hillside.

259

Honeymoon specials
Special wedding ceremonies arranged, which include dinner, champagne and complimentary fruit cocktails, traditional dance and music, and a videotape of the occasion.

Sightseeing and leisure
Jeep safaris, helicopter tours, snorkelling and scuba diving, shark feeding, parasailing, nature walks and many other excursions and tours. Car and bike rental. Massage.

US$540-688 (30 bungalows)

US$55-80

US$20

Information & Reservations
UK 0870 606 1296
INT. +44 870 606 1296

Aitutaki Lagoon Resort

PO Box 99
Aitutaki
Cook Islands

✈ Aitutaki 7 mins

tel +682 31 201
fax +682 31 202

260

This beautiful, romantic tropical island hideaway gives you the chance to truly get away from it all. The island is located 140 miles north of Rarotonga, the capital of the Cook Islands (approximately 45 minutes by air) and is one of just 15 in the Cook Islands' group. The resort is located on a secluded inlet linked by a causeway to the main island.

You can choose from deluxe beach, lagoon view or garden accommodation, all with secluded private terrace, plus mod cons such as fridge, direct dial phones, mini-bar and en suite bathroom. For the ultimate in relaxation, enjoy drinks at the beach bar or swimming pool, dance to the island's string band, immerse yourself in the culture of the islands with twice weekly cultural shows, or try the famous seafood buffet every Wednesday night.

A range of watersports is also available. Choose from snorkelling, diving, windsurfing, game fishing and kayaking. For exploring this luscious island there is a lagoon cruise and organised island tours. If you would rather explore on your own, hire a car, or perhaps rent a bike and cycle your way round.

NZ$305-665 (25)

NZ$665 (5)

NZ$12-45

NZ$16.50-25

Honeymoon specials
Fruit bowl, flowers and champagne on arrival.

Sightseeing and leisure
Complimentary snorkelling, kayaks, canoes and windsurfing. There is a golf course 10 minutes from the resort and the locals are often willing to lend guests their golf clubs, balls, etc. A bustling market is nearby. Boat trips to feed the fish in the lagoon and island tours can be arranged.

Information & Reservations
UK 0870 606 1296
INT. +44 870 606 1296

Turtle Island Resort

Fiji

✈ Viti Levu 45 miles

c/o Turtle Island Holidays
Level 1, Rialto North Tower
525 Collins St, Melbourne
Vic 3000 Australia

tel +61 3 9 618 1100
fax +61 3 9 618 1199
USA contact: +800 255 4347
info@turtlefiji.com.au
www.turtlefiji.com

Tour operators:
UK Seasons in Style
Tailor Made Travel

Member of:
Small Luxury Hotels of the World

Turtle Island, Fiji, has been voted one of the 'Top 10 Most Romantic Resorts Worldwide' and has recently won the 1999 British Airways 'Tourism for Tomorrow Award' (Pacific) and the '1999 Green Hotelier Award' for environmental achievement.

A five-star resort on a 500-acre privately owned Fijian island, it is an unspoiled tropical treasure and a journey into Fijian culture. Situated on the famous Blue Lagoon, it is home to just 14 couples. Fourteen separate powder sand beaches and 100 friendly Fijian staff make this an island jewel.

The charming Fijian-style two-room cottages (*bures*) situated alongside the Blue Lagoon have a four-poster bed, verandah with day bed for napping in the sun-flecked shade of the palms, and an indoor jacuzzi which set the scene for romance.

Guests can enjoy world-class cuisine with a gourmet picnic on a private beach or dinner on a pontoon under the stars. Exquisite food, all drinks including French champagnes, all activities and use of entire island are included in the pre-paid tariff.

Turtle Island is more than a honeymoon. It is a life experience. It is where you bathe in the delights which have been lost to modern society… the warm Fijian staff, the beauty of an island untouched by industry, where the ecology is a primary concern and where people understand that your honeymoon is special and can never be recreated.

261

from US$545* pppn (14)

included

included

(incl)

Honeymoon specials

Grand Wedding package includes marriage license, transport along the lagoon to open-air chapel by *billi billi* (wedding raft), wedding bouquet, Fijian apparel, flower leis, choir, minister, video, Fijian band, Kava ceremony, wedding feast and cake, beverages, film and Tapa bound wedding album. Price: US$2,000 fully inclusive. Seaplane transfers US$690.
*All prices subject to 10% tax.

Sightseeing and leisure

Turtle Island is one of the most secluded and romantic islands in the South Pacific. All activities – deep sea fishing, diving, horseriding, mountain biking, snorkelling, jungle and mountain walks, windsurfing, private beach picnics, sailing, fly fishing, tours, sunrise champagne breakfasts, Kava ceremonies and more are included in the price. Also, visit the local village church or school or take a sunset champagne cruise.

Information & Reservations
UK 0870 606 1296
INT. +44 870 606 1296

Vomo Island Resort

PO Box 5650
Lautoka
Fiji

✈ Nadi Int. 30km

tel +679 668 133
fax +679 668 500

vomo@is.com.fj
www.vomofiji.com

262

Vomo and Vomo Lailai islands cover approximately 90 hectares, all of which are exclusively for Vomo Island Resort guests. This resort lies among exotic mango forests, coconut groves and golden unspoiled beaches with stunning reefs.

There are only 30 spacious villas, some nestled in tropical gardens just steps away from the beach, and others are located on the slopes of Vomo's mountain. Inside, guests can enjoy the luxury of exquisite hardwood flooring, tropical furniture and original oil paintings and each villa opens onto its own private *lanai* where you can enjoy incredible ocean views. Each villa also has its own jacuzzi.

Three restaurants offer imaginative dining in natural settings and live music can be enjoyed at both the Reef Lounge and the Rocks Bar.

There are plenty of opportunities to keep entertained as well, with spectacular snorkelling and scuba diving around the abundantly populated reefs, as well as deep sea fishing, windsurfing, sailing and a host of dry-land sports.

For the ultimate in luxury and romance, guests can order a gourmet picnic basket and explore Vomo Lailai, or if that all sounds too energetic, deluxe double hammocks are scattered along the beaches to encourage some serious relaxation.

🛏 US$660-770 (28)

US$1,150-1,350 (1)

🍽 included

☕ included

Honeymoon specials

Bottle of wine on arrival. Fruit bowl. Upgrade subject to availability. Picnic to own private honeymoon island subject to availability.

Sightseeing and leisure

There is a beauty therapy centre on site, plus a wide range of water and land sports including a par-3 golf course. Guests can also explore the island with trips to a Fijian village or join the turtle watching programme.

Elegant Resorts

Your honeymoon is a once-in-a-lifetime experience. We at Elegant Resorts know this only too well and go to the ends of the earth to create and offer you blissful, tailormade honeymoons to some of the most exotic destinations around the world.

Our philosophy is to provide the finest quality holidays backed by a personal service that is second to none.

We pride ourselves on offering a unique collection of some of the most splendid destinations – some wild, some remote and simple, others sophisticated and opulent, and with every conceivable amenity.

Whether your dreams take you off on a yacht around the Caribbean, a romantic tour of Tuscany, a city break to Prague, a skiing trip to the picture-postcard Rockies, or an exotic adventure in Southeast Asia, we will take care of every detail, leaving you free to concentrate on the details of the big day, and more importantly, on each other. Our team of experts, with their highly creative approach, extensive knowledge of worldwide venues and unrivalled attention to detail, can provide a programme tailormade to meet your every need.

All our brochures (*listed to the right*) reflect the exclusivity of our holidays and each one is full of imaginative ideas for discerning travellers.

CONTACT
Call for a copy of one of our brochures and let Elegant Resorts make your dream a reality.
- Caribbean
- Worldwide
- Europe
- Skiing
- Villas Caribbean
- Villas Europe

tel +44 (0) 1244 350408
fax +44 (0) 1244 897750
enquiries@elegantresorts.co.uk
www.elegantresorts.co.uk

263

New Zealand

New Zealand

flying time
To: Auckland
London: 24 hrs
NY: 18 hrs

**climate/
when to go**
Weather conditions
can change rapidly
and dramatically, but
on the whole it is
pleasant year-round.
The South Island has
a wet climate to the
west and is dry to
the east. Both islands
receive snow in
winter, which falls
June-Aug. Summer
runs from Dec-Feb.

264

currency
NZ dollar

language
English

getting around
Most forms of travel
are affordable, safe
and clean. There is
an extensive bus
network, trains are
modern and
comfortable and
car and bicycle hire
is popular and
recommended. You
can also get some
great deals on
internal flights,
worthwhile for the
views alone.

A land of dramatic contrasts, New Zealand is also one of the most relaxed places on earth, the perfect place to unwind and enjoy life.

The rolling green hills of the North Island with its stunning lakes and clear rivers gives way to dramatic alpine and fjordland scenery of the South Island.

This is the land of adventure sports. Bungee jumping was invented here, while heli-skiing is a way of life in the mountains. Take to the skies again to discover the dramatic scenery in either the North or South island before taking a four-wheeled drive vehicle to reach the most inaccessible and romantic of the lakes and mountains.

Bathe in hot springs or just gaze in awe at the bubbling mud pools and spouting geysers. Discover tumbling waterfalls, icy glaciers and meandering rivers. Relax beside Lake Taupo, New Zealand's largest lake, formed in a volcanic crater or head to the dizzy heights of the country's tallest mountain, Mount Cook.

The coastline is as stunning as the interior with wonderful, wide sunswept beaches, rocky headlands and tiny, secluded coves. Swim, sail or just simply lie on the sand and watch the world go by.

Sample wines from some of the world's most celebrated vineyards or discover old gold towns, Art Deco architecture and picturesque harbour towns. Learn of the ancient Maori culture or indulge in a haggis and bagpipe evening in the 'Scottish' town of Dunedin. Its cities are fabulous, too. Tour the charming capital of Wellington or travel over the Canterbury plains to the garden city of Christchurch, before discovering the delights of the bustling harbour city of Auckland, known as the 'City of Sails'.

Huka Lodge

Information & Reservations
UK 0870 606 1296
INT. +44 870 606 1296

Huka Falls Road
PO Box 95
Taupo
New Zealand

✈ Taupo 8km

tel +64 7 378 5791
fax +64 7 378 0427

reservations@hukalodge.com
www.hukalodge.com

Member of:
Small Luxury Hotels of the World
The Leading Small Hotels of the
World

Truly get away from it all at Huka Lodge on the banks of the Waikato River above the mighty Huka Falls, where a natural paradise awaits. The lodge is set in seven hectares of park-like grounds and has just 27 guestrooms. These are all tucked along the riverbank for the ultimate in privacy and enclosed by towering trees.

The main lodge has an understated elegance and is a welcoming haven with blazing log fires. Antique country furniture is complemented by woven wool fabrics and carpets that reflect the richness of the surroundings. The intense deep greens and blues echo the river and forests, and touches of red mirror the spectacular southern sunsets.

Dining options are unlimited. Guests can eat where their mood takes them – the terrace, the library, the wine cellar, the garden – and an elegant setting will be specially arranged, for an intimate experience showcasing the very best of New Zealand's food and wine. To further enhance the experience, Huka's cellar contains over 30,000 bottles of fine wines from around the world.

Relaxation is the order of the day at this sanctuary. Try your hand at fishing, coupled with a wide variety of excursions – including heli-fishing – in outstanding wilderness surroundings.

265

NZ$480-1,080 (23)

NZ$790-1,770 (4)

NZ$150

NZ$40

Honeymoon specials

A complimentary copy of The Huka Lodge Dessert Cookbook.

Sightseeing and leisure

An enormous range of different fishing experiences are available, as are a myriad of other activities. Try horseriding, waterskiing on Lake Taupo, tandem skydiving, sailing or white water rafting. Wairakei International Golf Course is also nearby.

WEDDINGS ABROAD DIRECTORY

	Licensed for weddings	Wedding co-ordinator available	Prior registration with local authorities for wedding couples	Music for ceremony arranged	Photographs for ceremony arranged	Honeymoon packages	Wedding packages	Wine/champagne on arrival	All-inclusive	Reception facilities	24-hour room service	Limousine/car service for honeymooners	Special Honeymoon Suite	Beach wedding
Aitutaki Lagoon Resort, Cook Islands	●	●	★	●	●	●	●	●	●	●				●
Al Bustan Palace Hotel, Oman	●	●	●	●	●	●	●	●	●	●	●	●	●	●
Albergo Pietrasanta, Italy	●	●	★	●	●	●	●	●		●	●		●	
Arlberg Hospiz Hotel, Austria	●	●	●	●	●	●	●	●		●	●	●	●	
Ballylickey Manor House, Ireland								●		●				
Baron Resort, Egypt	●	●	●	●	●	●	●	●	●	●	●	●	●	●
Baros Holiday Resort, Maldives	●	●		●	●	●	●	●	●	●	●	●	●	●
Bay, The, South Africa	●	●		●	●	●	●	●		●	●	●	●	
Beaufort, The, England						●		●	●			★	●	
Begawan Giri, Bali	●	●	●	●	●	●	●	●		●	●	●	●	
Benguerra Lodge, Benguerra Island	★					★	★	●						●
Blue Waters Inn, Speyside, Tobago		●												●
Bora Bora Lagoon Resort, Fr. Polynesia		●				●	●	●	●	●			●	●
Brufani Palace, Italy						●		●		●	●		●	
Cambridge Beaches, Bermuda	●	●		●	●	●	●	●		●	●	●	●	
Casa No.7, Spain						★		★			★	★		
Charleston Place, South Carolina	●	●		●	●	●	●	●	●	●	●	●	●	
Château de Bagnols, France				●	●	●				●	●		●	
Château De Feuilles, Seychelles	●	★		●	●	●	●	●		●	●		●	
Château des Vigiers, France				●	●	●	●			●	●		●	
Château Eza, France				●	●	●					●		●	
Chewton Glen Hotel, England	●	●		●	●		●	●		●				
Ciragan Palace Hotel Kempinski, Turkey	●	●		●	●	●	●	●		●	●	●	●	
Colony Club Hotel, Barbados	●	●		●	●	●	●	●		●	●	●	●	●
Couples Negril, Jamaica	●	●	●	●	●	●	●	●	●	●	●	●	●	
Couples Ocho Rios, Jamaica	●	●	●	●	●	●	●	●	●	●	●	●	●	
Damai Lovina Villas, Bali	●	●	●	●	●	●	●	●		●	●	●	●	
Dan Eilat, Israel	●	●		●	●	●	●	●		●	●		●	
Datai Langkawi, The, Malaysia		●	★	●	●	●	●	●		●	●		●	
Dusit Laguna, Thailand	●		●	●	●	●	●	●		●	●		●	
Eilat Princess Hotel, Israel	★	●	●	●	●	●	●	●		●	●	★	●	★
Elounda Mare Hotel, Greece	★			●	●	●		●		●	●		●	
Excelsior Palace Hotel, Italy				●	●	●		●	●	●	★		●	
Four Seasons Hotel, Cyprus	●	●	★	●	●	●	●	●		●	●	●	●	★

Information supplied by hotels and correct at the time of going to press.
● Denotes the hotel provides the indicated service. ★ Please contact the hotel direct regarding this facility.

	Licensed for weddings	Wedding co-ordinator available	Prior registration with local authorities for wedding couples	Music for ceremony arranged	Photographs for ceremony arranged	Honeymoon packages	Wedding packages	Wine/champagne on arrival	All-inclusive	Reception facilities	24-hour room service	Limousine/car service for honeymooners	Special Honeymoon Suite	Beach wedding
Fulbari Resort, Nepal	•	•	•	•	•	•		•		•	•	•	•	
Full Moon Beach, Maldives						•		•		•	•		•	
Funzi Keys, The, Kenya						•		•	•					
Furama Resort Danang, Vietnam		•		•	•	•	•	•	•	•	•	•	•	•
Galley Bay, Antigua	•	•	•	•	•	•	•	•	•	•		•	•	•
Glitter Bay, Barbados	•	•	•	•	•	•	•	•	★	•	•	•	•	•
Grand Hotel Excelsior Vittoria, Italy	•	•	•	•	•	•	•	•		•	•	•	•	
Grand Hotel Fasano, Italy										•	•	•	•	
Grand Hotel Villa Igiea, Italy			•	•	•	•		•		•	•	•	•	
Grand Hotel Zermatterhof, Switzerland			•	•	•	•		★		•	•	•	•	
Half Moon Club, Jamaica		•		•	•	•	•	•		•			•	•
Hermitage, The, Nevis	•		•	•	•	•	•	•		•	•	•	•	
Hide Safari Camp, The, Zimbabwe	•	•	•	•	•			•		•			•	
Horizons and Cottages, Bermuda	•	•	•	•	•			•		•	•		•	
Hotel Alfonso XIII, Spain		•		•	•	•		•		•	•	•	•	
Hotel Casa Del Mar, California	•	•		•	•			•		•	•	•	•	★
Hôtel de la Cité, France		•	•	•	•	•				•	•		•	
Hotel du Palais, France		•		•	•	•	•			•	•		•	
Hotel Gabbia D'Oro, Italy	★	•		•	•	•	•			•	•		•	
Hotel Guanahani, St Barts		•		•	•			•		•	•		•	•
Hotel Hoffmeister, Czech Republic		★	★	•	•			•		•	•		•	
Hotel Im Palais Schwarzenberg, Austria		•		•	•			•		•	•		•	
Hotel La Bobadilla, Spain	•	•	•	•	•	•	•	•		•	•		•	
Hotel L'Archipel, Seychelles	•	•	•	•	•	•		•		•			•	★
Hotel Londra Palace, Italy			•	•	•			•			•		•	
Hotel Lungarno, Italy		•		•	•			•		•		•	•	
Hotel Makanda by the Sea, Costa Rica	•			•	•			•					•	•
Hotel Martinez, France								•		•	•		•	
Hotel Monasterio, Peru					•			•		•	•		•	
Hotel Pariz, Czech Republic	•	•	•	•	•	•	•	•		•	•	•	•	
Hôtel Plaza Athénée, New York	•	•	•	•	•	•	•	•		•	•	•	•	
Hotel Puente Romano, Spain				•	•	•		•		•		•	•	
Hotel Punta Islita, Costa Rica	•	•	•	•	•	•	•	•	•	•			•	•
Hotel Quinta do Lago, Portugal	•	•		•	•			•		•	•		•	

Information supplied by hotels and correct at the time of going to press.
• Denotes the hotel provides the indicated service. ★ Please contact the hotel direct regarding this facility.

	Licensed for weddings	Wedding co-ordinator available	Prior registration with local authorities for wedding couples	Music for ceremony arranged	Photographs for ceremony arranged	Honeymoon packages	Wedding packages	Wine/champagne on arrival	All-inclusive	Reception facilities	24-hour room service	Limousine/car service for honeymooners	Special Honeymoon Suite	Beach wedding
Hotel Royal Monceau, France						●	●	●	●	●	●		●	
Hotel Schloss Monchstein, Austria	●	●	●	●	●	●	●	●		●		●	●	
Hotel Splendido & Splendido Mare, It.			●	●	●	●	●	●		●		●	●	
Hotel Tugu Bali, Bali	●	●	●	●	●	●	●	●		●		●	●	●
Hotel Villa del Sol, Mexico	●	●	●	●	●	●	●	●		●		●	●	●
Hotel Yak & Yeti, Nepal		●		●	●	●	●			●	●		●	
Hoteldorf Gruner Baum, Austria	●	●	●	●	●	●	●	●		●		●	●	
Huka Lodge, New Zealand	●	●		●	●	●	●			●			●	
Imba Matombo, Zimbabwe		●	★	●	●	●	●			●			●	
Jerusalem Hotel, Israel				●	●	●	●			●	●		●	
Kempinski Resort Hotel Estepona, Spn.		●	●	●	●	●	●	★		●	●	★	●	
Kinasi, Ma'fia Island, Tanzania	●	★	★	●	★	●	●		●	●	★		●	★
Kivotos Clubhotel, Greece	●	●	●	●	●	●	●	●		●	●		●	●
Krone Assmannshausen, Germany				●	●	●	●			●			●	
La Digue Island Lodge, Seychelles	●	●		●	●	●	●			●			●	●
La Mamounia, Morocco				●	●	●		●		●	●	●	●	
La Samanna, St Martin	●	●	●	●	●	●	●	●		●	●	●	●	●
Laguna Beach, Maldives						●	●			●			●	●
Lapa Palace, Portugal	●			●	●	●	●	●		●	●	●	●	
Lapa Rios, Costa Rica	★		★	★	★		●	★	●	●			●	●
Las Brisas Acapulco, Mexico	●	●		●	●	●	●	●		●	●	●	●	●
Las Dunas Beach Hotel & Spa, Spain				●	●	●	●	●		●	●	●		
Le Meridien Fisherman's Cove, Sey.	●	●	●	●	●	●	●	●		●				●
Le Meridien La Cocoteraie, Guad.			●	●	●	●	●	●		★		●	●	●
Le Meridien Limassol, Cyprus		●	●	●	●	●	●	●		●	●	●	●	★
Le Prince Maurice, Ile Maurice, Mauritius	●	●		●	●	●	●			●	●	●	●	●
Le Royal Mer. Baan Taling Ngam, Thai.	●	●	●	●	●	●	●	●	●	●	●	●	●	●
Lemuria Resort of Praslin, Seychelles	●	●	●	●	●	●	●			●			●	●
Litchfield Plantation, South Carolina	●	●	●	●	●	●	●			●			●	
Little Palm Island, Florida	●	●		●	●	●	●			●			●	●
Longueville Manor, Jersey			●		●		●			●	●		●	
Mago Estate Hotel, St Lucia	●	●	●	●	●		●		●	●			●	●
Mahaweli Reach Hotel, Sri Lanka		●	●	●	●	●	●			●			●	
Marbella Club, Spain		●	●	●	●	●	●	●		●	●	●	●	●

Information supplied by hotels and correct at the time of going to press.
● Denotes the hotel provides the indicated service. ★ Please contact the hotel direct regarding this facility.

	Licensed for weddings	Wedding co-ordinator available	Prior registration with local authorities for wedding couples	Music for ceremony arranged	Photographs for ceremony arranged	Honeymoon packages	Wedding packages	Wine/champagne on arrival	All-inclusive	Reception facilities	24-hour room service	Limousine/car service for honeymooners	Special Honeymoon Suite	Beach wedding
Mas de Torrent, Spain	●	●	●	●	●	●	●	●		●	●	●	●	
Matahari Beach Resort, Bali	●	●	●	●	●	●	●	●		●	●	●	●	●
Mauna Lani Bay, Hawaii	●	●	★	●	●	●	●	●	●	●	●	●	●	★
Migration Camp, Tanzania	●	●	●	●	●	●	●	●	●	●	●		●	
Mombasa Serena Beach Hotel, Kenya	●	●	★	●	●	●	●	●		●	●	●		★
Montanus Hotel, Belgium	★	●	★	●	●	●	●	●		●	●	●	●	
Monte Do Casal, Portugal						●	●			●	●		●	
Montpelier Plantation, Nevis	●	●	●	★	●	●	●		★	●	●		●	●
Mwagusi Safari Camp, Tanzania							●	★			★		★	
Nakatchafushi, Maldives						●	●			●	★		●	
Nusa Dua Beach Hotel & Spa, Bali		●	●	●	●	●	●	★		●		●	●	
Nusa Lembongan Resort, Bali		●	★	●	●	★	★			●			●	●
Ottley's Plantation Inn, St Kitts	●	●	●	●	●	●	●	●	★	●	●	★	●	
Oustau de Baumanière, France	★	★	●	●	●	★	★	●		★		★	★	
Palace Hotel Gstaad, Switzerland		●	●	●	●	●	●			●	●		●	
Palm Island, St Vincent & Grenadines				●	●	●	●	●	●	●			●	●
Palmetto Beach Hotel, Barbuda	●	●	●	●	●					●			●	●
Pamushana, Zimbabwe						●	●		●	●			●	
Paphos Amathus Beach Hotel, Cyprus		●	●	●	●	●	●	●		●	●	●	●	●
Paradise Beach Resort, Thailand		●	●	●	●	●	★	●		●	●		●	●
Paradise Cove Hotel, Mauritius	●	●				●	●	●		●	●		●	●
Park Hotel Delta, Switzerland	●	●				●	●			●	●		●	
Pelangi Beach Resort, Malaysia		●	★	●	●	●	●			●	●	●	●	★
Penang Mutiara Beach Resort, Malaysia	●	●	●	●	●	●	●	●		●	●		●	●
Reid's Palace, Portugal						●	●			●	●		●	
Residence, The, Mauritius	●	●	★	●	●	●	●	●		●	●		●	★
Romantik Hotel le Silve, Italy						●	●			●	●		●	
Romantik Hotel Poseidon, Italy			●			●	●			●	●		●	
Royal Hotel, Italy	★	★	★	●	●	★	★	★		●	●		★	
Royal Pavilion, Barbados	●	●	●	●	●	●	●			●	●		●	●
Saman Villas, Sri Lanka	●	●	●	●	●	●	●	●		●	●		●	
San Domenico Palace, Italy	●	●		●	●		●			●		●		
Santa Marina Hotel, Greece	●	●	●	●	●	●	●			●	●		●	●
Sanyati Lodge, Zimbabwe		●	●	●	●	●	●	●	●	●			●	

	Licensed for weddings	Wedding co-ordinator available	Prior registration with local authorities for wedding couples	Music for ceremony arranged	Photographs for ceremony arranged	Honeymoon packages	Wedding packages	Wine/champagne on arrival	All-inclusive	Reception facilities	24-hour room service	Limousine/car service for honeymooners	Special Honeymoon Suite	Beach wedding
Secret Harbour Resort, Grenada	●	●	●	●	●	●	●	●		●				
Selous Safari, Tanzania	★	★				●	★	●	●	●			●	
Shutters on the Beach, California	★			●	●	●	★	●		●	●	●	●	●
Siboney Beach Club, Antigua	●	●		●	●	●	●	●		●				
Sofitel Coralia Motu Bora Bora, Fr. Poly.								★						
Soneva Fushi Resort, Maldives						●				★	●			
St James's Club, Antigua	●					●	●	●	●	●	●			●
St Nicolas Bay, Greece		●	●	●	●	●	●	●		●	●	●	●	
Stanley & Livingstone, Zimbabwe		●	●	●	●	●	●	●	●	●			●	
Sunset Marquis Hotel & Villas, California		●	●	●	●	●	●	●		●	●	●	●	
Suvretta House, Switzerland		●	●	●	●	●	●	●						
Swept Away, Jamaica	●	●	●	●	●	●	●	●	●	●			★	●
Taplow House Hotel, England	●	●	●	●	●	●	●	●		●			●	
Tsitouras Collection, The, Greece	●	●	●	●	●	●	●	●		●				
Thurnhers Alpenhof, Austria	●	●	●	●	●	●	●	●	●	●	●		●	
Tiger Tops Jungle Lodge, Nepal	★													
Tongsai Bay, The, Thailand	●	●	●	●	●	●	●	★		●			●	
Trident Villas & Hotel, Jamaica	●	●	●	●	●	●	●	●	●	●			●	●
Turtle Island Resort, Fiji	●	●	★	●	●	●	●	●	●	●	★		●	★
Victoria Falls Hotel, Zimbabwe	●	●						●		●	●			
Vomo Island Resort, Fiji	●	●	●	●	●	●	●	●	★	●			●	
Waka Nusa, Bali						●	●						★	
Waka di Ume, Bali						●	●						★	
Waterloo House, Bermuda	●	●	●	●	●	●	●	●		●			●	●
Windsor Court Hotel, Louisiana		●	●	●	●	●	●	●		●	●	●	●	
Xara Palace, The, Malta			●	●	●		●			●	●	●	●	
Zanzibar Serena Inn, Tanzania	●	●	●	●	●	●	★			●			●	●

Information supplied by hotels and correct at the time of going to press.
● Denotes the hotel provides the indicated service. ★ Please contact the hotel direct regarding this facility.

www.SpecialHotels.com

Want to know **more** about some of the

special hotels featured

in this **collection?**

Why not use our new on-line

interactive brochure...

- Guided tour of each hotel with more pictures and detailed information of facilities, colourful travel pieces, itineraries and up-to-the-minute weather reports.

- Instant email link-up and on-line booking facilities.

- Choose your favourite hotels and create a personalised shortlist, and enjoy exclusive benefits by becoming a registered user of www.SpecialHotels.com.

- Read what our writers have to say about their travel experiences. Why not let us know of your experiences by using our 'Feedback' facility?

- www.SpecialHotels.com is the easy route to making your world-class hotel reservation today.

INDEX

272

273

Travel Agents and Tour Operators
United Kingdom & Ireland

Abercrombie & Kent
tel +44 (0)20 7730 9600
fax +44 (0)20 7730 9376

Africa Archipelago
tel +44 (0)20 7471 0780
fax +44 (0)20 7384 9549

Africa Connection
tel +44 (0)1244 355 330
fax +44 (0)1244 355 255

AGA Tourism
tel +44 (0)1462 713 100
fax +44 (0)1462 713 200

Airwaves
tel +44 (0)20 8875 1188
fax +44 (0)20 8871 4668

Amathus Holidays
tel +44 (0)20 7831 2383
fax +44 (0)20 7831 9697

American Way
tel +44 (0)20 8686 9566
fax +44 (0)20 8239 7950

Art of Travel
tel +44 (0)20 7738 2038
fax +44 (0)20 7738 1893

Austravel
tel +44 (0)20 7584 3355
fax +44 (0)20 7838 1022

British Airways Holidays
tel +44 (0)1293 723 161
fax +44 (0)1293 722 624

Cadogan Holidays
tel +44 (0)1703 828 313
fax +44 (0)1703 228 601

Caribbean Connection
tel +44 (0)1244 341 131
fax +44 (0)1244 310 255

Caribtours
tel +44 (0)20 7581 3517
fax +44 (0)20 7225 2491

Carrier
tel +44 (0)1625 582 006
fax +44 (0)1625 586 818

Cazenove & Loyd Safaris
tel +44 (0)20 8875 9666
fax +44 (0)20 8875 9444

Connect AB
tel +44 (0)1753 684 810
fax +44 (0)1753 681 871

Cox & Kings
tel +44 (0)20 7873 5000
fax +44 (0)20 7630 6038

Cresta
tel +44 (0)870 161 0999
fax +44 (0)870 169 0797

Cyplon Holidays
tel +44 (0)20 8340 7612
fax +44 (0)20 8348 7939

Elegant Resorts
tel +44 (0)1244 897 011
fax +44 (0)1244 897 760

Gold Medal Travel Co.
tel +44 (0)1772 766 014
fax +44 (0)1772 251 188

Grenadier Safari
tel +44 (0)1206 549 585
fax +44 (0)1206 561 337

Group Promotions
tel +44 (0)20 8795 1718
fax +44 (0)20 8795 1728

Harlequin Worldwide Travel
tel +44 (0)1708 850 300
fax +44 (0)1708 854 952

Hayes & Jarvis
tel +44 (0)20 8222 7833
fax +44 (0)20 741 0299

Indian Ocean Connection
tel +44 (0)1244 355 320
fax +44 (0)1244 355 309

Int. Travel Connections
tel +44 (0)1244 355 400
fax +44 (0)1244 355 419

Italian Expressions
tel +44 (0)20 7435 2525
fax +44 (0)20 7431 4221

Kirker Holidays
tel +44 (0)20 7231 3333
fax +44 (0)20 7231 4771

Kuoni Travel
tel +44 (0)1306 740 500
fax +44 (0)1306 744 222

Leisure Direction
tel +44 (0)20 8324 4013
fax +44 (0)20 8324 4010

Made to Measure Holidays
tel +44 (0)1243 533 333
fax +44 (0)1243 778 431

North Am. Travel Service
tel +44 (0)1132 461466
fax +44 (0)1132 440481

Pan Pacific Worldwide
tel +44 (0)20 7323 2133
fax +44 (0)20 7323 1791

Premier Holidays
tel +44 (0)1223 516677
fax +44 (0)1223 516615

Prestige Holidays
tel +44 (0)1425 480 400
fax +44 (0)1425 470 139

Seasons in Style
tel +44 (0)151 342 0505
fax +44 (0)151 342 0516

Tailor Made Travel
tel +44 (0)1386 712000
fax +44 (0)1386 712071

Thomson a la Carte
tel +44 (0)990 502 555
fax +44 (0)121 236 7030

Tim Best Travel
tel +44 (0)20 7591 0300
fax +44 (0)20 7591 0301

Tropical Locations
tel +44 (0)20 8427 7300
fax +44 (0)20 8427 7400

TTI Ltd
tel +44 (0)1367 253 810
fax +44 (0)1367 253 812

Unique Hotels
tel +44 (0)1453 835 801
fax +44 (0)1453 835 525

Utell
tel +44 (0)20 8661 2263
fax +44 (0)20 8661 1234

Whole World Golf Travel
tel +44 (0)20 8741 9987
fax +44 (0)20 8741 1171

Hotel Groups

USA & rest of the world

Abercrombie & Kent
tel +630 954 2944
fax +630 954 3324

Africa Travel Inc.
tel +818 507 7893
fax +504 596 4407

African Portfolio
tel +800 700 3677
fax +212 737 6930

**Classic Safari Camps
of Africa**
tel +27 11 465 6427
fax +27 11 465 9309

Concorde Hotels
tel +800 888 4747
fax +212 319 5172

Explorers World Travel
tel +847 295 7770
fax +847 295 8314

Frontiers Int. Travel
tel +724 935 1577
fax +724 935 5388

Fun Safaris
tel +800 323 8020
fax +630 529 9769

GoGo Tours
tel +201 934 3812
fax +201 934 3793

International Lifestyles
tel +954 925 0925
fax +954 925 0334

Islands in the Sun
tel +310 536 0051
fax +310 643 9609

Liberty GoGo
tel +212 689 5600
fax +212 545 8050

The Meridien Group
tel +757 340 7425
fax +757 340 8379

Nature Encounters
tel +213 852 1100
fax +213 852 1101

Pan Pacific Worldwide
tel +212 757 4938
fax +212 757 4637

Quest of the Classics
tel +353 754 8891
fax +353 754 8891

Travel Impressions
tel +516 845 8000
fax +516 845 8095

Tropic Travel
tel +33 1 42 3623 88
fax +33 1 42 3623 66

Utell Int.
tel +402 398 3200
fax +402 398 5484

Accor Hotels
tel +44 (0)20 8283 4500
fax +44 (0)20 8283 4650

Best Loved Hotels
tel +44 (0)1454 414 786
fax +44 (0)1454 415 796

Charming Hotels
tel +39 06 8711 940
fax +39 06 8711 955

**Classic Safari Camps
of Africa**
tel +27 11 465 6427
fax +27 11 465 9309

Concorde Hotels
tel +33 1 40 71 21 21
fax +33 1 40 71 21 31

Elegant Hotels
tel +44 (0)20 7495 5588
fax +44 (0)20 7495 1444

GHM Hotels
tel +65 221 5250
fax +65 221 6272

Halcyon Hotels
tel +44 (0)1453 890 885
fax +44 (0)1453 890 885

**Hospitality in
Historic Houses**
tel +39 05 77 63 22 56
fax +39 05 77 63 21 60

ITT Luxury Collection
tel +353 (0)21 359 353
fax +353 (0)21 359 352

**Johansens Recommended
Hotels**
tel +44 (0)20 7490 3090
fax +44 (0)20 7490 2538

**Kempinski Hotels
& Resorts**
tel +44 (0)20 8307 7693
fax +44 (0)20 8544 9893

**Le Meridien Hotels
& Resorts**
tel +44 (0)20 7301 2000
fax +44 (0)20 7301 2011

**The Leading Hotels of
the World**
tel +44 (0)800 181 123
fax +44 (0)20 7493 7773

**The Leading Hotels of
the World (USA)**
tel +800 223 6800
fax +212 758 7367

Orient-Express Hotels
tel +44 (0)20 8568 8366
fax +44 (0)20 7493 0755

Preferred Hotels
tel +44 (0)20 8348 0199
fax +44 (0)20 8347 8998

Relais & Châteaux
tel +44 (0)800 960 239
fax +44 (0)800 968 152

Sina Hotels
tel +39 06 48 70 222
fax +39 06 48 74 778

**Small Luxury Hotels of
the World**
tel +44 (0)800 525 48000
fax +44 (0)1372 361 874

SRS Hotels
tel +44 (0)800 898 852
fax +44 (0)20 7323 0129

Swiss Deluxe Hotels
tel +41 (0)1 389 8021
fax +41 (0)1 389 8030

Turin Hotels
tel +39 11 51 51 911
fax +39 11 56 17 191

Universal Enterprises
tel +960 323 080
fax +960 322 678

The Wren's Hotel Group
tel +44 (0)1753 831 616
fax +44 (0)1753 855 909

Zimbabwe Sun (HMI)
tel +44 (0)20 8908 3348
fax +44 (0)20 8904 0094

www.SpecialHotels.com

Want to know **more** about some of the

special hotels featured

in this **collection?**

Why not use our new on-line

interactive brochure...

- Guided tour of each hotel with more pictures and detailed information of facilities, colourful travel pieces, itineraries and up-to-the-minute weather reports.

- Instant email link-up and on-line booking facilities.

- Choose your favourite hotels and create a personalised shortlist, and enjoy exclusive benefits by becoming a registered user of www.SpecialHotels.com.

- Read what our writers have to say about their travel experiences. Why not let us know of your experiences by using our 'Feedback' facility?

- www.SpecialHotels.com is the easy route to making your world-class hotel reservation today.